Dodson, Leonidas
Alexander Spotswood

ALEXANDER SPOTSWOOD

GOVERNOR OF COLONIAL VIRGINIA

1710-1722

By

LEONIDAS DODSON

AMS PRESS
NEW YORK

Reprinted from the edition of 1932, Philadelphia
First AMS EDITION published 1969
Manufactured in the United States of America

Library of Congress Catalogue Card Number: 76-91784

AMS PRESS, INC.
NEW YORK, N.Y. 10003

PREFACE

THE field of American biography is rich in the opportunities which it offers to the investigator. Many of the more dramatic figures in our history have their biographers, but this is more true of the national than of the colonial period. The men of the latter period who have received most attention are on the one hand the founders who ushered in the era, and on the other the revolutionary leaders who compassed its termination. Yet the intervening years were not without noteworthy men.

Historians of the last century were wont to mete out scant justice to the royal governor. Regarding the colonial period from the viewpoint of the American Revolution, they too often depicted the king's governor as an agent of British tyranny whose conflicts with the colonists were the outcome of the resistance of patriots to an external and arbitrary control. From such a pillory several worthy colonial executives have but recently been rescued. No such task, however, confronts the biographer of Alexander Spotswood. With him American writers have from the first dealt kindly. Nor is it difficult to see why this should be the case.

Spotswood resembles another Briton who left his mark on the history of Virginia in that our most fruitful source of information concerning him is the product of his own pen; and if the egotism of the *Trewe Relaycion* and the *Generall Historie* is the more patent, Spotswood's correspondence is far from depicting its author at his worst. Again it must be conceded that the justice of much of his self-praise gives Spotswood another point in common with John Smith. He was cast in a more heroic mould than the common run of governors, and the historian must need recognize in his administration policies both wisely conceived and vigorously pursued. Moreover, his administration ended, Spotswood cast in his permanent lot with Virginia. His grandson and namesake was a general in the patriot army during the War of Independence, and his numerous progeny occupies an honorable place among the "first families" of the commonwealth which he administered. Spotswood has thus been accepted as one of America's own. Perhaps he has received no more than his due. Yet he is the victim of no gross injustice. The satisfaction of a revolutionary appraisal is thus denied his biographer, who must find his *raison d'être*, if he finds it at all, in the need for a fuller and more unified account of one of the most colorful and significant personalities of the colonial period.

My thanks are due first and foremost to Professor W. T. Root of the University of Iowa. Not only did he suggest the subject of the present study but at all stages the work has been forwarded by the advice, encouragement, and direct aid which he has given so unstintingly. Grants to cover traveling expenses from the American Council of Learned Societies and from the Graduate School of the University of Iowa have made accessible manuscript material essential to the completion of the study. The author is deeply grateful to the officials of the Library of Congress, the Huntington Library, the Virginia State Library, the Virginia Historical Society, and the Historical Society of Pennsylvania, and to the clerk of the Orange County Circuit Court for the liberal assistance which they rendered. Professor T. J. Wertenbaker of Princeton University had the unusual kindness to place at the disposal of an unknown graduate student from another institution transcripts which he had made at great labor of material in the Public Record Office. The helpful criticism of Professor W. P. Hall of Princeton has recast many an unhappy phrase. Professors H. V. Ames and W. E. Lingelbach of the University of Pennsylvania have been so good as to read the manuscript, while Dr. Lingelbach and Mr. Phelps Soule of the University of Pennsylvania Press have done much to smooth out the difficulties attending the problems of publication. Dr. A. C. Bining has made some useful suggestions concerning the iron industry, and Messrs. A. E. Hutcheson and T. R. Schellenberg have kindly assisted in reading the proof. The aid which my wife has rendered, through encouragement, criticism, and stenographic work, has taught me that intramarital acknowledgments are not necessarily trite formalities.

L. DODSON.

Philadelphia, 1932.

CONTENTS

PARTIAL LIST OF ABBREVIATIONS

B. T. Jour.: Journal of the Commissioners for Trade and Plantations.

Cal. State Paps., Col.: Calendar of State Papers, Colonial Series.

C. O.: Colonial Office Papers.

Ex. Jour. Coun.: Executive Journals of the Council of Colonial Virginia.

Hening: Statutes at Large.

Jour. Burg.: Journals of the House of Burgesses of Virginia.

Leg. Jour. Coun.: Legislative Journals of the Council of Colonial Virginia.

Letters: Official Letters of Alexander Spotswood.

N. C. Col. Recs.: Colonial Records of North Carolina.

N. Y. Col. Docs.: Documents Relative to the Colonial History of the State of New York.

Pa. Col. Recs.: Minutes of the Provincial Council of Pennsylvania.

Perry: Historical Collections Relating to the American Colonial Church.

Chapter I

BEGINNINGS

1676! THE year brought excitement to the little colonial capital of Jamestown. Her streets were invaded by armed men, uncouth fellows for the most part, frontiersmen, small planters, debtors, freedmen—colonial discontent of all shades marshaled under the leadership of Nathaniel Bacon. Their presence was a protest against His Majesty's governor, Sir William Berkeley. For sixteen years no election had been held, and a systematic use of patronage, it was claimed, had made this colonial long parliament the tool of the prerogative rather than its scourge. Sir William, to whom the trade in skins and furs brought profit, had avoided strong measures for the protection of the frontier for fear of disrupting commerce with the Indians. Another grievance, if it could not be laid strictly to Sir William's charge, was felt to emanate from the authority which he represented. The price of tobacco was declining, and the consequent economic distress was blamed, rightly or wrongly, upon the system of trade regulation which officials at home had been evolving during the past two decades. Virginians were not of the stuff which bears wrongs with meekness.[1]

In all this there was nothing particularly un-English. Resistance to constituted authority had been an old story in England. Bacon himself was a Virginian of scarcely two years' standing. Yet three thousand miles of ocean necessarily affected the situation. The prerogative, although not lacking colonial underpinning, emanated primarily from England, while the basis of popular government was perforce in America. And thus, thanks to geography, a struggle which

[1] Evarts Boutell Greene, *The Foundations of American Nationality*, pp. 82-84; Thomas Jefferson Wertenbaker, *The American People*, pp. 28-30.

would normally have resulted in the gradual evolution of popular government culminated in those "human events" in the course of which, just one hundred years after Bacon's time, it became "necessary" for the colonies to declare at an end their political union with the land of their fathers.

The grievances of Bacon and his followers were three-fold. Relations between governor and assembly were unsatisfactory. The colony was ill defended. And the acts of trade and navigation were deemed irksome. These three problems created the essential difficulty of British rule in America. Something more than the will to power was involved in the conflict between governor and assembly, for the former was more than the executive of a province; he was the representative of an external authority. Problems of every category, important or trivial, local or continental, from the bounding of a parish to the winning of an empire, were apt to put him at loggerheads with the representatives of the people.

No satisfactory solution of the problem of defense was to be made during the colonial period. The mother country could not assume the entire burden, yet no effective plan was devised whereby all would contribute to a cause from which all benefited. The "requisition" system was notoriously ineffective.[2] Colonies exposed to Indian attack were all too often refused aid by those more sheltered commonwealths whose battles they were actually fighting. The solution of the problem seemed to lie in the development of an American nationalism equipped with the agencies of common action, but what would then become of British rule?

The lack of coordinated political institutions was partly offset by the general acceptance both in England and in the

[2] In 1721 Spotswood received from Governor Burnet of New York a letter demanding for the erection of forts there the sum of £900 "being the Quota appointed to be furnished by this Colony, and wch he by his Majesties Instructions is directed to demand in case of Necessity." The council declared that the burgesses had twice rejected such a demand and were not likely now to comply since "the same reasons that swayed them then do still subsist." *Executive Journals of the Council of Colonial Virginia*, H. R. McIlwaine, ed. (4 vols., Richmond, 1925-1930), III, 544, 545.

colonies of certain broad principles. These furnished a *modus vivendi.* Thus the regulation of their commerce by England was regarded by the colonies as the price which they paid for those military, naval, and diplomatic establishments which were maintained at Britain's sole expense, but the benefits of which were enjoyed by the empire as a whole. The monopoly of the British market which was accorded to colonial tobacco probably came close to offsetting less favorable features of the system so far as the Chesapeake colonies were concerned.[3] And it may be said that however irksome the colonists found certain provisions, the acts of trade imposed by England were more in accordance with the best thought of that age than the present self-imposed commercial restrictions are with that of today. Yet the acts of trade and their enforcement proved fruitful sources of friction between Britain and her dominion in America.

Again 1676. The scene is laid in the town of Tangier, dominating from the African side the Straits of Gibraltar. An English garrison is in possession, for Tangier had been part of the dowry which Catherine of Braganza brought to Charles II fourteen years before. A position of great strategic value, this, in the days before England held the famous Rock opposite, but one which in the face of Moorish hostility sorely taxed the resources of the Merry Monarch. The governor and garrison were served by a physician, one Robert Spotswood who, if his interminable quarrels with his neighbors count for anything, was an irascible man. To Dr. Spotswood, in the year of grace of which we speak, was born a son. Child of a contentious parent, his early years spent amid scenes of violence, the boy seemed destined for a stormy career. But perhaps his mother, the former Catherine Elliott, provided a calming influence.

He inherited a tradition both royalist and Anglican. The Spotswood of five generations before, William Spottiswood of Spottiswood, had fallen in the Scottish ranks at Flodden. His son, John Spotswood, championed the Reformation in

[3] *Infra,* p. 40.

Scotland. Admitted to orders by Cranmer, he was a close associate of Knox. The line between church and kirk was not then as distinct as it later became. He was deputed by the general assembly upon the birth of the future James the Sixth of Scotland and First of England, to congratulate the queen and request that the prince "might be baptized according to the form issued in the Reformed Church." Her Majesty received the congratulations but not the advice. After Mary had fled to England, however, Spotswood had the satisfaction of officiating at the coronation of the young king at Stirling the following year, doubtless a good Presbyterian affair.

His son and namesake, the great-grandfather of the object of this study, was archbishop of St. Andrews and historian of Scotland. When the breach developed between James and the kirk he sided with the former, and in later years seconded Laud's efforts to introduce the prayer book into Scotland. He it was who attempted to still the commotion at that service at St. Giles which has been made forever memorable by the story of Jenny Geddes and her stool. The grandfather, Sir Robert Spotswood, had been secretary for Scotland. Strongly opposed to the Covenanters, he became anathema to the Presbyterian party, by whom he was put to death in 1646. In the father the family descended to a humbler station of life, though whether from loss of fortune during the civil war or from infelicity of disposition is not known.

In 1684 the English abandoned the outpost which had been held at such cost of blood and wealth against the onslaughts of Mulai Ismail. The Tangier regiments returned home in time to do bloody work for King James when in the following year Dorset and Somerset rallied to the banner of Monmouth. The child, who was named Alexander, was brought to England by his mother in October 1683. Of the next ten years of his life there seems to be no record.[4]

[4] *Dictionary of National Biography*, *s.v.* Spotswood; Hume Brown, *History of Scotland* (3 vols., Cambridge, 1905), II, 301; J. S. Corbett, *England in the Mediterranean* (2 vols., London, 1917), II, 298-419, *passim.*

In 1693 Alexander Spotswood became an ensign in the Earl of Bath's regiment of foot then stationed in Flanders, and three years later he was promoted to the rank of lieutenant. In 1698, after the Peace of Ryswick, the regiment was ordered for Ireland and presumably Spotswood accompanied it thither. The outbreak of the War of the Spanish Succession found him once more in Flanders, serving as lieutenant quartermaster-general under Lord Cadogan, at first with rank of captain, later rising to that of lieutenant colonel. He was wounded at Blenheim, though if the story be true that he retrieved the offending cannon ball as a souvenir, his hurt cannot have been critical.[5] At Oudenarde he seems to have been captured, for a month after the battle we find Marlborough negotiating his exchange. Three months later he was back again at his post, superintending the transportation of grain. If we know our colonel, the quartermaster-general found in him an efficient aide.[6]

Meanwhile the war dwindled to a close. Mrs. Masham had the ear of Queen Anne. The Tory star was ascendant and peace impended. Britain would stand in less need henceforth of the men who had fought for her in Flanders. An army officer might now well consider a civil career, the better to serve his country—and himself.

[5] Keith says that he was "dangerously wounded." *History of the British Plantations*, p. 172.

[6] *Dictionary of National Biography*, *s.v.* Alexander Spotswood, Sir Bevil Granville; *Marlborough Dispatches*, Sir George Murray, ed. (5 vols., London, 1845), IV, 169, 180, 300, 307; *The Official Letters of Alexander Spotswood*, R. A. Brock, ed. (Richmond, 1882-1885; hereinafter cited as *Letters*), II, 298, 332.

Chapter II

THE COLONIAL GOVERNOR

On the twentieth day of June in the year 1710 her Majesty's ship the *Deptford* passed between the Capes of Virginia and dropped anchor in Hampton Roads. She had come to convoy the homeward bound tobacco fleet across seas infested with enemy privateers, and was thus welcome enough. Of more interest to Virginia, administered now for four years by president and council, was the presence on board of Alexander Spotswood, bearing the queen's commission as lieutenant governor. The next day he landed at Jamestown and enjoyed that night at Green Spring the not altogether disinterested hospitality of Philip Ludwell. Two days later the council met, the royal commission was published, and Spotswood assumed the office which he was to fill with varying fortunes for the next twelve years.

Governor in all but title and emolument,[1] Spotswood was the deputy of George Hamilton, Earl of Orkney, who had been granted the government of Virginia, tacitly as early as 1705, officially in 1710.[2] It was understood that Orkney should remain in Britain and receive half the governor's salary while a deputy administered the province. No active participation in the affairs of Virginia was expected of the Scottish earl, who received this sinecure possibly as a reward for a creditable military record; more likely in return for his support of the Act of Union which in 1707 joined England and Scotland in the kingdom of Great Britain. Momentous event for the mother country, the union was scarcely less significant for America. Scotch administrators were soon doing much, Scotch settlers more, to render the

[1] It has seemed best in the present work to refer to him as governor.
[2] See Appendix 1.

empire British in fact as well as in name. Rich indeed was the heritage which the colonies had from north of the Tweed. Perhaps the salary paid gratuitously to Orkney for thirty years was after all not a bad investment for America.

One of the first Scotchmen to fill an administrative post in the colonies was Orkney's deputy. As we have seen, his military record was creditable, and the good account which Orkney received of him, coupled doubtless with a prepossession on the earl's part in favor of one like himself a soldier and a Scot, led to his appointment.

The opportunities whereby the shrewd servant of the East India Company might in a few years become the wealthy nabob were not for the royal governor in America. Appointments to needy scions of great families were not unknown, and the hope of recouping a depleted fortune will occasionally account for the presence in the colonies of an incompetent executive. Nor was Spotswood's decision to exchange the career of an army officer for that of a colonial governor on half-pay uninfluenced by the prospect of bettering his circumstances. Yet such a career, vital to the empire and not without a measure of honor, promised more of travail than of reward. Responsibility it entailed in full measure; the power which in theory accompanied that responsibility was in practice seriously restricted.

The governor was the chief executive of the province and the dignified head of its government. His duties were many and as varied as colonial life itself. As commander-in-chief he supervised defense of the colony by land and sea, against hostile Indians and European fleets, revolting Negroes and pirates. He appointed, sometimes in conjunction with the council, most of the subordinate officials in the colony, and the supervision of their activities fell to his lot. The rôle of mediator in the internecine quarrels of a neighboring province, of godfather at the christening of an Indian girl, of explorer of the unknown west, cajoler of assemblies, or advocate of a fallen servant woman—these and many others were germane to his task. He warded off Indian raids by diplomacy, and epidemics by proclaiming days of prayer and fasting.

It must not be inferred from the multifarious activities of the governor that all important functions of government devolved in their fulness upon him. Not the least of his difficulties arose from the necessity of working both with and against other branches of the government. In the typical royal colony the chief organs of the provincial government were those which united to compose the assembly—governor, council, and popularly elected lower house. The services of the governor alone were strictly professional. The appointee of the crown, he was expected to find in his salary and perquisites his means of livelihood. If he chanced to have other sources of income within the colony he usually refrained from advertising the fact in England.

The council was also appointed by the crown. Since the salaries of a dozen full-time officials of suitable parts were altogether too heavy a charge upon the civil list, it was necessary to utilize in this important work the amateur talent of substantial colonial gentlemen, who served at a nominal stipend. The governor's nomination was the usual basis for selection, but it by no means followed that the councillors were mere henchmen of his. Composing as they often did the best that the colony could show in wealth, intellect, and social standing, they were the leaders of a self-conscious colonial aristocracy. They had come to regard themselves as possessed of powers which they were prepared to defend to the utterance, even against the representative of majesty. The function of councillors was three-fold: legislative, executive, and judicial. They constituted the upper house of assembly; in executive session they acted with the governor, their actions often transcending the merely advisory; and they were *ipso facto* members of the general court, the highest judicial body in the colony, the governor sitting with them as *primus inter pares.*

The voice of the people was made articulate in Virginia through the house of burgesses. Few countries in the early eighteenth century could boast so popular a body, for the bare freehold qualification required of voters was not hard to meet where land was plentiful. Happily exempt from borough mongers and governmental patronage, those banes of free government in the Britain of that day, Virginia's lower house reflected with fair accuracy the attitude of the province.

Two considerations ever limit the executive of a constitutional state with an exchange economy—the need for authority to act and for money to finance the action. So far as routine matters went Virginia's governor found himself reasonably well supplied with both. Viceregal powers were conferred upon him by his commission, and while these were considerably circumscribed by his instructions, there was much that he might do without colonial assent. Moreover, many functions of government were provided for by colonial law, the product of a century of experimentation in government where it was not derived from the still richer experience of the mother country, and this law might not be repealed without the governor's assent. Then too, the royal government in Virginia was favored above that of other colonies in having two funds independent of the caprice of the legislature. The quit rents might indeed be spent only as directed by the treasury in England, but the revenue from an export duty of two shillings a hogshead on tobacco was at the disposal of governor and council. There was thus in Virginia no struggle over a civil list such as embroiled governor and assembly in the other colonies, and the executive was strengthened through the inability of the legislature to penalize the king's officers by withholding their salaries.

Favorable though his position thus was, his Majesty's governor in Virginia fell far short of independence of the assembly. The ever changing problems of a young and growing commonwealth were constantly demanding new legislation and the voting of special appropriations. The permanent revenue was thus insufficient to defray the normal expenses of government and, despite admonitions from England, the colonists persisted in meeting problems which were both basic and permanent by means of temporary laws. Thus the governor stood in constant need of legislative support, and every session found him proposing, rebuking, encouraging, endeavoring to secure the passage of "government measures." The rôle of lobbyist must be added to the governor's repertoire.

Legislative cooperation, so essential to effective administration, was often dissipated by conflict between governor and assembly. This is the crux of the problem of royal government in America. Underlying the various temporary forms which this struggle might assume were two fundamental constitutional issues, the one local, the other imperial, blended in their manifestations and incapable of complete separation. In the first place there was ever present the question of division of power within the colony. The struggle between legislature and executive in Virginia was of course merely an old drama in a new setting. The diffused responsibility which numbers conferred upon the assembly was in this case accentuated by provincialism and by the colonial proclivity to reduce governmental activity to a minimum. The governor, with a wider outlook and a responsibility that was distinctly personal, could be counted upon to sponsor a more comprehensive program. In the inevitable conflict the control of the purse strings was likely to give the legislature the whip hand. That the popular body did not entirely prevail as in England was due in large measure to the fact that the governor's arm was strengthened by the mother country, and out of this arises the second issue between him and his assembly.

As the king's representative in Virginia the governor drew unto himself a prestige greater than that of a mere colonial executive. Not infrequently did he find it expedient to fortify his position by drawing around it the skirts of majesty. Yet this relationship was not all gain for the governor, for he encountered many of his severest problems in the course of defending, in a period of flux, that intangible entity—the royal prerogative. The "Old Dominion" had been a royal province since 1624. With the exception of a few concessions which had been granted by the emasculated charter of 1679, the political privileges of the Virginians had their rise in law from the governor's commission and instructions, which the crown might modify at will. While the royal prerogative might thus appear omnicompetent, a great gulf lay between abstract law[3] and practical expediency. Commission and instructions were issued from time to time with but slight modifications, and many of their provisions had come to be regarded as a permanent heritage. Providing at best but a skeleton constitution, they had been augmented by colonial law and precedent. Virginia had a constitutional development of her own, and like that of the mother country it was essentially a common law development. Virginians did not scruple to plead "what hath been the ancient custom" even against the royal instructions.

That colonial institutions could be modified in accordance with royal caprice was under these circumstances unthinkable. While this was principally due to their being so well established that they could not be molested without precipitating a crisis, the political thought of the time ran counter to the theory of the complete supremacy of the crown over any part of the empire. Yet here lay another menace to colonial autonomy, for the spirit of the age speaking through the revolution of 1689 had substituted for the senile royal power the virile authority of parliament, an authority as embracing as the empire itself. The full import of this constitutional change at home was not at once recognized in the colonies. Nor was colonial reasoning always clear and colonial action always consistent. Thus it was that the colonies, not seeing the logical end to which such a course of action would eventually lead, recognized the binding force of acts of parliament which made specific mention of them. Yet it was unquestionably the sense of the colonies that their assemblies, not par-

[3] If this indeed was the true law of the case. See in this connection C. H. McIlwain, *The American Revolution, a Constitutional Interpretation* (New York, 1923).

liament, were the legatees of much of the relinquished power of the crown. That their powers were coordinate with those of parliament was an assertion which colonial assemblies were not yet prepared to make, and Spotswood might still chide the burgesses with impunity for arrogating unto themselves all the rights of the House of Commons. Yet that this reproof was not inapt shows the direction in which the wind was blowing. Herein lay the seeds of an irreconcilable conflict which would bear fruit whenever the colonies found parliamentary control unduly irksome.

As yet, however, the outlook of parliament was anything but imperialistic. When it included the colonies at all it thought in terms of mercantilism. Active participation in colonial affairs amounted to little more than the regulation of industry and commerce in a rather loose and general way. Parliament seemed well content to leave to the crown the knotty problems of colonial administration.

The brunt of colonial administration devolved upon the Lords Commissioners of Trade and Plantations, trade before plantations be it noted. For we find the board composed of orthodox mercantilists for the most part, thinking in terms of the trade of Great Britain, and apt to regard the touchstone of the balance of trade as the measure of all things. Yet it would be unfair to brand the board of trade as narrow and doctrinaire. Fully persuaded that a flourishing empire was essential to Britain's commercial prosperity, there was little which affected colonial welfare which did not receive its careful attention. For the board was a conscientious body. Unhappily it lacked direct authority. An advisory committee to the privy council, it could only recommend. And while its recommendations were usually acted upon by ministers of state as a matter of routine, the delay necessarily slowed up the all too sluggish machinery of imperial control.

Alexander Spotswood was but one royal governor among many. British government in America did not stand or fall by his administration. Yet his problems were typical, and the course of events in Virginia for twelve years may well suggest the destiny of a continent. Is it possible to hazard a date for the beginning of the American Revolution? Was it already under way in 1710? Certainly the record of the preceding years augured none too well for effective royal control in Virginia. Sir Edmund Andros, that tactless executive, had been checkmated and removed, and a similar fate had befallen the far more efficient Francis Nicholson. The death of Edward Nott in 1706, after a brief and colorless administration, had been followed by an interregnum of four years, during which the government had been administered by the president of the council and his colleagues. The council had thus acquired a feeling of self-sufficiency which might prove inimical to the governor's authority. And then came Spotswood, energetic, courageous, able. That he intended to govern in accordance with the views of the authorities in England cannot well be doubted. To what extent was it possible to assert the power of the crown upon the continent of America? The fortunes of this young man of thirty-four may answer the question, in part at least.

Chapter III

CAROLINA

No ASSEMBLY had met in Virginia since Governor Nott's time. "But as soon as a governor comes," Robert Quary had remarked to the board of trade, "an Assembly must be called, who will find work enough for him, and the Honble. ye board of Trade too."[1] He was right. Much business had accumulated during the interregnum. Public claims remained unpaid; the work of building the governor's mansion was at a standstill; laws disallowed by the crown needed to be reenacted in revised form; not a few propositions and grievances from the people would have to be considered; and the governor himself had legislation to propose.

It will be remembered that Britain was still at war with France and Spain. It was natural, therefore, that Virginia's soldier governor should urge measures for the better defense of the colony. Fortifications, where there were any, were in disrepair. War supplies were similarly deficient in quantity and quality. And with one so recently an officer in Flanders the militia as then organized could scarcely hope to pass muster. Nor did the governor have sufficient authority to take emergency measures in time of crisis. These problems were to beset Spotswood throughout his administration.[2]

In much that related to her own protection Virginia acted as an independent unit. She had her own commander-in-chief, her own militia, and her own administrative system. Yet she was one of a number of British colonies clinging to the fringe of the North American continent, none of which could hope to withstand unaided the attacks of its potential foes. Nor, indeed, were these colonies as a group capable of guarding

[1] Quary to B. T., Dec. 2, 1709, *C.O.323/7*, K. 1. Quary was surveyor-general of the royal customs in America.

[2] A fuller discussion of the problem of defense is given in Chapter x.

their homes, protecting the shipping upon which their prosperity depended, and breaking through the barrier of French settlements which threatened to confine them to the narrow strip of seaboard east of the Alleghenies. Like all newly settled regions they lacked the accumulated capital and the surplus manpower necessary for a standing army and navy. For these they had to look to Great Britain. Only by close cooperation with the mother country and with one another could the colonies hope adequately to defend themselves.

Centrifugal forces were powerful. The colonies did not spring from a single settlement, but were for the most part founded by distinct expeditions from England to widely separated points. Between the infant colonies communication was infrequent. In course of time their expansion brought them in contact one with another. But where such contact led to disputes over boundary lines or trading privileges it created an atmosphere anything but neighborly.

Hugh Jones, a clergyman who had resided for some years in Virginia, has given classic expression to the particularism of the English colonies in America. "If *New England,*" he wrote in 1724, "be called a Receptacle of Dissenters, and an *Amsterdam* of Religion, *Pensylvania* the Nursery of Quakers, *Maryland* the Retirement of *Roman* Catholicks, North Carolina the Refuge of Run-aways, and *South Carolina* the Delight of Buccaneers and Pyrates, Virginia may be justly esteemed the happy Retreat of *true Britons* and *true Churchmen.*"[3] So it went. Common origin, united purpose, kindred interest, common destiny; a sense of these things our fathers lacked. Petty disputes over a few square miles seemed more important than the winning of a continent; trivial differences of creed and custom frequently obscured those larger problems of cultural and institutional development in which the interests of all were identical.

Virginia's neighbor to the south was the struggling colony of North Carolina, whose scattered inhabitants were still liv-

[3] Hugh Jones, *Present State of Virginia* (London, 1724; Sabin's Reprint, New York, 1865), p. 48.

ing the life of the frontier. There was good soil and abundant pasture, and the people lived in primitive plenty. Yet the lack of good harbors made communication with the outer world difficult, and North Carolina thus lacked markets for her surplus products. The produce of northeast North Carolina found an outlet through Norfolk, Virginia, whose trade lay chiefly in the exporting of flour, beef, pork, and lumber to the West Indies.[4] Since, however, Virginia prohibited the importation of tobacco from any territory outside the Capes, and North Carolina lacked harbors to accommodate ocean-going ships, her tobacco trade was monopolized by New England vessels engaged in the coastwise trade. Many of her inhabitants therefore appear to have raised only what they needed for their own consumption. Her government was of the flimsiest, her church all but non-existent. This uncouth neighbor was regarded by Virginia with a patronizing air which at times approached the supercilious.[5]

A boundary dispute had long disturbed the relations between Virginia and Carolina. According to the Carolina charter of 1665 the boundary extended from "the north end of Currituck river or inlet, upon a strait westerly line to Wyonoak Creek, which lies within or about the degrees of thirty-six and thirty minutes, northern latitude; and so west in a direct line, as far as the south seas."[6] Framed with that indefinite geographic knowledge which characterized the royal grants of the period, its ambiguous terms gave room for various interpretations. The chief bone of contention was the identity of Weyanoake Creek. Virginia declared it to be Wicocon[7] Creek, Carolina asserted that it was Nottoway River. Both streams flowed into Chowan River, but their

[4] *The Writings of William Byrd*, J. S. Bassett, ed. (New York, 1900), p. 28.

[5] Jones, *Present State of Virginia*, pp. 78, 79; Byrd, "History of the Dividing Line," *Writings*, pp. 3-255, *passim; Letters*, I, 35; H. L. Osgood, *The American Colonies in the Eighteenth Century* (4 vols., New York, 1924), II, 385.

[6] *Colonial Records of North Carolina*, William L. Saunders, ed. (10 vols., Raleigh, 1886-1890), I, 102, 103.

[7] Sometimes called Wicconse.

mouths were some fifteen miles apart, and thus a strip of land of this width, extending indefinitely westward, was claimed by both provinces. For a time nothing was done, but the rapid expansion of both colonies brought the dispute to a head.

The proprietors granted land upon easier terms than the crown in Virginia, where thanks to differences over terms the issuing of patents was for a time suspended altogether. The result was that many prospective settlers forsook Virginia for Carolina, while those settling within the area in dispute took out patents from the latter province. An agreement to refrain from making grants in the contested territory had the same effect, for although adhered to by Virginia it was constantly broken by Carolina. Spotswood discovered several Carolina patents even north of the mouth of Nottoway River. Jealous of their titles, the settlers naturally hoped to see the controversy settled in favor of Carolina, especially since, with the true frontiersman's objection to external control, they preferred her lax rule to the better organized administration of Virginia. Many were content to owe allegiance to neither government. The crown was thus, so it seemed, losing a considerable part of its quit rent revenue, while inhabitants of Virginia were barred from taking up land rightly a part of the Old Dominion. Those settling in that area did so either without patents, or with titles which might prove invalid when the line was eventually run.[8]

Intercolonial cattle lifting complicated the problem, as did also the presence of Indians. These Indians, the Nansemond and Meherrin, were tributaries of Virginia. A treaty of 1677, guaranteeing to them the land within three miles of their settlement, had long been respected. But with chaos reigning in the disputed region, white men seized Indian land and the tribesmen retaliated upon the property of these intruders. Replying to a protest from Governor Hyde, Spotswood ex-

[8] *Letters*, I, 44-47, 160, 161, II, 71, 72, 141, 142; *C.O.5/1316*, O. 16, 65, 129; *C.O.5/1363*, pp. 256, 258; *Ex. Jour. Coun.*, III, 316, 317, 367; Byrd, *Writings*, pp. 22, 23, 73.

pressed regret that the Indians should molest any of the king's subjects, but made it clear that he considered justice to be with the former. He had heard, he said, that an attack upon the Indians was being projected in Carolina. Such an act of bad faith might succeed once, but would leave a legacy of distrust and suspicion greatly to the disadvantage of the English. So long as the boundary line remained undetermined, the status of the Indians was also unsettled. In 1713 the Meherrin were ordered by the Virginia council to refuse the demands of North Carolina for men and tribute. In 1719 they complained that a Carolina patent encroached on their lands, and Spotswood promised his good offices with the governor of North Carolina to obtain redress. When two years later the Nansemond made a similar complaint, the council brusquely ordered the sheriffs to destroy all improvements made by settlers upon Indian land. By the time the boundary was finally determined the Meherrin had been practically exterminated by war and pestilence. Doubtless not all the right was with them. "If the complaint of these Indians were true," wrote Byrd, "they are hardly used by our Carolina Friends. But they are the less to be pitied, because they have ever been reputed the most false and treacherous to the English of all the Indians in the Neighborhood."[9]

In 1710, at the instance of the board of trade, commissioners were appointed to determine the boundary. Philip Ludwell and Nathaniel Harrison represented Virginia; Edward Moseley and John Lawson the lords proprietors. The conference was futile. The conflicting opinions as to the identity of Weyanoake Creek left no common basis upon which to work. If we may believe the Virginia commissioners, a further obstacle was encountered in the dilatory conduct of the Carolinians. Both Moseley and Lawson, so it was charged, had speculated in land titles in the disputed area and would be losers if the boundary were settled in favor of Virginia. Mose-

[9] *C.O.5/1316*, O. 77, 129; *Letters*, I, 25, 45, 47, 48; *Ex. Jour. Coun.*, III, 352, 521, IV, 2, 3; *Calendar of State Papers, Colonial Series*, 1710-1711, pp. 411, 412; Byrd, *Writings*, p. 89.

ley, besides neglecting to keep appointments, even those of his own making, failed to bring any instruments of his own, contenting himself with criticizing those of the Virginians. In this he was not without justification, as later events were to show.[10]

Upon learning of this *impasse* the board of trade recommended the appointment of a joint commission upon terms calculated to prevent further delay from North Carolina. Its report was to be submitted to the crown for final determination, and meanwhile no further grants were to be made in the disputed area. An order in council was issued to this effect. The board notified Spotswood, but since the proprietors took no action matters remained at a standstill.[11]

In the meantime Hyde declared his willingness to stop all grants in the disputed territory, and doubtless lent his best efforts to that end. However, as Spotswood wrote to the board of trade, "he is upon so precarious a footing there, and his Authority so little, that he is forced to submit his own Judgment to others whose interests are likely to suffer by an equitable determination of the controversy." Upon Hyde's death in 1712, the grants appear to have continued as before. Even in Virginia the government experienced difficulty in keeping settlers out of the forbidden area.[12]

In the spring of 1714 Spotswood decided to act. Not even the bounds of the disputed area were clearly defined, and thus people of Virginia were kept from settling upon land admittedly within that province. He therefore proposed to the council that both lines be surveyed, Virginia running the northern and North Carolina the southern. If Carolina did not comply within six months, Virginia was to run both. All persons be-

[10] *Ex. Jour. Coun.*, III, 276, 277; *Letters*, I, 22; *Virginia Magazine of History and Biography*, IV, 30-42, V, 1-21; Byrd, *Writings*, pp. 23, 24, 88.

[11] *C.O.5/1316*, O. 65; *C.O.5/1363*, pp. 252-261; *Journal of the Commissioners for Trade and Plantations* (hereinafter cited as *B. T. Jour.*), 1709-1715, pp. 240, 241, 246; *Acts of the Privy Council of England, Colonial Series*, II, 588, 593; *Cal. State Paps., Col.*, 1710-1711, p. 423; *Ex. Jour. Coun.*, III, 256-259.

[12] *C.O.5/1316*, O. 77; *C.O.5/1364*, p. 22; *Letters*, I, *passim*, II, 26, 27; *Cal. State Paps., Col.*, 1710-1711, p. 412; *Ex. Jour. Coun.*, III, 316, 317.

tween these lines were to be removed forthwith and no more permitted to settle there until the dispute was finally determined. By thus cutting off the proprietors' revenue it was hoped to dispose them to a speedy settlement. John Allen, surveyor of Surry County, was therefore ordered to run the line from the mouth of Nottoway River to the Roanoke. Rangers were ordered to attend him. Apparently opposition was anticipated. Within three months he had completed his task and the land north of the new line was open to settlement. Upon the expiration of the six months, North Carolina requested the suspension of the Virginia order until the pleasure of the proprietors was known. The council voted to allow another six months, provided North Carolina promised not to enter or survey any land north of Wicocon Creek.[13]

1715 saw a real advance. An agreement was reached between Spotswood and Governor Charles Eden. Beginning from the north shore of Currituck Inlet the boundary was to run due west until it intersected Chowan River or its extension the Blackwater. If it intersected the Blackwater north of Nottoway River it was to descend the former as far as the junction of the two streams. From that point it was to run due west. Similarly, if it intersected Chowan River south of Wicocon Creek it was to ascend as far as the mouth of the latter. If the line passed between Nottoway River and Wicocon Creek, it was to continue in a due westerly direction. This settlement, promptly approved by the Virginia council, was the basis upon which the line was finally run. The rivers in the case were separated from Currituck Inlet by some of the wildest country on the continent, including the famous Great Dismal Swamp. Thus Spotswood's sole basis for determining where the line would come out was the latitudes of the mouths of Wicocon and Nottoway as determined by the former Virginia commissioners. Had these been correct, the line would have cut Chowan some miles south of Wicocon and the disputed area would have fallen in Virginia. When run in 1728,

[13] *C.O.5/1316*, O. 171; *Ex. Jour. Coun.*, III, 367, 368, 374-376; *Letters*, II, 71, 72.

it cut Blackwater half a mile north of Nottoway, giving the region to North Carolina.[14]

The proposals agreed to by Spotswood and Eden were sent to the board of trade, which forwarded them to the proprietors. The proprietors approved them and notified their governor, who appointed commissioners for North Carolina. Administrative bungling did not end here. The proprietors failed to inform the board of trade of their move and the crown, awaiting their action, did not approve the agreement until 1727. The line was finally run the following year. In the meantime Virginia adopted the policy of permitting persons wishing to take up land in the disputed area to lodge petitions in the council office. These were to give them prior right if the land were found to be in Virginia.[15]

As already stated, the government of North Carolina exercised but slight authority. Confusion, violence, and intermittent anarchy seemed to characterize that province. Under these conditions an attempt to fasten the Anglican establishment upon a population composed largely of dissenters meant trouble. The issue was not one of conscience alone; for to support the clergy taxation was necessary. The Quakers found an additional grievance in the oath of allegiance which excluded them from office. The religious issue has already agitated North Carolina for a decade when Edward Hyde, newly appointed deputy governor, arrived from England in 1711.[16]

Hyde found the government in the hands of Thomas Cary who "supported by the interests of the Quakers, and assisted by a Rabble of loose and profligate persons," had seized control. The death of Governor Tynte of South Carolina from whom he was to receive his commission left Hyde without

[14] *C.O.5/1317*, pp. 329, 330; *Letters*, II, 141, 142; *Ex. Jour. Coun.*, III, 415; Byrd, *Writings*, p. 88.

[15] *Letters*, II, 229; *Ex. Jour. Coun.*, III, 454, 496, 519, 520, 546, 547, IV, 148, 149; *C.O.5/1365*, p. 257; *Acts of Privy Coun., Col.*, III, 135-137.

[16] H. L. Osgood, *The American Colonies in the Seventeenth Century* (3 vols., New York, 1904-1907), II, 244-249; Charles Lee Raper, *North Carolina, a Study in English Colonial Government* (New York, 1904), pp. 8-14.

legal authority. The council, satisfied that the proprietors intended him to be governor, urged him to assume the administration as president until his commission arrived. But in the assembly which he summoned, Cary and his supporters found themselves in the minority. Afraid of being called to account for "many unwarrantable Actions and Oppressions," they questioned the legality of a body thus irregularly convened. The assembly ordered their arrest, whereupon Cary collected an armed force of some sixty men and openly defied the government. The assembly retaliated with legislation which it was quite unable to enforce, but which helped to bring matters to a crisis. Cary declared himself president and was upon the point of ousting Hyde and his council. Such, at least, was Spotswood's account of the course of events which led the government of North Carolina to appeal to Virginia for assistance.[17]

Spotswood first attempted a reconciliation until the matter could be determined by the proprietors. Sending John Clayton with letters both to Hyde and to Cary he proposed that the harsh laws against the latter be abrogated and that both parties disband their military forces. Clayton carried a second letter to be delivered to Cary in case he remained contumacious, in which Spotswood made it clear that, if necessary, Hyde would be aided by a military force from Virginia. Both parties accepted his good offices and a meeting was accordingly arranged. Discovering that this was only a ruse on Cary's part to lure his opponents into a trap, Clayton, after some further efforts at mediation, delivered Spotswood's second letter. Cary thereupon threw temporizing to the wind and the Hyde group, badly frightened, renewed its appeal to Virginia.[18]

Clayton's report convinced Spotswood and the council that action against Cary was necessary. The threats of his party that they would enact another Antigua tragedy[19]; the recol-

[17] *Letters,* I, 81-83, 91, 92.

[18] *C.O.5/1316,* O. 98, 99; *Letters,* I, 83, 84, 93, 100, 101.

[19] Daniel Parke, governor of the Leeward Islands, had but recently been murdered in Antigua. This event doubtless created much feeling in Virginia, for Parke, a former councillor, had connections with that province.

lection of Bacon's rebellion; the evidence that Cary was endeavoring to bring the Tuscarora Indians down on the province; the fear that he would incite the slaves to revolt; all doubtless were considerations of weight. Spotswood was enjoined by his instructions to assist other plantations in distress upon the application of their governors. It was therefore resolved to send a body of militia against Cary by land and to detach some marines in boats to Chowan Sound. The militia of the frontier counties was accordingly mustered, not without opposition from the Quakers. But the news arrived that Cary, following an unsuccessful attack upon Hyde, had retired to Pamlico where he could be reached only by water. The militia was therefore disbanded, and such marines as could be spared from the guardships (the commodore of the homeward-bound fleet declined to cooperate) were dispatched to Carolina.[20] With their arrival the opposition to Governor Hyde appears to have collapsed without letting of blood.

From the meager and inflamed accounts available it is not easy to reconstruct with any exactness the circumstances of Cary's Rebellion. Of considerable interest are the reports of the warlike activities of the North Carolina Quakers, so at variance with the usual conduct of that sect. The desire of these people to destroy the Church and Church government in North Carolina was given as one of the principal causes of unrest. Spotswood stated repeatedly that it was from the Quakers that Cary obtained his chief support. The bitter letters of John Urmiston, a "Missioner" of the Venerable Society, are to the same effect. The resentment against the Quakers may well be understood. The view that they were endeavoring to overthrow society was by no means limited to North Carolina. But it is difficult to believe that they were advocates of violence and champions of loose living.[21]

Cary and some of his fellow conspirators fled to Virginia

[20] *Letters*, I, 84-86, 93-95, 101, 102; *Ex. Jour. Coun.*, III, 279, 280.

[21] *Cal. State Paps., Col.*, 1711-1712, pp. 32-35, 74-77; *N.C. Col. Recs.*, I, 763-775.

and tried to secure passage on the homebound fleet. They were evidently anxious not to be sent back to North Carolina. Spotswood, doubting the sincerity of their intentions to stand trial in England, sent five of them, Cary included, thither under arrest. He sent accounts of the whole affair to the board of trade, to the proprietors, and to the Earl of Dartmouth, enclosing his correspondence with Carolina. But his failure to send affidavits or other legal evidence against the prisoners[22] brought a rather sharp rebuke from the board of trade, and he was instructed never again to send prisoners to England without full proof of their crimes. Similar instructions were sent to the other colonial governors.[23] A year later, after some rather feeble attempts to get at the bottom of the matter, the proprietors permitted Cary and his colleagues to return to Carolina.[24] The board of trade commended Spotswood for his conduct in assisting Hyde, while the lords proprietors sent him a cordial note of thanks.[25] The Cary episode convinced Spotswood (the conclusion was not original) that orderly government could not be maintained in North Carolina "without their Governor be invested with a greater Authority than the Lords Proprietors can confer," and he proposed for that colony a deputy governor commissioned by the crown and supported by the authority of royal Virginia. This officer might assume the government of Virginia if upon an emergency it became vacant, and thus obviate administration by the president of the council, so inimical to British interests and to the prerogative.[26]

Scarcely had the Hyde-Cary episode ended when a still greater calamity fell upon North Carolina. The Tuscarora Indians made a sudden attack upon the settlements of Swiss

[22] This omission was doubtless due to the fact that the fleet sailed before they could be prepared. *Cal. State Paps., Col.*, 1711-1712, p. 76.

[23] *C.O.5/1316*, O. 91, 129; *C.O.5/1363*, pp. 331, 332, 413; *B. T. Jour.*, 1709-1715, pp. 300, 301, 377; *Ex. Jour. Coun.*, III, 281, 283, 284; *Letters*, I, 102, 106, 107.

[24] *N. C. Col. Recs.*, I, 818, 819; *Cal. State Paps., Col.*, 1711-1712, pp. 171, 172; 1712-1714, p. 90.

[25] *Cal. State Paps., Col.*, 1711-1712, pp. 211, 243.

[26] *Letters*, I, 107-109.

and Palatines recently established by Baron de Graffenried upon the Neuse and Pamlico rivers. The baron himself was captured and over two hundred settlers lost their lives. The attack swept all along the North Carolina frontier, but spent most of its violence in the south where the large grants recently made to de Graffenried encroached upon Indian land. To the horror of war were added famine and pestilence. Internal commotion earlier in the year caused the planting of a short crop, a dry summer reduced it further. Refugees crowded into unsanitary enclosures to escape the Indians, only to provoke the dreaded yellow fever. The sadly distracted colony could not cope with the calamitous situation. Hyde's best efforts to arouse the people to measures for protection availed little in a colony unschooled in habitual obedience to authority. The government lacked both supplies and money; external help was imperative if the province was to be saved. Urgent were the appeals for aid to Virginia and South Carolina.[27]

Spotswood's first care was to send out detachments of militia to prevent the tributary Indians from joining the Tuscarora. Finding that only a part of the Tuscarora nation had been concerned in the massacre, he promptly entered into negotiations with the rest. By making a display of the military strength of Virginia, and playing upon their desire to continue trade with her, he obtained their promise to help in extirpating the assailants of North Carolina, to secure the release of de Graffenried, and to deliver hostages.[28]

Another foe had to be guarded against. That summer, 1711, a British expedition had sailed against Quebec, and the Chesapeake guardships had accompanied it. The fear of a counter attack by the French fleet necessitated the strengthening of the coast defenses. Here again the governor had made some provision. He now called upon the assembly which met

[27] *Letters*, I, 116, 119, 132, 133. Spotswood intimated and Hyde asserted that Cary's intrigues with the Tuscarora were at the root of the massacre. *Cal. State Paps., Col.*, 1712-1714, p. 11.

[28] *Letters*, I, 117, 119.

that autumn to assume the burden of expense already incurred and provide for what was further necessary.

The council approved both the wisdom and frugality of the measures taken by Spotswood. The burgesses, too, endorsed his conduct, but they allowed him payment only for those expenditures which he was specifically authorized by law to make, and declined to provide for the maintenance of Indian hostages at William and Mary College. As to assisting North Carolina, they asked for an account of his negotiations with the Indians and requested the governor to declare war on the Tuscarora. Promising hearty cooperation, they asked for an estimate of the cost of prosecuting this policy for six months. Governor and council decided to prepare for war against the Tuscarora, and Spotswood sent the house the desired estimate in the hope that sufficient encouragement would be given to produce the necessary number of volunteers, as he had no relish for leading a detachment of impressed men upon such an enterprise.

The burgesses, with suspicious generosity, voted to raise £20,000. This they proposed to do by laying a duty of ten per cent *ad valorem* upon all goods imported from Europe for one year, and by duties upon corn, wheat, pork, pitch, tar, and skins for periods varying from one to three years. The bill passed the house without a dissenting vote. This action was over-hasty and probably insincere. The duty on European goods would give offense in England; that on pitch and tar ran counter to the British policy of granting bounties upon those commodities. And it was doubtful if the skin trade could bear an additional tax. Efforts of the council to render these duties more equitable were met with the declaration by the house that it could not permit the council to amend money bills, while its refusal to discuss the matter in joint conference was declared by the council to be a breach of the privileges of the upper house. The question of privilege once raised, a deadlock was inevitable; and the burgesses refused to consider other means of relieving North Carolina. Christmas Eve arriving, the governor gave the assembly a month's recess, hoping that their resolutions might thereby "be more quickened." Upon reassembling the house showed no greater disposition to enter into Spotswood's plans, and after sitting a week the assembly was dissolved with a sharp rebuke from the governor. The two houses had not reached an agreement upon the book of claims and the public creditors therefore went unpaid.[29]

Throughout the session Spotswood had the support of the council. The opposition of the house, so he told the board of trade, he attributed to the choice as burgesses of "persons of mean figure and character."[30] The board in turn desired him, after taking the advice of the council, to propose to the assembly the further limitation of the qualifications both of electors and of those elected.[31] When the board's letter was laid before the council, it was quick to demonstrate that however ready it might be to assist the governor in curbing the excesses of the representatives of the people, it was none the less opposed to any modification of the popular basis of Virginia's political institutions. Some declared that the time was not ripe for such a move, others were outspoken in favor of the current practice, but all seemed united in the opinion that they could not advise the governor to propose any alteration in the method of election.[32] By this advice Spotswood appears to have abided.

Meanwhile the Tuscarora crisis had to be met without legislative support. The two shillings a hogshead was already in arrears, but William Byrd offered to advance £500 to enable the governor to fulfil the treaty with the friendly Tuscarora. It was hoped that if the Indians performed their part of the engagement, North Carolina would need no further assistance. Indeed, so low was the Virginia exchequer that the coun-

[29] *Journals of the House of Burgesses of Virginia*, 1619-1776, ed. by J. P. Kennedy and H. R. McIlwaine (13 vols., Richmond, 1905-1915), 1702-1712, pp. 301-356, *passim; Legislative Journals of the Council of Colonial Virginia*, ed. by H. R. McIlwaine (3 vols., Richmond, 1918-1919), I, 515-533, *passim; Ex. Jour. Coun.*, III, 298; *Letters*, I, 129-132, 144.

[30] *Letters*, I, 19, 132.

[31] B. T. to Spotswood, April 23, 1713, *C.O.5/1363*, p. 485.

[32] *Ex. Jour. Coun.*, III, 392.

cil declared further measures impossible. The protection of Virginia herself was to devolve upon the militia. But repeated appeals for help came from North Carolina and the conviction grew that the friendly Tuscarora could not be relied upon. It was decided to send one hundred English and as many tributary Indians to the relief of North Carolina, who was to provide food for this force. The expense of equipping and paying it was to be met temporarily out of the quit rents. If Carolina could not pay this back, the Virginia assembly was to be asked to make it good. Powder was sent to the militia of the frontier counties, and the arrest was ordered of several persons suspected of trading with the Tuscarora. The North Carolinians declined to pay the Virginia troops or to furnish them with provisions, doubtless for the simple reason that they had neither money nor supplies at their disposal. But if, as Spotswood implied, it was their intent to impose a duty of ten per cent upon supplies furnished the troops from Virginia, there was some justification for the umbrage of Virginia's governor at their failure to cooperate. He countermanded his order for sending the troops, and the council approved his action, declaring that North Carolina had herself to blame if further misfortune befell her.[33]

Misfortune would indeed have fallen upon that province in full measure had not timely aid arrived from South Carolina under the leadership of John Barnwell. Barnwell met with fair military success, but patched up a peace without winning a decisive victory. For this, and for failing to keep faith with the Indians, he was censored by Spotswood,[34] while he in turn criticized the part played by Virginia.[35] The Virginia council replied in kind.[36] Upon one thing at least Barnwell and the Virginia authorities were agreed; that North Carolina

[33] *Ex. Jour. Coun.*, III, 299-303, 313.

[34] According to Spotswood, Barnwell broke faith with the Indians by attacking them after the conclusion of this treaty. To this Spotswood attributed the renewal of the war by the Indians. *Letters*, I, 170, 171.

[35] The "Journal of John Barnwell," giving his account of the expedition, is printed in *Va. Mag. Hist.*, V, 391-402, VI, 42-55.

[36] *Ex. Jour. Coun.*, III, 318, 319.

ill deserved their assistance. "I have such a tale to tell of the barefaced villainys daily committed here," wrote Barnwell to the governor of South Carolina, "as will make y^r Hon^r for the future use this country as Virginia does."[37]

No sooner had the South Carolina forces withdrawn than the Indians renewed their incursions. The death of Governor Hyde in September increased the confusion. The Virginia election of 1712 brought about a change in fourteen of the fifty-one seats and, according to Spotswood, boded ill for the relief of North Carolina, the "Mob" having succeeded in returning members of its own choosing. One return certainly sounded a note of opposition. George Marable, recently removed for misconduct from the commission of the peace of James City, was chosen to represent that county.[38] However, the reelection of Peter Beverley as speaker was satisfactory to Spotswood. The governor informed the assembly that his chief motive for calling it was to secure the payment of the public debts. But the burgesses, clinging to the policy which they had adopted the previous session, turned a deaf ear to the pleas of governor and council.

The house was in session when, in the fall of 1712, a second appeal for help was made by North Carolina. This time the assembly voted a modest, but genuine appropriation for the aid of Virginia's war-swept and pestilence-ridden neighbor, £1000 to be applied as the governor saw fit, and enough "Duffells" to clothe 300 men. The assembly also continued acts for the appointment of rangers and for the security and defense of the country, and voted £900 towards finishing the governor's house.[39] Spotswood was disposed to meet them

[37] *Va. Mag. Hist.*, VI, 54, 55.

[38] *Letters*, II, 1, 2; *Jour. Burg.*, 1702-1712, p. ix; 1712-1726, p. vii; *Ex. Jour. Coun.*, III, 316. It would be instructive to know more of the characters in this political drama. An affidavit made in 1706 depicts Marable in his rôle of justice of the peace defending an indentured servant against cruel treatment. *Calendar of Virginia State Papers*, ed. by Wm. P. Palmer, *et al.* (11 vols., Richmond, 1875-1893), I, 99. It is altogether possible that he was a genuine tribune of the people, rather than the leader of the rabble depicted by Spotswood.

[39] *Jour. Burg.*, 1712-1726, pp. 14-42, *passim*.

halfway. He passed an act concerning the lapsing of land despite the fact that he considered it an infringement on the prerogative for, so he told the board of trade, the burgesses were set upon it, and he was "unwilling to Sower their temper by contending with them in an indifferent matter." He added, however, that he deemed it more advisable that concessions from the crown be extended to the colonists as the benefits of the habeas corpus act had been, that is to say by means of the royal instructions, since he had "observ'd whatsoever fav'rs are allow'd to pass in an Act of Assembly are seldom reckon'd by the people on this Climate as gracious concessions."[40] Spotswood also showed his moderation by acquiescing in the burgesses' refusal to pay the disputed claims and in their referring to the next session of assembly a message of his concerning the low state of the standing revenue of the government.[41] His conciliatory attitude in these matters was wise, and was rewarded by the harmonious cooperation of the burgesses during the two remaining sessions of his second assembly.

Spotswood now entered into negotiations with North Carolina to concert some plan of joint action. Thomas Pollock, president of the council and acting governor since Hyde's death, seems to have been too distracted to formulate any effective program. The cloth was delivered to him, but the troops which it was intended to clothe "had all either deserted the governm't, absconded in it, or shelter'd themselves under ye Masque of Quakerism to excuse their bearing arms." He was unwilling that the £1000 be laid out in much needed provisions for the troops which had arrived under Colonel James Moore from South Carolina. He proposed instead that a Virginia force be held in readiness in case Moore failed. Supplies for the Virginia troops could not be provided with £1000, and North Carolina declared its inability to furnish any. But without them Spotswood would do nothing for, as he informed Pollock, he had "not been used to make war after the Indian manner without any measures concerted or prom-

[40] *Letters*, II, 11, 12.

[41] *Jour. Burg.*, 1712-1726, pp. 41, 42; *Leg. Jour. Coun.*, I, 554.

ises Regarded." He offered to apply the quit rents of Virginia to this purpose if the deputies of the proprietors would pledge all lands north of Roanoke River and Chowan Sound as security for the repayment of the crown within three years. This the deputies declared they had no power to do, and this rather shabby attempt to settle the boundary dispute in Virginia's favor came to nought. Spotswood and his council thereupon decided to concentrate their energies upon the Virginia frontier, blaming their inability to aid their neighbor upon the smallness of the grant made by the assembly and the failure of North Carolina officials to cooperate.[42]

For a second time North Carolina's only hope lay in the assistance sent by her sister province to the south, this time a detachment of several hundred Indians and a bare handful of whites under the command of Colonel James Moore. Moore's task was difficult. North Carolina made no provision for the rationing of his troops and had none of her own to cooperate with him. He also had trouble in controlling his savage allies, who were said to create even greater destruction than the enemies which they had come to subdue. Spotswood saw full well that if Moore met with a reverse the consequences would be grave. But happily Moore was able, in March 1713, to inflict a crushing defeat upon the Tuscarora. Realizing that Moore's volatile force, having obtained its booty of scalps and slaves, could no longer be relied upon, Spotswood counseled a peace upon lenient terms. North Carolina thereupon concluded a treaty with "King" Blunt of the Tuscarora, who had never been actively hostile. At Spotswood's suggestion, Blunt was recognized as king of his nation. But the treaty made no mention of Virginia. Annoyed, the Virginia council decided to maintain an attitude of hostility and non-intercourse towards the Tuscarora until Blunt should come to Virginia and make his peace. There is no evidence that he did so, but normal conditions eventually returned.[43]

[42] *Letters*, II, 4, 6, 7; *Ex. Jour. Coun.*, III, 331, 332; *Cal. Va. State Paps.*, I, 156-163.

[43] *Letters*, II, 4, 6, 11, 12, 24; *Cal. Va. State Paps.*, I, 165-167; *Ex. Jour. Coun.*, III, 347.

That the spirit of intercolonial cooperation was weak the Tuscarora War clearly shows. It demonstrates with equal clarity the inability of a colonial executive to take effective action without the support of his legislature. Convinced that North Carolina's troubles were the fruit of her own dissentions, Virginians were reluctant to render aid. Spotswood was doubtless not far from the truth when he declared himself to be "the only Person of this Governm't that ever proposes giving any Assistance to No. Carolina in its distresses."[44] Under these circumstances he probably did all within his power, and his conduct was approved by the board of trade.[45] Yet Spotswood is not to be commended for his harsh criticism of the conduct of Carolina officials laboring under difficulties very much greater than those which beset him, criticism which descended at times to trivial carping. This episode also reveals how sluggish the machinery of imperial control could be in face of an emergency. An account of the matter had been sent by the board of trade to Lord Dartmouth to be laid before the crown. The matter was then referred to a committee of the privy council. In March 1712 action was suspended pending the arrival of further information. If North Carolina had depended upon the mother country for aid she would have succumbed before its arrival.[46]

Had the Tuscarora succeeded in exterminating the English settlements in North Carolina and thus driven a wedge between South Carolina and Virginia, the consequences would have been serious. Shortly thereafter a still greater menace threatened the security of the plantations. In 1715 the Yamasee Indians and allied tribes precipitated an attack upon South Carolina, the object of which was to wipe out that province. Since there was reason to believe that the Indian tribes extending along the back of the entire area of British settlements were in consultation with one another, a con-

[44] *Letters*, II, 7, 10.

[45] *C.O.5/1363*, pp. 483, 507, 508.

[46] *B. T. Jour.*, 1709-1715, p. 317; *Cal. State Paps., Col.*, 1711-1712, pp. 170, 180; *C.O.5/1316*, O. 109; *Acts of Privy Coun., Col.*, II, 657, 658.

certed attack was feared. Each province felt itself in danger. Therefore when Spotswood sent prompt notification of the disaster to his fellow governors, urging that each both guard his own frontier and send aid to South Carolina, it was the former admonition which was heeded. North Carolina was reluctant to send aid, "alledging that their own danger requir'd not to weaken themselves." The Maryland council, confronted with an alarm from the frontier counties that the Potomac Indians were on the warpath, sent to London for arms and ammunition, and made other military preparations. Despite at least two appeals from Spotswood, however, no aid was afforded South Carolina. Governor Hunter wrote that the northern Indians had become very turbulent and ungovernable and evidently gave Spotswood to understand that no assistance was forthcoming from New York. That Pennsylvania would do anything was not to be expected.[47]

Spotswood wrote to Lord Stanhope, secretary of state, that although the crown doubtless expected the other English colonies in America to aid South Carolina in this emergency, unless specific instructions were sent to the various governors "some may probably think that ye providing for ye Security of their respective Provinces is all y't is incumbent upon them; or, w't is still more likely, their Assemblys will incline to Act up y't principle." He therefore proposed "that his Maj'tie may be moved to give some particular Orders for countenancing the proceedings of his Governors when ye common safety is concern'd, at least in y't of raising Men, tho'," he added significantly, "I do not offer at ye other of raising money to pay them, it being the liberty of ye Subject."[48]

Yet Spotswood was not alone in seeing the very grave consequences which might attend the success of the Yamasee onslaught. South Carolina was able to muster but 1500 fighting

[47] *Letters*, II, 124, 125; B. C. Steiner, "The Restoration of the Proprietary in Maryland" in *Annual Report of the American Historical Association*, 1899, I, 261.

[48] *Letters*, II, 124, 125.

men, while it was declared that the Indian nations known to be actively hostile could bring 8000 braves against her. Apprehension that other powerful tribes in the vicinity, notably the Choctaw, might enter the conflict was heightened by the belief that French and Spanish intrigue was rife among the southern Indians. Spotswood declared to Stanhope that if Charleston were attacked in its then weakened condition by either the French or the Spanish it must inevitably fall, since all the English were on the frontier fighting Indians. A foothold in Carolina would enable the French to open a new line of communication with the newly-formed settlements upon the Mississippi, "and by being at hand to support and encourage these Indians, who have now broke with the English, they might perpetuate a War w'ch would grievously disturb all these Colonys and put them Continually at a vast Expence to guard their Frontiers." Furthermore, the use of Charleston and Port Royal as bases for French privateers would be such a menace to colonial commerce that in time of war a squadron of men-o'-war would be required to guard the Chesapeake Bay and its trade. Even if the French and Spanish had no hand in inciting the attack of the Yamasee, the extermination of an English province would have an unfortunate effect in increasing the morale of the Indians and decreasing that awe of the fighting powers of the European which "has hitherto been our main Security."[49]

Upon an appeal from Governor Craven for arms, 160 muskets were promptly sent him from Virginia by order of governor and council. Ammunition was also supplied through the medium of the Virginia Indian Company. An agreement was reached with Arthur Middleton, an agent of South Carolina, that 300 men should be equipped and transported to Charleston by Virginia, after which they were to be supplied by Carolina with food and whatever additional clothing they required. Carolina was to pay them 22*s.* 6*d.* Virginia currency per month while they were in her service and was to send to

[49] *Letters,* II, 122, 123.

Virginia a corresponding number of slaves to be employed in their place. The first detachment of 118 men was speedily sent, and others followed, to the total number of 150. The acceptance by Middleton of such hard terms seems to indicate either a very urgent need of assistance, or a lack of intention to carry out the bargain. Measures were at the same time taken to prevent the weakening of Carolina by the desertion of inhabitants over the border into Virginia. Guardships were also sent from Virginia, Captains Mead and St. Loe entering into the plans of the governor with a readiness not always shown by British naval officers in colonial waters.[50]

The political situation in Virginia in 1715 was such that Spotswood would gladly have dispensed with an assembly, but the crisis in South Carolina left him no choice. He therefore called what proved to be the most hostile legislature of the administration. Spotswood estimated the expense of enlisting, equipping, and provisioning the three hundred men at thirty shillings a man. The burgesses voted to raise £450, but tacked this appropriation as a rider upon a bill to repeal the tobacco acts of 1713 and 1714. There was no chance that such a bill would pass either governor or council. The tobacco acts were cherished measures of Spotswood's, and the council was still in their favor. In any event the governor's instructions restrained him from assenting to a bill dealing with such unrelated subjects. The *impasse* was complete. A bill was passed, however, exempting the volunteers from the payment of levies for the current year, and remitting the duty on the slaves to be sent from Carolina, provided these were not sold in Virginia. By neither entreaty nor invective could Spotswood induce the burgesses to do more.[51]

In October 1715 Colonel George Evans and Robert Fenwick arrived from South Carolina in the hope of securing a further contingent. Spotswood had already written to the

[50] *Letters*, II, 119, 120, 126, 127, 136, 164, 238; *Jour. Burg.*, 1712-1726, p. 134; *Ex. Jour. Coun.*, III, 399, 400, 402.
[51] *Jour. Burg.*, 1712-1726, pp. 131-166, *passim.*

board of trade that since South Carolina had disregarded the agreement concluded with Middleton, it would be impossible to induce any more men from Virginia to go to her relief. Carolina's conduct was deemed the less excusable since the Virginia contingent had been of vital service at a critical juncture, having, Spotswood declared, repulsed an attack against Charleston from the south when the Carolina troops were occupied on the northwest frontier. With the governor, the one man in the province likely to have much interest in sending aid to Carolina, in this frame of mind, further relief was out of the question. Virginia was indeed of assistance in a vital, if indirect, manner in winning over some of the western Indians who had been in league with the Yamasee.[52] Correspondence between the two governments, however, degenerated into a series of recriminations.

The men who had gone to Carolina seem to have been largely debtors and indentured servants. The large pay and the promise that Negroes would be sent to work in their stead had served as the main inducements for their going. No slaves were sent from Carolina, and it was claimed that the Virginia troops were forced to accept for nine or ten months' service four pounds in South Carolina currency, about twenty shillings in Virginia money. It was also declared that instead of keeping the Virginia contingent together, as had been promised, Craven had ignored Spotswood's commissions and scattered the Virginians among the South Carolina troops. The promised supplies of clothing and provisions had not been forthcoming.

In his efforts to raise the contingent, Spotswood appears to have supported the promises of South Carolina with some sort of a personal guarantee. He was now deluged with the demands of debtors trying to escape the clutches of insistent creditors, of poor men who by going to Carolina had been unable to raise their annual crop of corn and tobacco and

[52] *Ex. Jour. Coun.*, III, 416. Desire to reopen the fur trade constituted a strong motive for such action on the part of Virginia.

whose families were therefore destitute, of the widows of the fallen, of the masters of servants who had lost their services for a considerable period of time, and of the creditors of the debtors and the masters of the servants who failed to return. "I cannot conceal . . . the trouble it gives me," wrote Spotswood, "after having preserved for so many years among the Inhabitants of this Colony the Reputation of honesty and Candour, I should now be suspected of combining to kidnap its Inhabitants into the Service of another Province, upon imaginary Encouragements which were never designed to be performed."[53] It was doubtless the irritation caused by this embarrassing situation which led Spotswood to inveigh so strongly against the conduct of South Carolina.[54] The governor advanced £100 to pacify the various claimants, the council agreeing to repay him out of the two shillings a hogshead should South Carolina fail so to do.[55] Francis Kennedy was sent to South Carolina to endeavor to obtain redress, but without success, and upon his return the council decided to send him to represent the affair to the authorities in England. Spotswood's experience with colonial legislatures made him realize that this process would not be speedy. He therefore proposed that in the meantime £500 be granted out of the quit rents to relieve the sufferers by the expedition. There is no evidence that the crown did this.[56] Spotswood also failed to secure an appropriation from the assembly, the burgesses declaring that it would be a hardship upon the government of Virginia to relieve those suffering because of a breach of faith upon the part of South Carolina.[57] Some relief was granted out of the two shillings a hogshead, while Kennedy

[53] *Letters*, II, 241.

[54] Popple to Shelton, Aug. 17, 1716, *C.O.5/1364*, p. 412; *Letters*, II, 164-166, 228, 238-240. The council made a rather petty retaliation by ordering that the slaves of refugees from South Carolina, which had been allowed to enter Virginia duty free should not be exported. This order was shortly rescinded. *Jour. Burg.*, 1712-1726, pp. 129, 135; *Ex. Jour. Coun.*, III, 416, 418.

[55] *Ex. Jour. Coun.*, III, 422, 423.

[56] *Ibid.*, pp. 440, 441; *Letters*, II, 228, 240-242.

[57] *Jour. Burg.*, 1712-1726, pp. 187, 195.

was allowed £250 out of the quit rents.[58] The lack of cordiality between the two governments was doubtless accentuated by a dispute over the Indian trade.[59]

Spotswood's letters concerning the Yamasee War do not contain those charges of inefficiency which he brought against North Carolina officials during the Tuscarora crisis. Craven was evidently a leader of ability, and Spotswood's comments upon his actions, the treatment of the Virginia troops excepted, were uniformly favorable. As in the Tuscarora War, Spotswood's activities in protecting the Virginia frontier and sending aid to Carolina were commended by the board of trade. His policy was one of enlightened self-interest for, as Lord Carteret remarked before the board of trade, it was prudent upon his part to aid Carolina, and thus fight the enemy at a distance rather than within his own government.[60] The whole episode left an aftermath of bad feeling between the two provinces. War against a common foe is not apt to increase mutual respect among the allies.

[58] *C.O.5/1318*, p. 97; *Ex. Jour. Coun.*, III, 461, 472, 493, 505.

[59] *Infra*, p. 81.

[60] *C.O.5/1364*, pp. 238, 239, 252, 253; *B. T. Jour.*, 1715-1718, p. 55.

Chapter IV

THE COMMERCE OF VIRGINIA

In more recent times political institutions may have been the handmaidens of trade, but in the sixteenth and seventeenth centuries the situation was reversed. Trade was begun and colonies founded to strengthen the body politic. It went without saying, therefore, that the mother country would be jealously watchful lest the trade of her colonies, instead of contributing to her strength, should add to that of her rivals. Free trade was thus out of the question, and the commercial activities of the subject both at home and abroad were restricted by a maze of regulations.[1]

In such an atmosphere Virginia, the oldest successful colony of England, had her origin. During the first five decades of her history, the mother country was too engrossed with constitutional struggles at home to pay much attention to her. With the Restoration,[2] however, the problem of regulating trade with the colonies was taken up and actively pursued until, by the dawn of the eighteenth century, Virginia and her sister colonies were part of a far-flung commercial system.

The economic prosperity of Virginia depended upon one staple product, tobacco. At first the profits derived from the sale of this newly found commodity in Europe were great.

[1] The modern appraiser of the mercantile system will do well to remember that its objectives were different from those towards which modern society is (in name at least) striving. The welfare of the individual was of little concern, in fact a large population at subsistence wages was considered desirable. Furthermore, relative rather than absolute national prosperity was the goal. England might be willing to sustain an economic loss, as for example by foregoing the cheap carrying service of the Dutch, if by so doing she could deal her adversary a blow heavier than that which she herself sustained.

[2] Some beginnings were made during the Interregnum, and England was made the staple for Virginia tobacco as early as 1621. C. M. MacInnes, *Early English Tobacco Trade* (London, 1926), p. 144.

But as time wore on and an ever-increasing acreage in Virginia and Maryland was planted with tobacco, overproduction had its inevitable result. Prices came down and profits were reduced to a narrow margin. Moreover, the Chesapeake colonies encountered the competition of tobacco produced elsewhere. That within the empire was indeed slight. The raising of tobacco in the mother country was forbidden by law,[3] and the plantations were given the monopoly of the home market, foreign tobacco being excluded by prohibitively high duties, while little tobacco seems to have been grown in British possessions other than Virginia and Maryland. But the production of tobacco now exceeded the consumption in England. The prosperity of the planter therefore depended upon the export trade to the continent of Europe, and here very serious competition was encountered.[4] By the turn of the century the planting of tobacco was flourishing in Holland, Germany, and other European countries. In 1700 the Dutch output was estimated at 10,000,000 pounds. Six years later it had grown to 27,000,000. Of this nearly half was exported, largely to the Baltic countries. France, too, consumed a mixture of Dutch and Virginia tobacco, and the market was further congested by the Dutch practice of flattening Virginia stems and making them up with a mixture of Dutch leaf into a cheap grade of cut tobacco, which because of its low price and hot, dry taste (said to be agreeable to the northern palate) found ready sale. Three million pounds of this tobacco was said to be exported annually to the Baltic, Flanders, Friesland, Münster, and Westphalia. British merchants who had formerly supplied Riga and the contiguous territory with between 800 and 1,000 hogsheads of roll and cut tobacco found themselves undersold by the Dutch. By 1714 the production of tobacco in Holland was said to be double that of 1706.[5]

[3] 22 and 23 Car. II, c. 26.

[4] It was estimated that the tobacco trade between Britain and foreign countries had formerly yielded a favorable balance of £250,000. Hyde and Perry to the Board of Trade, 1714, C.O.5/*1316*, O. 160.

[5] Representation of the Board of Trade to the House of Lords, *C.O.5/1364*, pp. 34-38.

The market for Virginia tobacco was further curtailed by the wars then raging in Europe. The struggle between Peter the Great and Charles XII during the first two decades of the new century jeopardized the Baltic trade; while the Anglo-French conflict, which lasted intermittently from 1689 to 1713, closed the routes of commerce to France and the territory under her control.[6] Tobacco being non-contraband, however, an attempt was made to revive the trade with France during the war. An order in council of February 20, 1708, directed that neutral ships be encouraged to carry tobacco from England directly to France, instructions to commanders of men-o'-war and privateers being modified to permit this trade.[7] English merchants were anxious that when peace was concluded with France the right to carry tobacco thither should be granted to the subjects of both nations under as low a duty as possible.[8]

Conditions such as these made it imperative that British tobacco be available for the continental market at as low a price as possible. In order to understand the forces militating against this, it is necessary to consider the influence of the acts of trade and navigation upon the commerce in tobacco.

Tobacco was an "enumerated" commodity, that is to say, masters of ships trading to the plantations were under bond to take all tobacco directly to England.[9] Here, a high import

[6] A printed paper, *The Present State of the Tobacco Plantations in America*, stated that before the war of the Spanish Succession, France and Spain imported nearly 20,000 hogsheads of Virginia and Maryland tobacco. Richard Perry declared that the trade with France had sprung up in the years of peace after Ryswick. *C.O.5/1316*, O. 12; *B. T. Jour.*, 1709-1715, p. 36.

[7] *C.O.5/1316*, O. 1.

[8] *B. T. Jour.*, 1709-1715, pp. 36, 403. The former duty on tobacco imported into France was said to have been 40 sols (about 1*s*.7*d*.) per pound.

[9] Except those plying an intercolonial trade. A bond of £1000 for each ship under 100 tons and £2000 for each over that burden had to be given both in England and in the colonies. The effectiveness of this regulation was doubtless much impaired by the acceptance of bonds without secure backing, and the laxness of colonial officials in placing bonds in suit. *Va. Mag. Hist.*, XXII, 18, 19, 119-121. The royal commission and instructions of 1715, issued nominally to Orkney, have been reprinted in the *Virginia Magazine of History*. This version is the result of a series of transcriptions, and inaccuracies have crept in, e.g., "daily observed" for "duly observed" (XXI, 117), "refer any

duty was levied, amounting to six and a third pence per pound, due at various times within eighteen months after importation.[10] Most of this duty was rebated if the tobacco was reexported within eighteen months,[11] only a halfpenny a pound being retained by the crown. Even with this concession, the tobacco trade to Europe was considerably handicapped. The voyage had to be broken in England, and this involved the additional expense of port duties, warehouse charges, and of unlading and relading, not to mention the delay, which might be fatal when speed was necessary to take advantage of a brisk market.[12] Furthermore, considerable

---

minister to any ecclesiastical business" for "prefer any minister to any ecclesiastical benefice" (*ibid.*, p. 349).

[10] This was composed of five separate duties, the "old subsidy" of 1*d.* due at entry, the "additional duty" of 1*d.* due at the end of nine months (12 Ch. II, c.4), the "impost duty" of 3*d.*, due in eighteen months (1 Jas. II, c.4), the "new subsidy" of 1*d.*, due in three months (9 and 10 Wm. III, c.23), and the "new subsidy" or "one-third subsidy" of ⅓*d.*, due at the end of nine months (2 Anne, c.9). The statutes here given are those by which the duties were first levied. Where these were temporary, they were continued by later acts.

[11] The anomalous position of the Isle of Man, which was part of the patrimony of the Earl of Derby and, so far as the customs system was concerned, ranked as a foreign country, seems to have provided opportunity for abuses in securing debentures. Tobacco was reexported to the Isle of Man, and then smuggled back into England. It was estimated that the revenues sustained an annual loss of £16,500 because of this practice. *B. T. Jour.*, 1709-1715, pp. 133, 134, 241-257.

[12] In 1720 Micajah Perry and John Hyde were questioned by the board of trade concerning the price of tobacco in the colonies, and that at which it was available for exportation to Europe. Perry said that "the prime cost of tobacco in Virginia, with the charges there, is about 1¾d. per pound, and the freight and charges in Great Britain, (exclusive of the duty), is about 2¼d., so that Virginia tobacco for re-exportation may be valued on a medium at 4d. per lb." Hyde said that the cost of tobacco in Maryland was a penny and in Virginia a penny halfpenny a pound, "though in Virginia they call it 2d." He placed the freight to England at a penny a pound, and the charges there at as much again. Thus Maryland tobacco was available for exportation at threepence and Virginia at threepence halfpenny a pound. Hyde asserted, however, that little Virginia tobacco was reexported. It would thus appear that the market for tobacco of the best quality was found in England rather than on the continent. *B. T. Jour.*, 1718-1722, p. 210. That year Robert Carter was getting 11*d. and* 11½*d.* a pound for his tobacco in London, 10½*d.* at Liverpool, and 10*d.* at Bristol. He declared that "we don't know how to think of tob'o than eleven pence for our crops." These prices of course include the British duties. Carter to Messrs. Perry, July 22, 1720 and Jan. 17, 1721; to William Dawkins, July 22, 1720. *MS. Letter Book of Robert Carter*,

credit was required to furnish the bonds which had to be given for the payment of the duties if the tobacco remained in England. It had been the custom not to demand the actual payment of the duty until the period of eighteen months had expired. If the tobacco had in the meantime been reexported, most of the bond was canceled by the debenture, and the merchant merely paid the difference of a halfpenny a pound. If the tobacco remained in England, he paid his bond with interest from the time when the duties came due. In 1711, however, when the trade was at a very low ebb, the customs officers were ordered to demand the duty when due. This called for a supply of capital which in that period of depression the merchants were unable to command and a cry of protest arose. Many, unable to pay the duties, would be unable to unload their tobacco. The return of the fleet would thus be delayed and the plantations would lack the necessary supplies from Britain,[13] the shipping of next season's crop also being hindered. Merchants would be forced to reexport the tobacco to Holland immediately, in order to secure the debenture to cancel their bonds. They would thus flood the market and be obliged to sell at a sacrifice. The period of eighteen months, the merchants declared, was designed to allow them to supply the foreign market by degrees, by which method alone they could secure a price which would adequately remunerate the planter. The discouragement caused by the high duties to both planter and merchant was turning the plantations from the production of tobacco to manufacturing, thus greatly reducing exportation of woolen and other manu-

1720-1721, preserved in the Huntington Library (hereinafter cited as *Carter Letter Book*). As for freight, Carter refused in September 1720 to pay £8 and £9 per ton, though he had himself charged £10 two months before. The following February he refused to pay £10. By May freight to London had been reduced to £8 in York River, to £7 in James River. Carter to Dawkins, July 13, 1720 and May 27, 1721; to John Pemberton, Sept. 13, 1720 and Feb. 14, 1721. *Ibid.*

[13] In 1714 Richard Perry and other Virginia merchants informed the board of trade that several ships, containing between six and seven thousand hogsheads, had lain in the Thames for the past twenty months. *B. T. Jour.*, 1709-1715, p. 539. Shipowners charged 2*s.* a month storage per hogshead upon this tobacco. *C.O.5/1316*, O. 153.

factured goods to Virginia and Maryland. Thousands of hogsheads of tobacco, they declared, had been sold for less than the customs duties.[14] The board of trade, realizing the difficulties under which the merchants labored and fearing that if news of this dispute reached Virginia it would still further discourage the planting of tobacco, recommended that the merchants once more be allowed eighteen months in which to discharge their bonds.[15]

The planters in Virginia asked even more. They demanded that the duties be reduced and transferred from the importer to the consumer.[16] The merchants confined their demands to the changing of the mode in which the duties were levied, not that they liked them any better than the planter, but being closer to the situation in England they doubtless realized that there was little likelihood that the duties would be moderated.[17] This whole matter was definitely settled in favor of the merchants by an act of parliament of 1714 for encouraging the tobacco trade.[18] By this all duties were made payable at the end of eighteen months, a discount at the rate of ten per cent per annum being allowed for duties paid before the expiration of fifteen months. For the benefit of those merchants unable to furnish bonds upon good security, tobacco might be landed upon the payment of the 1*d.* old subsidy, and placed in warehouses furnished by the merchants under the royal lock and key, the merchant giving his own bond to pay the duties within fifteen months. At the end of that time the merchant was to pay the duties either by money or debentures or give good bonds for the payment of the duties at the end of eighteen months. Failing this, the goods were to be disposed of by public sale, any surplus above the duties be-

[14] *C.O.5/1316*, O. 92; *Cal. State Paps., Col.*, 1711-1712, p. 111.

[15] *C.O.5/1363*, pp. 340-342; *Cal. State Paps., Col.*, 1711-1712, p. 112. Whether the Treasury acted upon this recommendation is not known.

[16] Apparently they wished the substitution of an excise tax for the import duties.

[17] Representation of the Council of Virginia to the Board of Trade, Sept. 11, 1713, *C.O.5/1316*, O. 153.

[18] 12 Anne, Stat. 2. c. 8.

ing given to the owner.[19] Another serious abuse was ended by this act. It was found that at the very time when good tobacco found no market, damaged tobacco was bought up and brought to Britain. Here it was allowed to enter duty free, and was frequently reexported, being allowed debentures upon duties which it had never paid, and was marketed in Bilboa and other free ports of Spain, where it was in demand for the manufacture of snuff.[20] It thus competed with tobacco of good quality both at home and abroad at an advantage of nearly sixpence a pound. Such, at least, was the claim.[21] By the act of 1714 no tobacco was in future to be imported duty free. That which was of too poor a quality to pay duty was to be destroyed, the owner being allowed certain concessions because of the trouble of separating good from bad, the additional freight charges incurred, and so forth.

In view of these circumstances, it is no wonder that upon assuming the government of Virginia Spotswood found the economic life of that province in a very unsatisfactory condition. Many had abandoned the tobacco trade, and those who had continued to send consignments to England had been plunged in debt, the tobacco not bringing enough to pay freight rates and duties. The credit of the more prominent planters was greatly reduced, that of the smaller had vanished altogether. The importation of manufactured goods from England into Virginia and Maryland, which had amounted in former years to £300,000, had practically ceased. The poorer people were therefore compelled to manufacture clothing for themselves. The government was informed that in 1710 40,000 yards of cloth was made in one of the best

[19] The merchants did not like the provision for locking up the tobacco, but appear to have been well pleased with the act as a whole. *B. T. Jour.*, 1709-1715, p. 539.

[20] Apparently the outports and Scotland were most interested in this trade, though the London merchants were said to have a hand in it. It was said that sailors would pour salt water on tobacco to further reduce its quality.

[21] *C.O.5/1316*, O. 153; *B. T. Jour.*, 1718-1722, p. 275; *Cal. State Paps., Col.*, 1712-1714, p. 276.

tobacco counties. Spotswood was doubtless correct in saying that this was merely a makeshift to which people were driven by necessity, since they were so unskilled that it cost them more to make cloth than the usual price of the English goods.[22] But the idea that the decline of the tobacco trade was fostering manufactures in the plantations was used as a bogey to obtain concessions in England. The actual condition of the common people in Virginia during the latter years of the war seems to have been deplorable, many respectable families being reduced to poverty.[23]

That the decline of the tobacco trade was due in large measure to the war Virginians realized full well; nor was Spotswood able to dispel the belief that the high duties levied in Britain contributed to their difficulties.[24] These influences were beyond their control. The planters also recognized, however, that the decline in the price of their product was closely connected with the great increase in production. They therefore attempted to restrict the output of tobacco. The difficulty of the problem lay in the fact that the individual, in pursuing his own interests, was compromising those of the group. The individual planter could make a profit in face of constantly falling prices only by reducing the cost of production, and this was best achieved by cultivating upon a larger scale with a cheaper grade of labor, that of the African Negro. But from the point of view of the colony as a whole, and especially from that of the small yeoman farmer who was being pushed to the wall, the introduction of Negro slavery, with the consequent increase of output, was the root of the evil. Strenuous efforts were therefore made

[22] The governor suggested that those thrown out of employment by the decline of the tobacco trade might profitably engage in the production of naval stores. *Letters*, I, 73.

[23] *C.O.5/1316*, O. 12, 153, 160.

[24] *Jour. Burg.*, 1702-1712, p. 241. Just where the burden of the British duties fell, cannot positively be stated. Part, at least, was borne by the British consumer, and the producer of "alternative" commodities. But if the demand for tobacco was "elastic," which seems highly probable, the high retail prices which the duties entailed lessened consumption, and therefore reacted unfavorably upon the planter.

to restrict the importation of Negroes. The colonial assembly would gladly have prohibited the slave trade, during times of depression at least. But powerful interests in England profited from the traffic. His instructions restrained the governor from assenting to such a law,[25] which in any case would have been promptly repealed by the crown. The assembly had thus to remain content with placing upon the traffic duties as high as it thought the British authorities would tolerate. In 1705 a duty of 20*s*. was placed on all Negroes.[26] In 1710, while framing a bill to raise funds for completing the governor's mansion and other public services, the burgesses proposed to raise the duty to £5.[27] Spotswood remonstrated. But the assembly preferred the loss of the entire revenue bill to any moderation in the duties on slaves, and the governor had to give way. He consoled himself by reflecting that purchasing slaves to the limit of their credit had plunged the people so deep in debt that it was impossible for the slave trade to revive until that in tobacco prospered, while if the price of tobacco went up, slaves would be purchased regardless of the duty.[28] The act of 1710 was continued in 1714, and made more effective by giving officers right of search.[29] Upon the expiration of this act returning prosperity removed both the excuse and the occasion for the duty on slaves; but in 1723,

[25] *Va. Mag. Hist.*, XXI, 351.

[26] Hening, III, 233.

[27] At the instance of the council, infants were admitted duty free. The council also proposed a higher duty upon slaves from other plantations than upon those direct from Africa, since the former were usually transported because of crime or disease.

[28] *Jour. Burg.*, 1702-1712, pp. 281, 286-288; *Letters* I, 52, 53. The governor was doubtless correctly informed on both points. The royal instructions indicate that large sums were owed the Royal African Company for slaves sold on credit. (*Va. Mag. Hist.*, XXI, 351, 352.) With the return of prosperity, however, the slave trade became too profitable to be hampered materially by the duties. In July, 1720, Robert Carter could expect to realize from £1200 to £1300 from the sale of twenty Negroes, but the following May, when a period of depression was setting in, he stated that as fine slaves as had ever been seen in the colony were selling at Tindall's Point for from £16 to £18 a head. Robert Tucker and Robert Carter to Messrs. Chamberlayne and Stillwell, July 26, 1720; Robert Carter to Messrs. Perry, May 27, 1721. *Carter Letter Book.*

[29] *Jour. Burg.*, 1712-1726, pp. 97, 117.

a depression having again come in the tobacco trade, a duty was once more laid upon the slave trade.[30] It is doubtful if this legislation had much effect upon the importation of Negroes. Between 1699 and 1708 over 6600 were imported, while some 15,500 were brought to Virginia between 1710 and 1727.[31]

It was also sought to reduce the size of the tobacco crop, and at the same time to improve its quality, by passing laws against the tending of seconds, the sprouts growing on tobacco plants after the crop had been gathered. These grew to leaves nearly as large as the first, though far inferior in quality.[32] By an act of 1706 the tending of seconds was made punishable by a fine of 500 pounds of tobacco for every "tithable" employed upon the plantation. The penalty was insufficient; detection difficult. In 1720, therefore, the fine was doubled and planters were required to destroy all stalks, roots, and suckers within twenty days of the cutting of the crop. This act was to be read twice annually by each sheriff or his deputy at the June and July county courts.[33] Apparently efforts to restrict the tobacco crop in Spotswood's day were confined to orderly and legal methods. One finds no evidence of tobacco cutting riots, such as there had been in 1682.[34]

With the price of tobacco so sensitive to supply, a bumper

[30] Drysdale to the Board of Trade, June 29, 1723. *C.O.5/1319*, p. 223. This act was repealed by the crown. *C.O.391/34*, p. 128. Opinion in the colony upon the expediency of the duty on slaves, probably divided, certainly fluctuated with the tobacco market. In 1715 King and Queen County sent a representation to the burgesses demanding that the duty be abolished or lessened; Surry, on the other hand, proposed in 1720 that the importation of Negroes be prohibited, and in 1722, that a duty of £20 be imposed. *Jour. Burg.*, 1712-1726, pp. 137, 266, 339.

[31] *C.O.5/1316*, O. 22, 23; *C.O.5/1320*, pp. 9-19, 331-339. A few slaves were brought by the Royal African Company, but for the most part the trade was conducted by separate traders. York River received considerably more Negroes than the other naval districts of Virginia.

[32] Spotswood to the Board of Trade, March 6, 1712. *C.O.5/1319*, p. 90.

[33] Hening, III, 435, 436; IV, 87, 88; Spotswood to the Board of Trade, March 6, 1721, *C.O.5/1319*, p. 90; Jones, *Present State of Virginia*, pp. 117, 118.

[34] Philip Alexander Bruce, *Economic History of Virginia in the Seventeenth Century* (2 vols., New York, 1896), I, 405, 406.

crop was of but dubious benefit to Virginia. "Am afraid," wrote shrewd old Robert Carter, "the Blessing that attends us in a plentiful Year will have the Consequence of a decline upon our Markett wch of necessity must make us lower our Topsails."[35]

In accordance with the spirit and practice of the time a code of law regulated the tobacco trade of Virginia. In many cases the regulations were of benefit to the trade, enjoining improvements which it would have been difficult to secure through the cooperation of individuals. Such was the regulation of 1706 specifying the size of tobacco hogsheads. Tobacco might not be imported into Britain in bulk, for a law, designed to prevent the smuggling of small quantities of tobacco, required containers to hold at least two long hundredweight.[36] If, however, tobacco were packed in casks and chests of all shapes and sizes, it would be difficult to load ships economically. The inside diameter of the cask head was therefore fixed by law at thirty inches and the length of the staves at forty-eight.[37] The ships used in the tobacco trade were built to accommodate hogsheads of this size, the holds being designed to carry seven tiers. An act of Maryland, passed in 1704, allowing hogsheads to be two inches larger in the head was disallowed and regulations similar to those of Virginia were thereupon adopted.[38] The regulation of the size of tobacco hogsheads removed all just occasion for

[35] Robert Carter to Messrs. Perry, Sept. 19, 1720. *Carter Letter Book.*

[36] 10 and 11 Wm. III, c. 21. The colonial custom of reckoning 100 pounds to the hundredweight was termed an "evil custom" by one English critic, though Jones deemed it a virtue. *C.O.323/8*, L. 1; *Present State of Virginia*, p. 45.

[37] Hening, III, 437, 438. It is possible that another motive for this regulation was to prevent the reduction of the revenue of two shillings a hogshead, by the shipping of tobacco in oversize casks.

[38] *Archives of Maryland*, XXVI, 331; *B. T. Jour.*, 1709-1715, pp. 267, 268; *Acts of Privy Coun., Col.*, II, 630-632; *Cal. State Paps., Col.*, 1710-1711, p. 568, 1711-1712, p. 209. The argument made in behalf of a larger hogshead for Maryland was that her tobacco (apparently Oronoco) would not pack as tight as the sweetscented tobacco of Virginia. But, as the English merchants pointed out, the raisers of Oronoco in Virginia were under a similar disability. Only six tiers of the larger hogsheads could have been carried.

the practice of "cropping" by the shippers, that is to say the reduction of the size of the hogshead either by the removal of staves or by pressing the heads together with handscrews and cutting off the ends of the staves. Pressing the tobacco was likely to cause it to spoil, and when once a cask was cut, tobacco was likely to be lost, or purloined by the sailors. The discrepancy between the weight of cargoes upon leaving Virginia and upon entering at the British ports gave reason for belief that much of the tobacco removed from the casks was smuggled into Britain by the crew.[39] In 1710, therefore, an act was passed requiring every shipmaster engaging in the trade to give a bond of £200 that he would refrain from the practice of cropping. Naval officers permitting the loading of tobacco before this bond was given were liable to a fine of £200. Officers or mariners found guilty of cropping were to be fined £5, immunity being granted to those turning queen's evidence. Naval officers were given the right to search all ships while being loaded, resistance entailing a penalty of £10.[40] The act of 1710 being temporary, it was made perpetual by one of 1714.[41]

Tobacco was not only the staple product of Virginia, it was also her principal medium of exchange. It passed current according to weight, regardless of quality, and was legal tender for most public and private debts. Had tobacco been of uniform quality and of stable price the only drawback to this system would have been the bulkiness of the commodity, and even this could have been surmounted by means of certificates. But since it was subject to fluctuation in price, and varied in quality from the finest which the world produced to worthless trash, tobacco furnished a somewhat unsatisfactory currency. The former objection nobody attempted to regulate, nor is it conceivable that such a task could have been accomplished. Efforts were made, however, to keep up the

[39] The shrinkage on some hogsheads, it was said, was as much as fifty per cent.

[40] Hening, III, 497-499; *Letters*, I, 56, 57.

[41] Hening, IV, 57; *Jour. Burg.*, 1712-1726, pp. 103, 111, 117.

quality of tobacco. The act of 1705 which forbade the tending of seconds, and regulated the size of tobacco hogsheads, also required all hogsheads offered for sale or tendered in payment of debts to be honestly packed with tobacco of uniform quality, under penalty of 1,000 pounds of tobacco for every hogshead fraudulently packed. Provision was also made for obliging creditors to receive tobacco of good quality in payment of tobacco debts.[42]

When the assembly met in November 1713, peace had been made with France. To no other people could this event have been more welcome than to Virginia, bringing as it did promise of renewed trade with the continent. It was only to be expected, however, that the return of prosperity would be gradual; and there was one abuse which, in the governor's opinion, would not be remedied by the mere return of peace, to wit, the raising of a very inferior grade of tobacco merely for the payment of financial obligations. Spotswood therefore made what was perhaps the boldest stroke of his administration—he called upon the assembly to put a stop to this practice which, besides exercising a sinister influence upon both public and private finance, gave "an unhappy occasion to the breeding up too many persons in a fraudulent way of dealing."[43] A plan of regulation was adopted of which Spotswood claimed to be the sole author,[44] and which he declared, doubtless with truth, was "look'd upon to be the most Extraordinary one that ever pass'd a Virginia Assembly and such an one as those persons to whom I first communicated my thoughts, and to whom the Temper of these Assemblys are well known, believ'd I could never have compassed."[45]

[42] Hening, III, 436, 437. It seems likely that this provision was designed to prevent creditors from refusing payment when the price of tobacco was low. In 1710 a grievance praying that further care be taken to prevent the false packing of tobacco was rejected by the burgesses, on the ground that the law then in force was sufficient. *Jour. Burg.*, 1702-1712, p. 249.

[43] *Ibid.*, 1712-1726, p. 47.

[44] "And if it is likely that you will reap the Advantage, I hope no one will envy me the honour of the Project." Speech of Spotswood to the assembly at the close of the session. *Leg. Jour. Coun.*, I, 570. See also *Letters*, II, 49.

[45] *Ibid.*, pp. 49, 51; *Jour. Burg.*, 1712-1726, pp. 47, 54-68, 73.

This act, "for preventing frauds in Tobacco payments And for the better Improveing the Staple of Tobacco," provided for the erection of warehouses at convenient landing places in the various counties. To these tobacco was brought before it could be exported or offered as legal tender. Here it was examined by the agent, and if found of good quality received, the owner being given certificates specifying the weight and "species"[46] of the tobacco. These certificates were legal tender for all debts and public dues which by law were payable in tobacco. When presented for redemption they entitled the holder to the choice of any hogshead of the right species, chosen without being opened. Not all tobacco was handled in this way. Anyone wishing to export his own tobacco received a note which entitled him to the same hogsheads which he had delivered to the agent. The agent was allowed to surrender tobacco for immediate exportation only, thus reducing to a minimum the opportunity for subsequent fraudulent packing. No shipmaster might receive any hogshead which did not bear the agent's stamp. No one was eligible for the position of agent who had not resided in the colony at least seven years, this being considered the minimum time in which an expert knowledge of tobacco could be obtained. The agent, who had to post a bond of £2000, was paid either five shillings a hogshead or eight per cent of the tobacco handled, at the option of the owner. He received other minor fees and might charge storage on tobacco left with him after May 1.[47] That such sweeping regulations could be obtained from a Virginia assembly indicates the depths to which the tobacco trade had sunk.

The tobacco act had many good points. It insured the payment of quit rents, public levies, ministers' salaries,[48] officers'

[46] That is, whether Oronoco or sweetscented.

[47] *C.O.5/1386*, pp. 55-69.

[48] The convention of the clergy sent a delegation to thank the council and burgesses for the passage of this act, and presented an address to the governor in a body. *Ex. Jour. Coun.*, III, 388, 389. Not only did the act increase the value of the clergyman's salary; it relieved him of the necessity of traveling up and down his parish to collect it in kind. He now received certificates for tobacco deposited at the warehouse. *Letters*, II, 49.

fees, and other dues of a public nature payable in tobacco, in produce of a marketable grade in place of the trash which had often been proffered in the past. It seemed admirably calculated to prevent the exportation of inferior tobacco[49] and thus to reduce the size of the tobacco crop, since high-grade tobacco could not be produced upon all the land under cultivation.[50] By bringing the tobacco into warehouses upon the waterfront it enabled the crop to be laden on board the vessels in half the time formerly required to gather it up at the various plantation landings, and it gave collectors and naval officers an opportunity to supervise the trade such as they had never before enjoyed. It furnished a currency which filled a real need in the colony. Yet the act was not without defects. The task of bringing the tobacco to the warehouses and the charges for having it examined and stored[51] were heavy burdens, against which complaints soon broke out. There was also something to be said against the act from a political point of view. Through it the governor had at his disposal some forty agencies, which were expected, one with another, to yield an annual revenue of about £250 apiece. The governor made no secret of the fact that he proposed to grant these positions to burgesses who had supported the act[52]

[49] The British act of 1714, which went into effect about the same time, worked to the same end by putting a stop to the practice of admitting spoiled tobacco duty free.

[50] The argument of the opponents of the act that it thus reduced the revenue from the trade, while doubtless true enough, can hardly be deemed a count against the act.

[51] Public warehouses, commonly called "rolling-houses," were not new in Virginia. An act of 1712 confirmed all rolling-houses within one mile of public landings, but provided for their future erection within half a mile. Provision was made for the construction of public landings and rolling-houses in the frontier counties, condemnation proceedings being authorized where necessary. The manner of computing storage charges was different from that prescribed by the tobacco act of 1713, but these seem to have been as high, if not higher. The difference was that the act of 1713 made the use of public storehouses obligatory. An act of 1720 made further provision for the convenient location of rolling-houses, and for their use as warehouses for merchandise unloaded from vessels. *Ex. Jour. Coun.*, III, 409-411; Hening, IV, 32-36, 91, 92.

[52] Nicholas Meriwether, burgess for New Kent, was removed from the commission of the peace for having endeavored to turn popular opinion in his county against the act. *Ex. Jour. Coun.*, III, 364.

and to other prominent men. Thus he hoped to enlist the influence of the leading men of the colony in all measures to improve the tobacco trade and to discourage the growth of other industries. There was perhaps nothing pernicious in this, but one sentence in a letter from the governor to the board of trade indicates the danger. "Thereby, I have, in a great measure, I think, clear'd the way for a Gov'r towards carrying any reasonable point in the House of Burgesses."[53] Spotswood can hardly be blamed for endeavoring to remove that thorn in the flesh of all colonial governors, the opposition of the lower house. Yet executive control of the legislature by means of patronage was a menace to healthy political development.[54]

The adoption of the bill by the council was unanimous,[55] but it was passed through the lower house only "w'th some Address and great struggle." Indeed, "the Vulgar's Standard of Right and Wrong" had prevailed so long, that it was not to be expected that all elements in the colony would accept the new regulations with meekness. "He is ye lover of this Country," confided the governor to the board of trade, "who in all Controversies justifies the Virginian, and [in] all Dealings is ready to help him overreach the Forreigner; He is the Patriot who will not yield to whatever the Governm't proposes, and can remain deaf to all Argum'ts that are used for ye raising of Money, and lastly, him they call a poor man's Friend who always carries Stilliards to weigh to the needy Planter's advantage, and who never judges his Tobacco to be Trash." Evidently there was already opposition enough to elicit from the governor typically vigorous invective. The opposition was destined to stiffen; the invective to become more vigorous still.

[53] *Letters,* I, 49. In 1714 twenty-seven burgesses, a clear majority, were tobacco agents, as was also the clerk of the house. *Va. Mag. Hist.,* II, 2-15. The governor was not in complete control of the situation, however. Save when guilty of a misdemeanor no agent might be removed without the assent of the council.

[54] A paper, probably from the hand of William Byrd, criticizing the act clause by clause, is to be found in *C.O.5/1317,* pp. 347-349. See *B. T. Jour.,* 1715-1718, p. 137.

[55] *Letters,* II, 50.

A number of petitions were received by the assembly of 1714 against provisions of the act. It was demanded that packing of good cut and stemmed tobacco be permitted, in place of the requirement that all tobacco be left on the stem and tied in bundles, that exemption be granted from the obligation of carrying tobacco to the public warehouses, that agents be forbidden to engage in trade either as principals or factors, that an extension of time be granted for exporting tobacco under the old regulations, and that other products might be enumerated and valued for the payment of public dues. All these were rejected.[56] The proposition that debts contracted in the past but coming due in the future be paid in the tobacco that was legal at the time that the debt was contracted, or that the difference between the two standards be allowed the debtor, received more favorable consideration. The crops both of tobacco and corn were small in 1714, and shipping appears to have been scarce, so at the instance of the governor an act was passed suspending for a time the operation of parts of the law, and allowing the poorer people more time in which to pay their public dues.[57] The tobacco act of 1713 was continued,[58] but the passage of another act to prevent the malicious burning or destroying of public storehouses of tobacco agents points plainly to the strong opposition against the new regulations.[59]

The storm of opposition against the tobacco act broke with full force when the newly-elected assembly convened in August 1715. Grievances from all but four of the twenty-five counties demanded the repeal of the act, in part or entirely. A bill was thereupon brought in and passed to repeal the act of 1713 and the three acts of 1714 relating to it. All petitions praying for relief under the act were rejected, as was a

[56] *Jour. Burg.*, 1712-1726, pp. 81-86, 91.

[57] *Ibid.*, pp. 81, 87, 97, 100, 116. That this was not designed to reverse the governor's plan, is indicated by the fact that this act imposed a penalty upon the exportation of unstamped hogsheads.

[58] The act went into effect on Nov. 10, 1714 for a period of three years. A motion to continue it for five years was lost. *Ibid.*, p. 91. It was continued to Nov. 10, 1718. *C.O.5/1364*, p. 474.

[59] *Jour. Burg.*, 1712-1726, pp. 83, 116.

bill sent down from the council remedying certain inconveniencies in the tobacco act, and on two different occasions motions to introduce a similar measure into the house were lost. The house was evidently determined to be satisfied with nothing less than outright repeal. To this end they attached to the repealing bill a clause granting an export duty of a shilling a hogshead to furnish a fund for the relief of South Carolina, then in the throes of the Yamasee War. They also passed a bill disabling all persons holding offices of profit under the government from being members of the house of burgesses, the evident intent of which was to prevent burgesses acting as tobacco agents.[60] The repealing measure was rejected by the council, which held that tacking things of a different nature on to a money bill was a breach of the privilege of the upper house, and the disabling bill met with the same fate.[61]

The council, which seems to have given constant support to the new schemes, now made further regulations to be followed by the agents. These prevented an agent from purchasing tobacco brought to him, selecting the hogsheads of best quality. They required a distinctive mark for hogsheads rejected by the agent, and afterwards passed by "view,"[62] this distinction being also noted upon the certificate. Agents were required to keep adequate books and transmit to the naval officer invoices of tobacco delivered for loading on shipboard before the departure of the ships. Agents were restrained from diverting tobacco from other warehouses by passing it at less than the legal rate. The sums to be charged for storage were also regulated. William Bridger, an agent who had signed a grievance against the act, was removed by order of the council. The colonial executive evidently intended to see the new policy through.[63]

[60] *Jour. Burg.*, 1712-1726, pp. 132-147.
[61] *Leg. Jour. Coun.*, II, 599, 600, 603.
[62] That is, by a committee of three freeholders, "reputed to be Skilfull in tobacco."
[63] *Ex. Jour. Coun.*, III, 409-411, 413, 414.

The English merchants were for some time undecided whether to support the tobacco act or to demand its repeal. So great was the depression in the trade that they were ready to welcome any measure which promised relief. Many of them, therefore, were willing to wait and see if the act would raise the quality of Virginia tobacco. Apparently, however, poor-grade tobacco continued to be shipped. This may perhaps at first have been merely that for which certain exceptions had been made in 1714, but as late as 1717 tobacco of too poor a grade to pay customs in Britain continued to arrive. This appears to have been the decisive factor in turning the merchants against the act.[64] It was opposed largely by the same men who were hostile to the Indian act,[65] among them Micajah Perry,[66] John Hyde, and William Byrd.[67] Solicitor-General William Thompson held the act to be contrary to the governor's instruction against passing acts of an unusual nature, though the chief objection against it appeared to be that it was an act in restraint of trade. The board of trade accordingly recommended the tobacco and Indian acts of 1713 and 1714 for disallowance, Perry and Hyde urging haste. The repeal was announced by proclamation in Virginia on November 12, 1717. At the same time colonial governors were instructed not to give their assent to future laws affecting the trade of Great Britain without a suspending clause.[68]

[64] There is a possibility that the merchants, objecting to the other provisions of the act, exaggerated their accounts of the badness of the tobacco in order to secure its repeal. However the letter of Joseph Bentley, a surveyor of Liverpool, complaining to the commissioners of the customs of the trash which was arriving at Whitehaven, has an air of genuineness. *C.O.5/1318*, p. 149. See also B. T. to Gooch, May 27, 1731, *C.O.5/1366*, pp. 71-74.

[65] *Infra*, p. 89 ff.

[66] Perry's opposition may have been delayed by the fact that eighty pairs of scales for the use of the tobacco agents were purchased from him. The agents stood the expense of these scales, and the fact that they were held for money still due on them after the act was repealed may have antagonized the very men whom the governor hoped to win to his interest. *Ex. Jour. Coun.*, III, 370, 380, 445, 456, 457.

[67] *B. T. Jour.*, 1715-1718, pp. 137, 139, 142, 227-230; *C.O.5/1318*, pp. 7-16.

[68] *B. T. Jour.*, 1715-1718, pp. 240-244; *C.O.5/1318*, p. 457; *C.O.5/1364*, pp. 474-476.

The burgesses of 1718, still strongly antagonistic to the governor, refused to adopt any regulations in place of the repealed acts, although they petitioned the crown to reconsider its additional instruction, since this seemed to prevent the passage of revenue bills without a suspending clause.[69] Yet the evils of overproduction again became apparent in the early twenties. A proposition from Surry in 1722 that craftsmen be restrained from planting tobacco was doubtless typical of considerable sentiment in the colony. This was rejected, but an act was passed to prevent the production of trash tobacco.[70] The assembly of 1723 went further and attempted to restrict the tobacco crop by fixing the number of plants which each householder, laborer, and boy might cultivate.[71] This measure, enacted for three years, had the hearty support of both governor and council. Another act, with similar provisions in a somewhat more elaborate form, was passed in 1729. Neither of these acts had the scope of Spotswood's regulations, yet the planters' distaste for that of 1729 was great. In 1732 a Virginia clergyman wrote to the bishop of London that he feared its continuation in force would lead to some civil commotion.[72] It was evidently a Labor of Hercules to devise a set of regulations which would stop the raising of trash, prevent overproduction, and at the same time please both the colonial planter and the British merchant.

A duty of two shillings was levied for every hogshead or other container of tobacco exported from Virginia.[73] Ships stopping at Virginia either to load or discharge cargo were subject to a tonnage duty of one shilling and threepence per

[69] *Jour. Burg.*, 1712-1726, pp. 180, 183, 191, 207, 208.

[70] *Ibid.*, pp. 329, 353.

[71] An account of the tobacco raised in the various counties in 1724, pursuant to this act, was sent by Drysdale to the board of trade. The total output for the colony was 17,732 hogsheads of Oronoco and 17,252 of sweetscented. *C.O.5/1319*, p. 439.

[72] *Va. Mag. Hist.*, XX, 158-178; *Ex. Jour. Coun.*, IV, 45-51; *C.O.5/1319*, p. 227; *Fulham MSS.*, *Virginia 1st. Box*, No. 15.

[73] By Virginia statute a duty of 2*s.* was also imposed upon every 500 pounds of bulk tobacco exported, a provision presumably designed for the colonial trade, since bulk tobacco could not legally be imported into Britain.

ton burden.[74] A poll tax of sixpence was levied for every person, exclusive of the crew, on board incoming ships. All these duties, from which ships owned by Virginians were exempted,[75] were commonly known as the two shillings a hogshead. Compared with the duty levied in England they were a very light burden to trade and their significance is political rather than economic. For a fund was thus provided which was at the disposal of governor and council. Out of this the salaries of officials and the most pressing expenses of government could be paid without the concurrence of the burgesses.[76] Though acts were passed from time to time regulating the duty of two shillings a hogshead, it was a permanent revenue. The governor was obliged by his instructions to refuse his consent to any act which lessened or abolished it, and such act, if passed would have been sure of prompt disallowance in England.

On the other hand, the import duties which were from time to time levied on liquors and slaves were accounted for, not to the receiver-general, but to a treasurer appointed by the assembly, and were at the disposal of that body. Both in England and Virginia it was thought better to raise a revenue by this indirect method than by the ever unpopular poll

[74] This duty was levied regardless of the amount of goods taken aboard or unloaded, exceptions being made by order of the council only upon very rare occasions. *Ex. Jour. Coun.*, III, 332, 348, 501, 502, 513. It was therefore customary for vessels making up their cargo in both Virginia and Maryland to enter in one colony only, and send small vessels, which would pay only a small port duty, for the tobacco they wished to carry from the other. The Maryland authorities made it a practice to demand port duties only in proportion to the amount of tobacco laden in that province. Yet they levied full duties on the small ships taking tobacco to be laden in Virginia, while the Virginia officers appear to have been remiss in demanding duty from similar ships bound for Maryland. Masters therefore found it more profitable to enter in Maryland than in Virginia, even when a greater part of their freight was from the latter province. This situation coming to the attention of the Virginia council, the naval officers were ordered to demand port duties on all vessels carrying tobacco to ships entered in Maryland. *Ibid.*, p. 323; *Letters*, II, 21.

[75] Hening, III, 490-495; *Ex. Jour. Coun.*, III, 453, and *passim*.

[76] The receipts from the sale of treasury rights for land were accounted for with the two shillings a hogshead, since they were at the disposal of governor and council, whereas the quit rents could only be appropriated by warrant from the crown. A table of the revenue of two shillings a hoghshead is to be found in Appendix II.

tax. Instructions were given to the governor to recommend to the assembly a duty upon liquors, but that upon slaves was invariably added for reasons which have already been discussed. By an act of 1705, reenacted in 1710, a duty of fourpence a gallon was placed on distilled spirits imported directly from the West Indies,[77] sixpence a gallon if shipped from elsewhere. A duty of fourpence a gallon was placed upon wine, and one of a penny upon beer, cider, and ale. The exports of Great Britain were exempted from this duty.[78]

By an English statute of 1673, enumerated commodities exported from one colony to another were subject to a duty, roughly corresponding to the "old subsidy" levied in England. This in the case of tobacco amounted to a penny a pound. This duty appears to have been granted in 1711 to William and Mary College.[79]

To facilitate the administration of trade regulations and the collection of duties, Virginia was divided into six districts,[80] for each of which there was appointed a naval officer and a collector. The royal instructions forbade the union of these two offices in the same person, but since the perquisites of the naval officer were scant, he was also constituted receiver of Virginia duties.[81] Naval officers were ap-

[77] Virginia shipowners were allowed to import rum from the West Indies upon their own account at half this duty.

[78] *Hening*, III, 229-235, 482; *Va. Mag. Hist.*, XXI, 113. From 1710 to 1718 the duty on liquors and slaves yielded a revenue of £27,840.14.7 By the latter date so large a balance had been piled up that the duty was discontinued. *C.O.5/1318*, pp. 774, 775.

[79] Beer, *Old Colonial System*, Part I, Vol. I, 80-83; *Letters*, I, 80, 179. In 1720 the burgesses rejected a grievance from Northumberland, complaining of the importation of tobacco into that county from Maryland. It is very doubtful if this tobacco paid the penny a pound duty. *Jour. Burg.*, 1712-1726, p. 256.

[80] These were Upper James, Lower James, York, Rappahannock, Potomac, sometimes called South Potomac, and Accomac, sometimes called Eastern Shore.

[81] *Va. Mag. Hist.*, XXI, 356; *Ex. Jour. Coun.*, III, 249; *Letters*, I, 8. The naval officer was on this account also called "collector," and it is sometimes difficult to tell which officer is being referred to. The appointment of collectors of both the two shillings a hogshead and the duty on liquors and slaves was left by Virginia law to the governor, who was authorized to allow the collecting officer a commission not to exceed ten per cent for the former and six per cent for the latter. Hening, III, 235, 493. Collectors appear to have been appointed by the surveyor-general, the governor making temporary appointments

pointed by the governor with the advice of the council.[82] No member of the council was permitted to hold these posts,[83] and the governor was cautioned against appointing anyone much concerned in trade.[84] These officers were under oath to discharge their duties in person, deputies being permitted only in case of emergency. Naval officers had to be approved by the customs board in England and were required to give bond of £2000 to that body.[85] They were subject to oversight by the surveyor-general of customs for the southern district of America,[86] but since that officer's duties took him out of the colony most of the time, a large share of the actual supervision devolved upon the governor. The tenure of naval officers and collectors was indefinite, there being during Spotswood's time only three instances of removal.[87] Their terms

---

in the surveyor-general's absence. The final confirmation of the appointments rested with the commissioners of the customs.

[82] Spotswood frequently restricted the advice of the council to the formality of answering the governor's question whether they had any objection to his appointee. *Ex. Jour. Coun., passim.*

[83] During the latter part of the preceding century the councillors appear to have monopolized this office. *Ex. Jour. Coun., passim.* Presumably this practice had proven undesirable, for it was forbidden by the crown in 1699.

[84] Spotswood pointed out that a too rigid adherence to this principle would disqualify practically all men of parts, requiring as it did the "ill husbandry" of purchasing European goods in Virginia, at a greatly advanced price. *Letters*, I, 179. In 1717 the board of trade received a representation from several merchants, complaining that Daniel McCarty, collector of South Potomac, was himself engaged in trade, contrary to law, and to the prejudice of other merchants. *C.O.5/1318*, pp. 91, 92.

[85] *Va. Mag. Hist.*, XXI, 356; *Letters*, I, 80.

[86] Quary was *ex officio* member of the councils of the various plantations under his supervision, and upon his appointment Keith asked the same privilege. *C.O.323/7* K. 29.

[87] Gawin Corbin, naval officer of Rappahannock, was in 1711 removed for forging the date of a royal license, permitting the frigate *Robinson*, of which he was part owner, to sail without convoy. Corbin protested his innocence, and went to England to attempt to clear himself. *C.O.5/1316*, O. 89, 90, 95, 107; *Letters*, I, 77-79, 96; B. T. Jour., 1709-1715, pp. 291, 292, 325, 326; *Ex Jour. Coun.*, III, 269, 276. He failed to regain his position, Christopher Robinson being appointed to succeed him. *Letters*, I, 103. Corbin was later one of the governor's most violent opponents in the house of burgesses. John Luke, collector of Lower James, was either late in 1714 or early in 1715 removed for incompetence, while in 1719 Nathaniel Burwell, naval officer of York, was replaced for reasons which are not clear, but which were apparently connected with the dispute between governor and council. *Ex. Jour. Coun.*, III, 512; Robert Carter to Messrs. Perry, July 13, 1720. *Carter Letter Book.*

of office were usually ended by old age or death. They seem in general to have been prominent men of good estate.[88] The offices were not sinecures for, as we have seen, they had to be executed by the incumbent in person. Moreover, since they were far from lucrative, they hardly yielded enough for both sinecurist and deputy.[89] But this very fact raises the question how men of station could afford to devote their time to the execution of an office which brought such small returns. The offices appear to have been in demand and their bestowal regarded as a favor. While there is no evidence reflecting upon the integrity of most of these officers, it is not improbable that some, at least, found it possible to supplement their lawful receipts by a kind of blackmail levied upon illegal traders.

To what extent illegal trade was carried on in Virginia, and indeed in the American colonies in general, can never be known with any exactness. The illicit trader naturally saw to it that he left as few traces as possible; his records are not available, and statistical treatment of the problem is out of the question. Yet petitions of legitimate traders whose interests were being injured, complaints of royal officials who found the enforcement of the acts of trade beyond their power, instructions to governors urging them and their subordinates to renewed vigilance, together with occasional seizures and somewhat rarer condemnations, all point towards the existence of this trade. In 1709 the board of trade received a complaint of illegal trade between the British plantations in America and the Dutch West Indian Islands of St. Thomas and Curaçao. The memorialist declared that it was easy to "steal" a load of tobacco from Virginia, little attention being paid to small vessels running to and fro in the bay along both east and west shores. Most of the small West Indian traders, he said, had either two captains, or had the

[88] *Ex. Jour. Coun.*, III, 249, 365, 375, 428, 531, 532, 539; *Letters*, I, 8, 9 (where John Allen, mentioned in the notes, should be Arthur. See *Ex. Jour. Coun.*, III, 249), 80, 103.

[89] This was particularly true of the Eastern Shore, where, the Virginia duties amounting to about £50, the naval officer's share could not be more than £5. *Letters*, I, 80. His share of the two shillings a hogshead was not much greater.

register in the mate's name, the captain alone knowing the contents of the cargo and the mate swearing at the custom house to such accounts as the captain chose to give him. There were only four customs houses in Virginia, and these were kept by the collectors in their own homes, which were sometimes out of the way for trade. "Many Rivers have No officers to See what is Done by Shiping And But few Places in America But Shipes may land or take in Goods at. And should officers Be placed in all Such places in America 10,000 Men Could not performe it. To Keep Shiping from Landing And taking of Good by Stelth."[90]

After some further investigation, the board of trade gave instructions to Spotswood to do his utmost to prevent and discover this trade.[91] The governor innocently hoped that the trade could be discovered by comparing the clearings of vessels with the certificates of discharge returned from the ports to which they were bound, but he soon found out that vessels, particularly those from New England, made a practice of taking on more tobacco after they had cleared. By this means they not merely avoided paying the two shillings a hogshead, but obtained a supply of tobacco which they could dispose of at foreign ports before proceeding to the port for which they had cleared. The governor questioned seamen regarding clandestine trade, but received little information of value.

The district of Lower James appeared to be the seat of this trade, both by virtue of its proximity to the Capes and because of the incompetence, if not corruption, of its collector, John Luke. The governor thought that this trade might in large measure be prevented by a guardship,[92] and still more

[90] Memorial of Peter Holt, *C.O.323/6*, Bund I, 93.

[91] *B. T. Jour.*, 1709-1715, pp. 111, 114, 115, 121. About this time, at the recommendation of the board, instructions were sent to the governors of the plantations to take measures to stop the treasonable trade with the French West Indies under guise of exchanging prisoners under flag of truce. *Cal. State Paps., Col.*, 1710-1711, p. 85.

[92] The former guardship, H.M.S. *Garland*, had been wrecked upon the Carolina coast, and some delay intervened before H.M.S. *Enterprize* was sent out to replace her.

by a sloop, whose shallower draft would enable her to search inlets and shallows where the larger guardship could not venture.[93] But an even smaller craft was required to search the innumerable small channels and inlets where small trading craft might run ashore and load a few illicit hogsheads. Spotswood therefore submitted to the customs board a plan, approved by the council, whereby the three collectorships of York and James Rivers were to be combined, a single collector being stationed at Williamsburg, which was within a mile of navigable creeks leading to both rivers. The salaries of the other two collectors were to be applied to two searchers, one for York and James, the other for Potomac and Rappahannock.[94] With Surveyor General Robert Quary, to whom the matter was referred by the customs board, Spotswood finally worked out a scheme whereby William Buckner was to be appointed collector for York and James with residence at Williamsburg, at a salary of £100, and Nicholas Curle made searcher at the same salary. The searcher was to keep a shallop, equipped with sails and at least four men, constantly cruising in the bay to detect illegal traders. He was to receive a further allowance of £50 for building a house upon Point Comfort for the use of himself and his successors, this being the best base for his operations. It was thus hoped to render the whole system more efficient, and incidentally to get rid of the incompetent Luke.[95] But these suggestions from the men in touch with actual conditions were apparently disregarded, and things dragged on much as before.

Commerce between British and French colonies being contrary to a treaty of 1686 which went once more into effect after the Treaty of Utrecht, instructions were sent to the governors of the plantations to prevent all such trade. In

[93] *Letters*, I, 9, 10, 15, 18, 19, 87, 88.

[94] Among other things, they were to be provided with steelyards with which to discover hogsheads which had been entered at less than their true weight. But a thorough investigation would have necessitated unloading the entire cargo.

[95] *Ibid.*, pp. 75-77, 88, 112-115; *Cal. State Paps., Col.*, 1710-1711, pp. 242, 243.

the winter of 1714 a French ship, the *Galliard* of Rochelle, was driven into the James in an unseaworthy condition. Contrary to the orders of Spotswood, who feared that such a precedent might attract other foreign vessels upon pretext of distress, Luke authorized the sale of her entire cargo of cotton and indigo. He was thereupon suspended, the sale countermanded, and the French supercargo obliged to ship his goods to London on board a British ship. Nicholas Curle, naval officer of Lower James, had in the meantime died, and Spotswood filled the situation temporarily by the appointment of George Walker, a Quaker, who had acted as Curle's deputy during the latter's sickness. This Luke resented, doubtless because he found Walker's efficiency inconvenient. The governor, however, was well pleased with the Quaker and declared he would have continued him in that office if only he could have "prevail'd with him to lay aside that one Silly Scruple of the word Swear." As it was, he gave Walker a commission as searcher in Lower James district, and since there was no salary attached to that office, Walker petitioned the general assembly for an allowance of £24 per annum out of the duty on liquors to enable him to maintain a boat and four men. This rather modest proposal the burgesses rejected.[96]

Upon Luke's suspension, Keith appointed as his successor Francis Kennedy, who soon found himself in difficulties under the provisions of an act of 1705. This act imposed upon any

[96] *Letters*, II, 103-106, 108; *Jour. Burg.*, 1712-1726, p. 87. The prevention of trade with French colonies became still more urgent in 1717, when Martinique revolted against the French government. It was feared that if the rebels received supplies from the British colonies, amicable relations with France might be interrupted. By a proclamation of November 12, 1717, Spotswood declared that all ships engaging in trade contrary to the treaty would be confiscated. *Ex. Jour. Coun.*, III, 457, 609. The board of trade, however, cautioned him that while French ships trading to Virginia might be confiscated under the Navigation Act, it was its opinion that British ships could not be forfeited merely for trading with the French plantations contrary to treaty, unless such trade was also contrary to British or Virginian laws which imposed the penalty of confiscation. However, the governor was to discourage trading contrary to the treaty. How he was to do this when no penalty could be imposed, the board neglected to state. Board of Trade to Spotswood, July 4, 1718. *C.O.5/1365* pp. 62, 63, 198.

person holding public office in Virginia without three years' residence a penalty of £500, natives of Virginia and officers commissioned directly by the crown alone excepted.[97] Information was exhibited against Kennedy in the Virginia courts to recover the fine. An appeal was made to the customs board in England. The attorney-general declared the act of 1705 void as contrary to the British statute which empowered the commissioners of the customs to appoint any natural-born subject. The customs board recommended that the case be dismissed and the act of 1705 disallowed. When the board of trade investigated the matter Edmund Jennings, president of the council at the time the act passed, testified that it was designed to prevent a governor from disposing of the best positions in the colony to his favorites. The act, however, was not worded to this effect and the board of trade also recommended its disallowance though suggesting that some of its good features be reenacted. The case against Kennedy was thereupon dismissed.[98]

While tobacco was by far the greatest export of Virginia, the peltry derived from the Indian trade also figured in her commerce. The infant production of naval stores was now receiving considerable attention and, thanks to Spotswood's activities at Germanna, pig iron was being added to the list of Virginia's exports. That some corn was exported is indicated by the prohibitions placed upon that trade when the colony faced a shortage, but these same prohibitions bear witness to the fact that the surplus was not very great.[99] What there was, was doubtless sent to the West Indies. By far the greater part of Virginia's tobacco was sent to England, though some was sent to the British plantations and, as we have seen, there is reason to believe that a considerable quantity found its way surreptitiously to foreign ports. Peltry was probably sent mostly to Britain and naval stores entirely so, for only

[97] Hening, III, 250, 252. This act also barred from office former criminals, Negroes, mulattoes, and Indians.

[98] *C.O.5/1317*, pp. 1-4; *C.O.5/1364* pp. 208-212, 224-229, 253-255; *Letters*, II, 143.

[99] *Ex. Jour. Coun.*, III, 222, 374, 498, 499.

thus could the producers obtain the bounties which constituted their chief profit. It is evident that the bulk of Virginia's exports went to Great Britain.

Estimates of Britain's yearly imports from Virginia and Maryland for the period 1715-1723 averaged £310,907.1.6, while her exports to the Chesapeake colonies for the same period amounted to only £160,852.12.5 per annum,[100] leaving a balance of £150,054.9.1. to be accounted for.[101] Much of this balance was presumably absorbed by payments which the colonist made to his British creditor. A considerable part was doubtless canceled by the slave trade, it being likely that the Negroes were paid for either in tobacco, which was forthwith taken to England, or in bills of exchange upon England. Another means by which the colonial surplus was absorbed was the importation of liquors. The tobacco exported to the West Indies doubtless paid for the distilled spirits which Virginia received from thence, but the exportation of tobacco to the Madeiras and Azores was forbidden, and Virginia had to account for the wine which was imported from these islands under the provisions of the Methuen Treaty by some other means. The wine, which cost about seven or eight pounds a pipe, was usually paid for half in British goods and half in bills of exchange upon Lisbon. This was evidently a triangular trade, tobacco being taken to England and ex-

[100] This figure includes practically all legally imported European goods for these, with a few exceptions, had to be received by way of England. The freight from England to Virginia was probably low, being an example of "joint cost." The ships had to make the outward voyage in order to get the tobacco crop, which was bulkier than the manufactured goods which they took out with them, and competition between shippers would thus force the freight down. In fact, it was declared that the planter paid no freight on goods from London and but little from Bristol, it being understood that he would reward the obliging shipowners by consigning to them his tobacco. Jones, *Present State of Virginia*, p. 34.

[101] *British Museum Additional MSS.*, 14035, p. 26. Thus these colonies, like all others which specialized in the production of enumerated commodities, brought an unfavorable balance to the mother country in their direct trade with her. But it was expected that this would be more than counterbalanced by the reexportation of these commodities. This doubtless was what actually happened, for Britain's favorable balance for these years from her trade in general was placed at £19,409,203.15.7., or an average of £2,416,150.9.5. per annum.

changed for British goods and bills upon Lisbon. These were taken to the islands and exchanged for the wine which was brought back to Virginia. Judging from the number of passes which it was deemed necessary to send to Virginia and Maryland to protect vessels engaged in this trade from the attacks of Algerian corsairs (according to Blakiston, seventy, but placed at sixty by Micajah Perry) the commerce with these islands must have been quite extensive.[102] Madeira furnished the common grade of wine, the better qualities being imported from Europe by way of England. Chocolate, tea, and coffee were said to be cheaper in Virginia than in England, even when shipped by way of the mother country, because of the liberal debenture allowed upon reexportation.[103]

Spotswood found Virginia suffering from economic depression, and this condition continued for about four years after the beginning of his administration. There was then a decided change for the better, and during the latter half of his administration the colony enjoyed a very fair degree of prosperity. About the time of his removal another though less severe depression occurred.[104] It was natural, therefore, to associate good times with Spotswood's administration, and one writer, at least, has done this.[105] But the true cause of the economic revival is to be found in the restored peace of Europe and the consequent reopening of the markets for tobacco. The period under consideration was one of transition from the small holding tilled by white labor to the large plantation cultivated by Negro slaves. Such periods of transition are necessarily painful, and the discontented element in the colony, the "rabble" to which the governor referred at times in such deprecating terms, may have been recruited to no

[102] *B. T. Jour.*, 1715-1718, pp. 110-113; 1718-1722, p. 210; *Letters*, II, 138, 139. In 1718 the board asked Spotswood for accounts of the imports from these islands, which he sent them. Unfortunately, these have not been located. *C.O.5/1365*, pp. 41, 42, 202.

[103] Jones, *Present State of Virginia*, pp. 52, 53.

[104] Caused in part at least by the pricking of the South Sea Bubble. Robert Carter to his son John, Feb. 14, 1721. *Carter Letter Book.*

[105] Jones, in his *Present State of Virginia.*

small extent from the ranks of the small holders, who were being thrust to the wall by competition from the large plantations.[106] Yet the prosperity of the generality of the inhabitants of Virginia doubtless compared well with that of any other section of the globe at that time. How far this prosperity was curtailed by the acts of trade and navigation, it is impossible to say. The high duties in England, the prohibition of direct exportation to and importation from foreign countries, and the disqualification of foreign shipping[107] were all economic burdens. But it must be remembered that they were in accordance with the spirit of the times and were far more enlightened than those imposed upon the trade of the colonies of other powers. Nor must the economic aspect of the situation alone be considered for, to some degree, though in a clumsy way, these regulations enabled the mother country to protect her colonies, and by controlling the sea to keep open the channels of trade upon which the prosperity, if not the very existence of the colonies depended.[108] The ability of the mother country, by virtue of her greater prestige in international circles, to obtain by means of treaties concessions favorable to the trade of her colonies must not be overlooked. The Mercantile System cannot be regarded with approval by the modern student of economics, yet it was hardly the mere instrument of selfish tyranny. That it bore as hard upon the American colonist as upon the rank and file of the population at home appears highly improbable.

[106] The small holders controlled the house of burgesses, which was elected upon a bare freehold qualification. The actual representatives were indeed usually men of some standing in the community, but they were naturally obliged, in some measure, to reflect the views of their constituents.

[107] The navigation principle, confining all trade with the colonies to British or colonial built and owned ships of which the master and three-quarters of the crew were British subjects, had a very definite bearing upon naval power. The prime purpose for which it had been introduced, to break up the Dutch carrying trade, had long since been accomplished, however.

[108] It is futile to state the obvious truth that the same end might better have been accomplished by voluntary contributions on the part of the colonies or by their direct taxation by the mother country. The colonists were as quick to resent and resist the latter method as they were reluctant to resort to the former.

Chapter V

INDIAN RELATIONS

A PROTECTING wall of mountains spared Virginia the acute Indian problem which a more open frontier and the presence of powerful confederacies entailed upon some of her sister provinces. Indian fighting she had had, and to spare, but the power of the tribes between the Chesapeake and the Blue Ridge was now broken. Spotswood's survey of the natives living within the bounds of Virginia, which as ambitiously conceived by that government included a liberal slice of North Carolina, revealed nine petty nations, some 700 souls in all, with perhaps 250 warriors. These belonged to three distinct linguistic families, separated by differences in tongue and tradition. The Pamunkey, Chicahominy, and Nansemond were Algonquian, survivors of the powerful Powhatan confederacy. The Nottoway and Meherrin were Iroquoian, and were thus related to the Tuscarora of North Carolina and to the redoubtable Five Nations to the north. The Saponi, Totero, Occaneechi, and Stegaraki belonged to the great Siouan or Dakotan stock, which for the most part had moved west, fleeing before the fury of the Iroquois. Those remaining were hard pressed by their traditional foes. The Virginian Indians all recognized the authority of the government, and had accepted the status of "tributaries." The English had little to fear from them. Yet along the hither edge of the sheltering Blue Ridge ran the Iroquois war trail. Virginia could not be utterly indifferent to Indian affairs.[1]

Some years before Spotswood's time, Robert Boyle, the celebrated natural philosopher, had endowed William and Mary College with a fund of £200 for the education of Indian children. But faith had been broken, and children sold

[1] *Letters*, I, 167; Bureau of American Ethnology, Bulletins Nos. 17, 22, 30.

as slaves. So at least the tributaries affirmed in justification of their reluctance to send any more scholars to Williamsburg. It had therefore been the custom of the governors of the college to purchase children of distant tribes captured in war, so that the college might have the benefit of Boyle's donation. But this was a subterfuge. To Spotswood the education of their children would prepare the way for the civilization and conversion of the tributaries and in the meantime ensure their fidelity, the pupils being hostages for the good behavior of their elders. He set to work. Tidings of the Tuscarora attack upon North Carolina served to redouble his efforts.

Not all the Tuscarora had been concerned in the massacre. To keep disaffection from spreading, detachments of militia were sent among the tributaries. More constructive was Spotswood's scheme to secure as hostages two of the chief men's sons from each of the Indian settlements, somewhat pretentiously known as towns. A treaty with this as one of its provisions was negotiated with the eight friendly Tuscarora towns. To overcome the scruples of the tributaries Spotswood offered to remit the annual tribute of skins, a perquisite of the governors. For a while they hesitated, but by November 1711, the Nansemond, Nottoway, and Meherrin had complied. Thus began that confidence of the Indian in Spotswood which he seems never to have lost. Within a month the Pamunkey, apparently pleased with the treatment the others had received, sent twice the number required as hostages. The Boyle fund was quite inadequate to take care of so many and the house of burgesses signified no inclination to augment it. But the council thought it best to encourage the Indians, and advised that all the children be admitted, in the hope that an appropriation from the general assembly or private donations would enable the college to accommodate them. By December, when Chickahominy scholars arrived, Spotswood could inform the board of trade that there were now hostages from all the towns of the tributaries. The Tuscarora failed to comply with their treaty, but nevertheless the following summer found some twenty Indians at the college, including four who had been purchased before Spotswood's time.[2]

The scholars secured, how were they to be supported? Spotswood first appealed to the assembly, proposing to some of the burgesses "a Project whereby that may be done without any Charge to the Country." But thanks to the disagreement between the two houses over an appropriation to aid North Carolina, nothing was done to forward Indian education.[3]

Spotswood then turned to England. Appealing to both the bishop of London and the archbishop of Canterbury, he declared that it was necessary to have children from each town of the tributaries since, because of diversity of language, only thus could all benefit by their education. He begged that the Boyle fund might be augmented by donations from the Society for the Propagation of the Gospel. Nor was this all. He proposed that ministers be sent to two of the principal Indian towns to exercise the combined functions of missionary and justice of the peace, that a church or chapel and a schoolhouse be built at each, and that an allowance be provided for a schoolmaster. A Mr. Forbes, a clergyman lately arrived from England, was willing to become a missionary "and I know not a fitter person." He hoped that the Society would the more readily enter into these plans since this was the first appeal ever made to them from Virginia. It was unlikely that the assembly would contribute to the evangelization of the heathen "as they value themselves upon furnishing a handsome maintainance to a Number of the Orthodox Clergy equal if not exceeding all the other English plantations on ye Continent."

Henry Compton, the venerable bishop of London, caught the vision. He petitioned the crown for an allowance out of the quit rents for building the churches and for maintaining at least one minister and schoolmaster, hoping that the So-

[2] *Letters*, I, 121-174, *passim*; *Ex. Jour. Coun.*, III, 291-295.

[3] *Jour. Burg.*, 1702-1712, pp. 302, 332, 334; *Leg. Jour. Coun.*, I, 526.

ciety would make provision for the others. He also asked for an allowance sufficient to supply the deficiency in the Boyle fund. An ally was found in William Blathwayt, auditor-general of the plantations. He considered the scheme quite opportune, since France was making efforts to extend her influence among the Indians along the back of the English settlements, thus endangering not only the fur trade but the very security of the English. He thought that the undertaking fell within the province of the S.P.G. Yet, although the quit rents were far overdrawn, he approved of allowing £300 from that fund for building a church and maintaining the minister and his assistant for the first year, and endorsed a further allowance of £150 annually for carrying on the good work if the Society were unwilling to make an allotment for that purpose. The treasury took no action. Compton also pleaded the cause of the Virginia Indian before the S.P.G. They procrastinated. The aged bishop, now too infirm to attend the meetings, wrote to the secretary urging the necessity of immediate action. Nothing was done. Compton's death in 1713 was a severe blow to Spotswood's schemes, his successor John Robinson showing no such interest.[4]

But Spotswood was not discouraged. Lack of resources must be offset by thriftier management. In one direction retrenchment seemed feasible. It was customary in troubled times for troops of rangers to patrol the frontier. Upon the outbreak of the Tuscarora War in 1711, the council appointed an officer and ten men in each frontier county to range three days a week "above the inhabitants." When the assembly met, Spotswood's recommendation that these rangers be paid encountered the customary rejection accorded by the burgesses to debts incurred without their assent. But the assembly now authorized governor and council to appoint rangers, drafted if necessary from the militia. These were exempted from local taxes and paid out of the public levy. The frontier was accordingly divided into eleven districts,

[4] *Letters*, I, 156, 174-178; P. R. O.—*Treas.* 64/90, pp. 82-85; Perry, p. 192.

each with a lieutenant and eleven men. Conscription was not a tradition in Virginia, and the pay proving too small an inducement the government, rather than resort to the draft, encouraged volunteers by permitting them to take up wild horses within the limits of their range. The following year the pay was increased.[5] But the ranging service was unpopular, expensive, and ineffective. If one could convince the assembly that the frontier could be better defended at a smaller cost by the elimination of this distasteful system, surely they would cooperate. So thought the governor, and this time he was not to be disappointed.

His new plan was to consolidate the scattered communities of the tributaries. They would then be strong enough to resist attack, and the work of the missionary and the schoolmaster could be carried on among them more effectively. Conditions favored his policy. Fear of their Iroquoian foes had obliged the Siouan tribes to rely upon the English for protection. The Saponi, abandoning their exposed location at the foot of the mountains, had in 1708 been accepted by President Jennings as tributaries. They were settled on the Meherrin as a barrier against the Tuscarora. Similar motives induced them to unite with the other petty Siouan tribes. In December 1711, the Saponi, Occaneechi, and Stegaraki expressed a desire to live together, and petitioned for a tract of land north of the Meherrin River above the Tuscarora trading path. The following April the chief of the Totero received leave for the remainder of his nation to join them. All the Siouan peoples within the colony were now united, and may be referred to collectively as Saponi. This group, staunchly loyal to the English, provided the nucleus for the new order.[6]

At this juncture the Tuscarora again played a part, fleeting but decisive, in the evolution of Spotswood's Indian pol-

[5] *Ex. Jour. Coun.*, III, 286, 296; *Jour. Burg.*, 1702-1712, pp. 309, 310, 328, 330, 331; Hening, IV, 9-12.

[6] Jennings to Sunderland, Sept. 20, 1708, Huntington Library, HL2021; *Ex. Jour. Coun.*, III, 188, 296, 310.

icy. In March 1713, they sustained a crushing defeat at the hands of James Moore and his mixed force of whites and Indians from South Carolina. Large numbers fled to Virginia and were soon committing depredations along the Roanoke. The alarm which they created was heightened by the belief that they were in league with the northern Indians. Spotswood ordered out several parties against them without success. The governor then resolved to lead in person an expedition of 200 volunteers from the militia of the threatened counties. But the frontiersman's aversion to military expeditions was not to be overcome by "the encouragem't of 12d. a day pay, together with provisions and ammunition and the conveniency of Tents." To his great chagrin Spotswood was not able to induce even this modest number to follow him, and seeing the futility of attempting to subdue the Indians by force of arms, he sent out some fifty tributaries under the command of two Indian traders to locate the Tuscarora and make overtures of peace. They were found at the head of the Roanoke, without food, afraid to return to North Carolina, and eager to make peace as tributaries of Virginia. They numbered some 1500 souls, and the governor prudently realized the folly of imposing hard terms upon them, which might provoke them to acts of violence or drive them to unite with their kinsmen the Five Nations. He therefore agreed to receive their great men at Williamsburg.[7]

In the meantime the ranging service had proven far from satisfactory for, despite the number of parties engaged, some twenty inhabitants and tributaries had been killed or captured by hostile Indians. Spotswood hoped that the treaty with the Tuscarora would be concluded while the assembly was in session during the fall of 1713 but the Indians proceeded with the negotiations in their wonted leisurely manner, and the governor saw that the transition from one plan of frontier defense to the other could not come before the close of the session. Happily at this time the assembly was working

[7] *Letters*, II, 34, 37, 41, 42; *Ex. Jour. Coun.*, pp. 350, 351, 357, 358.

harmoniously with him, and he was given a free hand to carry out his plans. The act for appointing rangers was continued, but at his request the governor was authorized to disband them if he saw fit, and to apply the appropriation for their pay to other measures for the security of the frontier. He was also given the disposal of over £700, the balance of a fund raised for the relief of Carolina which, thanks to misunderstandings between the two governments, remained unexpended. "The two Points I will have in View," said Spotswood to the burgesses, "shall be the Lessening the present charge for future Years And the Setling the Indian Trade So as it may be free and Open to all persons," significant words in the light of future events, for in order to achieve the former end the governor found it necessary to forego the latter.[8]

By December the governor had disbanded five parties of rangers and reduced the rest to ten men each. In the meantime the council was discussing the details of the plan for colonizing the tributaries. At length, on February 26, 1714, the duly qualified deputies of the Tuscarora arrived at Williamsburg. The following day the government concluded three treaties, one with the Nottoway, another with the Saponi, a third with the Tuscarora. For each the governor was to a select a reservation the equivalent of six miles square, upon which the Indians might build a fort and town and make other improvements. Whenever the advance of the English settlements made it necessary for the Indians to move, they were to receive an equal reservation elsewhere, together with compensation for their improvements. The land was to be held in common and all leases and sales to the English were to be void. The governor, however, was empowered to set aside a tract not exceeding 2000 acres for the support of religious and educational work among them. If the Indians decreased in number their reservations might be reduced, but not below 100 acres per person. The Nottoway

[8] *Letters*, II, 43, 51; *Jour. Burg.*, 1712-1726, pp. 47, 63, 64, 67, 68, 70.

were to be located between the Appomattox and the Roanoke, the Saponi to the south of the James, and the Tuscarora between the James and the Rappahannock. These last were thus deliberately excluded from the Roanoke region, for it was felt that they could never be satisfactory tributaries of Virginia if they remained in contact with their old home, North Carolina. The Indians were given the right to hunt on the unpatented land in the colony, the Northern Neck excluded. All between the Rappahannock and the James was assigned to the Tuscarora; that between the James and the Roanoke was to be divided by the governor between the Nottoway and the Saponi.

The Tuscarora agreed to become tributaries of Virginia, to occupy their new reservation within seven months, and to deliver twenty hostages. Beyond this the three treaties were similar. The governor promised to negotiate a treaty with the Seneca[9] to secure the tributaries from attack. They in turn pledged themselves to hold no intercourse with foreign Indians without the governor's consent, to give the government timely warning of invasion or plot against it, and to hold themselves in readiness to march with the forces of Virginia against all enemies whatsoever. An officer and twelve men were to be posted at each fort. These, it was hoped, by acting as spies upon the movements of the Indians, would protect the frontier at one-fifth the cost of the ranging service, and when the civilization of the Indians had reached a sufficiently advanced stage, might be dispensed with altogether. No Indian was to leave the reservation or visit the towns of the other tributaries without permission. Public fairs were to be held at each settlement at least six times a year; they were to be open to all British subjects, and were to be supervised by the magistrates. When a minister and schoolmaster should be installed at these three settlements, all the children were to be instructed in the English language and the Christian religion. In the meantime

[9] This term seems sometimes to have been used to designate Iroquois in general.

the Tuscarora and the Nottoway were each to send twelve boys of their principal families to Saponi Town as soon as a school was established there. Indians guilty of felony were to be delivered up to be punished according to the laws of Virginia. Lesser offenses and petty disputes were to be tried by judges appointed by the governor. The governor remitted the annual tribute of skins, retaining only the nominal acknowledgment of three arrows.[10]

Within a month it was found necessary to revise the new plan. The Tuscarora, having patched up a peace with North Carolina, refused to deliver the stipulated hostages and returned, for the most part, to that province. This aroused the Viriginia ire against Carolina, but Spotswood by attempting to win the Tuscarora from their allegiance to Carolina had certainly placed himself in the wrong. The treaty indeed excluded from its benefits those concerned in the Carolina massacre and the murders committted since that time, and Spotswood wrote to Pollock that the Indians said they had been in Virginia since the outbreak of hostilities. But these seem mere sops to the Virginia conscience, for Indians recently hostile were evidently present in large numbers. Some Tuscarora remained and were given permission to incorporate with the Nottoway, with whom the Meherrin were also to be joined. They were to be settled between the Roanoke and the James, while the Saponi were to be located upon the Roanoke. The council decided to incorporate the Nansemond with the Saponi, but what success attended this attempt to merge Algonquian with Siouan is not known. The gap left by the departing Tuscarora was filled by the colony of Germans which Spotswood established that summer at Germanna.[11]

The summer of 1714 was a busy one. Spotswood spent

[10] *Cal. State Paps., Col.,* 1712-1714, pp. 306-312; *Ex. Jour. Coun.,* III, 363-366; *Letters,* II, 57, 58.

[11] *Letters,* II, 70; *Ex. Jour. Coun.,* III, 367, 368, 373; *Cal. Va. State Paps.,* I, 165 (where the date of Spotswood's letter to Pollock is obviously March 19, 1714, not 1713.)

eight weeks on the frontier, and traveled over eight hundred miles. When the assembly met in November he was able to report considerable progress. A fort had been erected at Christanna on the south side of the Meherrin River, and a tract laid out there for the Saponi. On the opposite bank a reservation was provided for the Nottoway and Meherrin, who had found the tract at the head of the James too barren to live upon. An officer and twelve men were stationed at the fort, who with an equal number of Indians were to perform the ranging service between the Roanoke and the Appomattox. Thus the region most subject to attacks from the Tuscarora was secured. The rangers for Prince George were disbanded, while the remaining troops, four in number, were reduced to six men each, and Spotswood could say that the cost of guarding the frontier had been cut one-third. At the same time its effectiveness had been greatly increased, the outlying settlements now being free from alarms. Spotswood pointed out that with a little care the strength of the barrier against attack might continue to increase at decreasing cost, for if the settlement of the Germans was sufficiently encouraged, more of their countrymen might be induced to join them, and when the tributaries were won over to Christianity, it would no longer be necessary to retain a troop of Europeans in their midst. This could not be expected at once, but Spotswood declared himself content "to think Posterity may Reap the benefit thereof."[12] The assembly seemed well pleased and promised financial aid for another year. But the governor informed them that this would not be necessary, since his economies had left a balance sufficient to pay for two years the officer and twelve men at Christanna and the other four troops of six rangers each. It would also suffice to defray the cost of the fortifications at Christanna and Germanna, of the road to the latter, of surveying the Indian reservations, of the Indian treaties, of the governor's expe-

[12] *Letters*, II, 99, 100; *Ex. Jour. Coun.*, III, 376; *Jour. Burg.*, 1712-1726, pp. 79-80; *William and Mary College Quarterly*, Ser. 2, III, 42.

dition that summer—in short, of the government's entire frontier activities.[13]

The phenomenon of a royal governor declining the proffered appropriation of a colonial assembly is sufficiently uncommon to demand explanation. While the house of burgesses then in session was friendly, Spotswood had reason to believe that its successor would be less tractable. By yielding a temporary grant he might secure a settlement which a future hostile legislature would be powerless to touch. The governor had two irons in the fire. The first concerned the permanent revenue of the government. The two shillings a hogshead had for some years shown a deficit, and it was now proposed that another grant be made to supplement it. But the burgesses scrupled to erect so powerful a buttress to the royal power in Virginia. The second measure, however, that more directly affecting the frontier, was acceded to. This was a project no less comprehensive than the erection of a monopolistic Indian company. By this means it was hoped not only to revive the fur trade, but to facilitate Spotswood's Indian policy and, most important of all, place it on a self-supporting basis.

Since the Virginia tributaries were few in number and their hunting grounds restricted by the mountain barrier to the west, the peltry which they were able to offer in trade was limited. By far the greater part of Virginia's fur trade was carried on with the tribes of the southwest, which could be reached only by passing through the back country of the Carolinas. Pack trains would set out carrying rum, coarse cloth, guns, hatchets, beads, powder, shot, and other goods of European manufacture, and would return laden with skins of bear, beaver, buck, fox, mink, muskrat, and raccoon.

Rum and bad faith were poor foundations for permanent trade relations. But the trader was not always farsighted. Regulation by mutually jealous provincial governments left much to be desired. Virginia had enacted in 1705 a rather inadequate code. South Carolina, to whom the preservation

[13] *Jour. Burg.*, 1712-1726, p. 103.

of friendly relations with the Indians was a very much more vital problem, made more sweeping regulations in 1707. This precipitated an intercolonial quarrel. From Carolina's viewpoint it might seem essential to peace that all traders proceed first to Charleston, there to pay an annual fee of £8 and post a £100 bond; and equitable that duties be paid by all upon both imported Indian goods and exported skins. To the Virginia trader the long journey to Charleston was as intolerable as the added financial burden. President Jennings complained to the board of trade which, predisposed in favor of a royal colony, urged Virginia's case in a representation to the crown. The Virginia trade was of long standing; the western Indians were not under the government of Carolina; intercolonial duties on European goods had ever been and should still be discouraged; Virginia's Indian goods were imported direct from England, whereas it was to be feared that those used by Carolina were secured through an illegal trade with Curaçao and St. Thomas in rum and spirits; lacking the shipping facilities of Virginia the Carolinians would have to drive harder bargains with the Indians; this would drive them to trade with the French on the Mississippi, a danger which the cheapness of British goods would avert if only free trade were preserved. An order in council was accordingly issued directing the proprietors of Carolina to instruct their governor to allow the Virginians freedom of trade. However, the Carolinians continued to seize the goods of such Virginia traders as failed to comply with their regulations. And, to leave no doubt as to its attitude, the legislature of South Carolina passed in 1711 an act specifically applying to the Virginia traders the provisions of that of 1707, which had not mentioned them by name. Spotswood complained to the board of trade, and the proprietors were again admonished, with apparently as little effect as before.[14]

The prevalence of trade with hostile Indians also oc-

[14] Hening, III, 464-469; Cooper, *Statutes at Large of South Carolina*, II, 309-316, 357-359; *Acts of Privy Coun., Col.*, II, 611-614; *B. T. Jour.*, 1709-1715, pp. 73, 397; *Letters*, I, 112; *C.O.5/1316*, O.25, 26, 47.

casioned intercolonial friction. Indians attacking one colony usually found it all too easy to secure supplies of war from another, and there was probably truth enough in Spotswood's statement that this led the Indians to believe that the colonies were not under separate governors only, but also separate sovereigns, and would therefore not aid one another. Carolina was accused by Spotswood of trading with "hostiles," and Virginia was certainly an offender in this respect. Nor did the menace lie solely in deliberate trading with the enemy, for caravans designed for friendly tribes might be captured by the Tuscarora and their confederates. Unable to secure legislation against trade with the Indians, the governor had to prohibit this traffic by proclamation; but the numerous complaints of illegal trade, orders for prosecution of illegal traders, and other attempts to abate the evil point to the futility of such proclamations. It was impossible to control the small traders backed, as they seem to have been, by public opinion. Indeed, as the governor and council saw full well, a prolonged prohibition of trade with all Indians whatsoever was likely to mean that Virginia would lose that trade altogether, for it was to be feared that South Carolina and, what was worse, the French, were improving this opportunity of diverting this profitable traffic toward themselves. In June 1712, therefore, a proclamation was issued permitting trade with the western Indians, each trader giving bond of £300 not to trade with the Tuscarora, and to observe whatever rules the governor should make. No trade in powder or shot was permitted with the tributaries except according to the licenses granted the respective nations. The tributaries were directed to seize all whites attempting to trade with the Tuscarora. An effort made in the fall of 1712 to pass an act prohibiting trade with this nation suffered the fate of former attempts.[15]

By 1714 Virginia's commerce with the Indian was at a

[15] *Letters*, I, 117, 118, 171; II, 18, 25; *Jour. Burg.*, 1702-1712, pp. 328, 329, 350, 355; 1712-1726, pp. 10, 21, 28, 29; *Ex. Jour. Coun.*, III, 315, 316, 324, 366; *C.O.5/1316*, O. 129.

low ebb. William and Mary College, deriving a considerable part of its revenue from an export duty on skins and furs, suffered in consequence. To revive the trade, and to forward Spotswood's other Indian reforms, the Virginia Indian Company was established.[16]

The idea of a company which would have a monopoly of Virginia's Indian trade did not originate with Spotswood. Nicholson, in so many respects Spotswood's prototype, had sponsored such a policy. In fact later, when the company was under fire, Spotswood declared that the project was none of his, but had been introduced by some of the Indian traders. It is difficult, however, to avoid the conclusion that the scheme took form in the fertile brain of the governor.[17]

By the *Act for the Better Regulation of the Indian Trade* all commerce between inhabitants of Virginia and the Indians, tributaries living north of the James alone excepted, was confined to Fort Christanna. A monopoly of this trade for twenty years was granted to the Virginia Indian Company, authorized by this act subject to final incorporation by the crown. In return the company was to undertake various public services, for the non-performance of which it might be heavily fined, or even dissolved. It was to contribute £100 towards building a magazine at Williamsburg, and was to take thence all the powder used in the Indian trade, returning in its place a like supply of fresh powder. It was to erect a schoolhouse for the Indian children at Christanna, and at the end of two years was to assume the entire burden of maintaining the garrison and keeping up the fortifications there. Indians who had received an education either at the college or at Christanna might be admitted to any place of trust or profit under the company. But there was no intent to lower racial barriers. No Indians without passports might come within 300 yards of an English house, and the English were forbidden to receive them. *Bona fide* traders from other colonies might par-

[16] *C.O.5/1316*, O. 26; *C.O.5/1317*, pp. 364, 365; *Letters*, 11, 19, 25.
[17] *Cal. State Paps., Col.*, 1689-1692, p. 381; 1699, p. 314; 1701, pp. 638, 639; *Jour. Burg.*, 1695-1702, p. 169; *Letters*, II, 230.

ticipate in the trade at Christanna. The governor was given wide discretion in establishing the new régime. He might at any time prohibit trade entirely, now with some prospect of success. Trading with hostile Indians was made treason.[18]

Spotswood, it would seem, had taken Albany as his model. He pointed out to the board of trade that by confining trade to one place where all transactions were to be in open market fraudulent dealings with the Indians would be prevented. The prospect of sharing in the trade would give the tributaries an incentive to settle upon the new reservations provided for them close to the fort. He added that it was impossible for the trade of Virginia to be revived by small traders with little or no capital who, purchasing their goods on credit at a high price, had to drive hard bargains with the Indians in order to make both ends meet. This could only be achieved by a company with a greater capital than any one person could command.[19]

Spotswood did not wait for the organization of the Indian Company to continue his activities upon the frontier. He secured the services of a schoolmaster, Charles Griffin, to work among the Indians at Christanna at a salary of £50 a year, which the governor paid out of his own pocket. All the Saponi children were to attend school, and twelve Nottoway scholars were to meet with them until a school was built at their town. The governor offered the Rev. Alexander Forbes, already mentioned, the salary of £80 to serve at Christanna, "but his retiring soon after into a married State, . . . chang'd his inclinations." He was also at this time discussing with the recently appointed bishop of London, John Robinson, the chartering of a Virginia branch of the S. P. G., to be composed of twenty-five of the most influential men in the colony. He renewed his applications for funds from the S. P. G. and also from the quit rents, pointing out that without such aid the work he had undertaken must fail as soon as he was removed from office. The desired subsidies in aid of

[18] *CO.5/1386*, pp. 80-83.
[19] *Letters*, II, 94, 95.

Christianizing the Indians were not forthcoming, but Spotswood assured the bishop that he had "not given over the prosecution of that design," and promptly renewed his requests that his lordship use his influence to obtain either from the crown or the S. P. G. "some Fund for carrying on y't work hereafter," for "tho' during my continuance here I shall very readily contribute my Assistance towards it . . . you know I am only here during pleasure." May 1716 found him asking again for a missionary and enlarging upon the eagerness of the Indians to receive instruction. A good glebe had been set aside, and many settlers, attracted by the fertility of the soil, were locating near Christanna, over sixty miles from any parish church. If a missionary were given the usual allowance from the S. P. G., contributions from these settlers and from the Indian Company would "make his Circumstances very easy."[20]

The task of settling three hundred Saponi at Christanna was rapidly performed, and the enrollment in Griffin's school soon exceeded seventy. The kindly pedagogue soon won the affection of the Indians. The children learned to read the Bible, to write, and to say their catechisms. The tradition of centuries was not overcome in a year. The war dance and the sweating house remained. What, indeed, had the medical science of the day to offer in place of the latter? And as to economic progress, Fontaine could write in 1716 that the Christanna Indians lived "as lazily and miserably as any people in the world." But a start had been made in the right direction.[21] The Nottoway and the Meherrin fitted less readily into the new order. These Iroquoian peoples, usually on good terms with their powerful kinsmen the Tuscarora and the Five Nations, had less occasion than the Saponi to be subservient to Virginia. Their settlements had now become surrounded by those of the English, and the consequent friction was a menace to peace. Spotswood had determined to

[20] *Letters*, II, 63, 64, 90-93, 138, 158, 159.

[21] *Ibid.*, pp. 113, 114, 141; Jones, *Present State of Virginia*, pp. 14, 15; Ann Maury, *Memoirs of a Huguenot Family* (New York, 1872), pp. 272-281.

isolate Indian from European, and the Nottoway and Meherrin were ordered to move to their new reservation at Christanna. Suspicious of the Saponi, they objected, and the government resorted to strong measures to compel them to obey.[22]

It was never intended that the Virginia Indian Company should place the fur trade in the hands of a clique of government favorites. The books were laid open for subscriptions on December 24, 1714, the day the governor assented to the act. The law provided that before March 1 not less than £50 or more than £100 should be received from any one person. Since the initial capitalization was to be £4000 (the company was empowered to increase it to £10,000), this would have meant a membership of between forty and eighty. Those formerly engaged in the Indian trade, with the notable exception of William Byrd, who was at this time about to leave for England, were urged to invest in the new enterprise. It would seem, however, that they declined so to do, and used their influence in dissuading others, so that by March 1 none of the stock had been taken. It was felt that the company had been placed under so many obligations that it could not be made profitable, or at least that private trading would yield higher dividends. Facing the prospect of the failure of his scheme, Spotswood appealed to the public spirit of a number of the leading men of the colony. Councillors, burgesses, and merchants responded—we know the names of twenty[23],—and the company was formed. His statement in 1713 to President Pollock of North Carolina that he deemed it "below the dignity of one of her Matys governors to be a Trader" notwithstanding, Spotswood invested £100, and was elected governor of the company. His enemies accused him

[22] *Ex. Jour. Coun.*, III, 396, 400, 401.

[23] The following are known to have been members of the Virginia Indian Company: John Baylor, Peter Beverley, Arthur Bickerdale, Richard Bland, Charles Chiswell, William Cocke, William Cole, William Dandridge, Cole Diggs, Nathaniel Harrison, John Holloway, Robert Innes, Henry Irwin, Thomas Jones, Edmund Kearney, Thomas Nelson, Mann Page, William Robertson, Alexander Spotswood, and E. Walker. *C.O.5/1317*, pp. 385-390; *C.O.5/1318*, pp. 61-90; *Fulham MSS. Virginia*, Box 1, No. 139.

of using the name of his housekeeper to obtained a larger holding. To this the governor returned an emphatic but ambiguous denial.[24]

The company was apparently an active organization from the first. The school at Christanna was promptly built and half the cost of the new powder magazine was paid to the treasurer of Virginia. Except for that used by the government of Virginia the company disposed of all powder from the magazine, even that supplied to the governments of North and South Carolina in 1715 passing through its hands. Various improvements necessary for the carrying on of the trade, such as warehouses, bridges, and roads, were constructed. After December 1716 the company assumed the cost of the fortifications and garrison at Christanna, and apparently also relieved the governor of paying Griffin's salary as school teacher. By promising the tributaries, and later the western Indians, goods at reduced rates, the company gave them an additional incentive to send their children to school.[25]

While thus performing valuable public services, the Virginia Indian Company could not forget that the foremost function of a trading company was commerce. The Yamasee War was impeding trade with the western Indians, many of whom had taken up arms against South Carolina. It therefore became of paramount importance to secure the allegiance of the western Indians, and Spotswood was expecting, as early as March 1715, to meet their deputies during the summer. The king of the Sara made two trips to Viriginia that year, asking permission to settle on the outskirts of Virginia, and seeking also for the Catawba a treaty which would establish free trade with Virginia. The governor declined to make peace until the chief men of that nation should themselves come to Virginia, fearing that otherwise the treaty might be disregarded and the supplies obtained from Virginia used against Carolina.

[24] *B. T. Journal*, 1715-1718, p. 165; *Letters*, II, 209; *C.O.5/1317*, pp. 385-390; *C.O.5/1318*, pp. 61-90; *Cal. Va. State Paps.*, I, 173.

[25] *C.O.5/1317*, pp. 385-390; *Letters*, II, 144, 145, 237, 238; *Ex. Jour. Coun.*, III, 399, 400, 402.

But the western Indians appeared to be tired of war, into which they said they had been drawn by the threats of the Yamasee, and the following April the king of the Sara returned with the great men of the Catawba and of some minor affiliated tribes. These peoples, who like the Saponi spoke a Siouan tongue, agreed to deliver up as hostages some of their children to be educated at Christanna as the price of being granted freedom of trade. Even before the treaty was concluded the council, hearing that peace had been made between South Carolina and all the western Indians except the Yamasee and the Creek, permitted the company to trade with all Indians not actually at war with South Carolina. At the same time, April 1717, the Sara, whose part Spotswood had taken the previous year in a quarrel with North Carolina, were permitted to settle at the head of Roanoke River, they delivering up the customary hostages to be educated at Christanna. When the Catawba finally arrived with the hostages at Christanna, an untoward event nearly brought negotiations to a disastrous close. The western Indians met the governor at the fort, and according to the usual custom gave up their arms, placing themselves under the protection of the English. They then camped outside the fort, where in the early morning they were attacked by a party of Mohawk, five being killed, two wounded, and five carried off as prisoners. The western Indians naturally thought they had been betrayed by the English, and it doubtless taxed the governor's ingenuity to persuade them to depart peacefully, leaving their hostages at Christanna. Even so, retaliation was feared and the company, which had prepared a trading expedition at an expense of nearly £3000, found it difficult to induce its men to set out, although they were to be at least forty strong.[26]

When the assembly met in August 1715, it proved hostile. While most of the opposition was directed against the governor's efforts to improve the staple of tobacco, nine counties

[26] *Letters*, II, 108, 109, 127, 128, 135, 236, 237; *Ex. Jour. Coun.*, III, 406-443 *passim*.

sent propositions and grievances against the *Act for the Better Regulation of the Indian Trade.* A bill was brought in to oblige the Indian Company to defray the whole cost of the trade, which it already did, to pay the Indian interpreters and other incidental charges, and "at their proper cost" to "defend the Country against the Invasions or Incursions of all Indians whatsoever." The bill passed the house unamended, but survived only one reading in the council, though not a member of the company was present. The action of the burgesses did not necessarily reflect their attitude toward the Indian trade. There were doubtless those, particularly would-be independent traders, who were opposed to the company, but the perfunctory manner in which the act was passed savors more of politics than of constructive legislation. In the famous speech which closed the session Spotswood declared that it was proposed "That the Act for Regulating Trade and Propagating the Christian Faith among the Indians, Shall be abrogated, the School for teaching their Children be Demolished, and the Gent'm at whose charge it was Erected, be Banished out of *America.*"[27]

More inimical to the Indian Company, which purchased its goods through its own factors in London,[28] was the opposition of English merchants who were thereby ousted from the lucrative rôle of middlemen. Those who, ignorant of the new regulations, sent cargoes of Indian goods to Virginia, had their resentment quickened by the dilemma of selling to a monopolist or reshipping to England. Many arguments against the company were presented to the board of trade. To monopolize trade, it was contended, violated the rights of the subject; to erect corporations, those of the crown. An unfortunate precedent was thus set for other colonies to follow. Monopolies were not the means whereby trade was revived, but were destructive to it. The company, formed like other monopolies for the purpose of extorting unreasonable gain, would, it was speciously argued, raise the price of its

[27] *Jour. Burg.*, 1712-1726, pp. 155, 158, 160, 167; *Leg Jour. Coun.*, II, 605.
[28] *B. T. Jour.*, 1715-1718, p. 230.

commodities so high that the Indian trade would be driven from the royal province of Virginia to the proprietary provinces of Maryland and Carolina, or even to the French. This, by lessening the consumption of British goods, would be a blow to British industry. The contribution of the company to the conversion of the Indians was liberally discounted. "Companys never Contributed much to the Propagating of Christian Faith as hath been Experienced by Our African Company, the Dutch East India Company, and others which might be enumerated, unless when they have gotten Possession of a Trade Exclusive of others, they Sett the Several Nations of Infidells to Warrs to destroy One another in order for Private Gain to the great dishonour of the very name of Christians." Surely the king's government could carry on this work as well as traders and planters. The education of Indians and the support of the college ought to be met, as formerly, by the duty on skins and hides. Things were at a pretty pass if the government could not control private traders or care for its munitions without the aid of a company. "Therefore We humbly Submit to Your Lordships Consideration whether there is or can be anything more in this intended Company but to introduce Stock-Jobbing and Monopolys into the Plantations to Serve Some few designing Men, and to Embroil and trick others through the Specious Pretence of Propagating Christian Faith, retrieving Commerce, Supporting a Colledge, and Securing the peace of a Collony." Nor was this all. "This Company (as We are informed) have and are fitting out Sloops to trade with the Dutch and French for Rum and Sugar, and . . . We are not without Apprehensions but that the Tobacco and the Rumm and Sugar Trade and going upon Wrecks, will all fall under this New Company's Management."[29]

It is to be doubted if such scurrility had much effect upon the board of trade, which seems to have sifted carefully the evidence presented.[30] Upon certain grounds, however, it took

[29] *C.O.5/1317*, pp. 185, 345, 351, 371-374, 405, 407; *C.O.5/1364*, pp. 294-298.

[30] *B. T. Jour.*, 1715-1718, p. 142.

exception to the act. It correctly regarded the strength of the French in Canada as being in a large measure due to their living among the Indians and intermarrying with them, and wishing the English to do likewise, it was opposed to the restrictions placed upon the intercourse between Indian and white. Upon his going to Virginia, Spotswood appears to have entertained similar views, but he was not long in discovering that "the inclinations of our people are not the same with those of that Nation, for notwithstanding the long intercourse between ye Inhabitants of this Country and ye Indians, and their living amongst one another for so many Years, I cannot find one Englishman that has an Indian Wife, or an Indian marryed to a white woman." He told the board that the frontiers were largely peopled by redemptioners who had served their time, adding "It is pretty well known what Morals such people bring with them hither, which were not like to be much mended by their Sictuation, remote from all places of worship." These people, he declared, by debauching and cheating the Indians, were the cause of most of the trouble on the frontier, for "it is a very generall observation, both here and the neighbouring Provinces, that no murders or hostilitys have ever been committed by the Indians unless where the English have given the first provocation." Indian attacks always descended upon those parts of a colony with which the natives were most familiar. "They have naturally an opinion of the power of the English, but when they are permitted to come frequently among the Inhab'ts, to see the weakness and scattering manner of living of many Familys on the frontier plantations, these Impressions wear off, and they become encourag'd thereby to all those bloody Attempts they have heretofore made." The recent attacks on North and South Carolina were, he declared, cases in point.[31]

An even more serious objection was seen by the board in the incompatibility of the bill with the 16th, 100th, and 101st clauses of the governor's instructions. Spotswood defended himself by declaring that the only unusual feature of

[31] *C.O.5/1364*, pp. 379, 380; *Letters*, II, 114, 226-228.

the act was the erection of the Indian Company, and the clause providing for this might be repealed by the crown without impairing the operation of the rest of the act. He denied that commodities had been engrossed otherwise than in accordance with the will of the majority of the inhabitants. To reconcile this act with the instruction that the Indian trade was to be free to all subjects in Virginia taxed the ingenuity of the governor, but he justified his action on general grounds of expediency, and said that, since investment in the company had been open to all, if any were excluded they had themselves to blame. Apparently forgetting that Sir Edward Northey had declared it inoperative in time of peace, the board also sent to Spotswood two clauses of the act for the encouragement of trade to America,[32] with which they evidently considered the Indian act incompatible. Spotswood's defense rested mainly upon the contention that the conditions of Indian trade to the far interior were different from those contemplated in the act. But he did not demonstrate why the governor and assembly of Virginia should exercise a power which the act appeared to deny to the crown, and this was doubtless the point which the board had in mind.[33]

The company was defended in London by its agent, Robert Cary,[34] and its members sent one memorial to Spotswood, which was forwarded to England, and another to the board of trade.[35] Many contradictory statements were offered by supporters and opponents regarding the former conditions of the Indian trade, the amount of money employed, the number of men engaged, and so forth. The truth of these it would be impossible to ascertain without a careful study of the history of the trade for a number of years previous to the erection of the company. The accounts of imports which the

[32] Apparently clauses 14 and 15 of 6 Anne, c. 37.

[33] Northey to B. T., Feb. 11, 1715. *C.O.323/7*; *C.O.5/1364*, pp. 430, 431; *Letters*, II, 230-235.

[34] *C.O.5/1317*, pp. 337-341, 367, 368; *B. T. Jour.*, 1715-1718, pp. 144, 149, 159, 160.

[35] *C.O.5/1317*, pp. 385-390; *1318*, pp. 61-90; *Fulham MSS., Virginia*, Box 1, No. 139.

board of trade secured from the inspector-general of the customs are inconclusive, but would seem to indicate that imports of skins and furs for both Virginia and Carolina were more affected by disturbed conditions in Europe and America than by the organization of the trade itself.[36] The objections offered against the company were sent to Virginia by the board of trade for the observations of governor and council. The latter insisted upon hearing the opponents of the bill, and prolonged its deliberations to such an extent that it appears doubtful if its report, which was entirely favorable to the company, reached the board in time to influence its decision.[37] When the Indian act was referred to the crown lawyers, Solicitor-General William Thompson returned a decidedly adverse report, holding it to be contrary to the governor's sixteenth instruction and to several acts of parliament. That it was an act in restraint of trade and established a monopoly seem to have been the chief counts against it.[38] Finally William Byrd, Micajah Perry, and John Hyde, another London merchant, threw their influence against the company. These men, after staying out of the controversy for some time, eventually opposed both the Indian and tobacco acts.[39] Indeed the fates of these two bills seem to have been closely interwoven. They were both recommended for disallowance in the same representation, the principal objection against them being that they were acts in restraint of trade. They were accordingly repealed by an order in council of July 31, 1717.

The wording of the Indian act of 1714 indicates that Spotswood realized from the first that the home government, while approving his Indian policy in general, might take exception to his monopolistic company. In such an event he expected that the crown would abolish the company but leave

[36] *C.O.5/1317*, pp. 355, 360, 361, 364, 365, 393-403; *B. T. Jour.*, 1715-1718, p. 149.
[37] *Ex. Jour. Coun.*, III, pp. 436, 439, 440; *Letters*, II, 229, 236; *C.O.5/1318*, pp. 37-39.
[38] *Ibid.*, p. 41.
[39] *B. T. Jour.*, 1715-1718, pp. 229, 230, 240-243.

in force the rest of the act, upon which he seems to have placed the greater value. In this he erred. Two separate acts should have been passed. The power of the crown to disallow part of an act of a colonial assembly was doubtful, and the only legal means to get rid of the company was to destroy the entire act. The board of trade thus dealt Spotswood a heavier blow than it desired. It indeed recommended, and in this it was backed by the crown, that the assembly regulate the Indian trade, and repay the company the outlay it had made for the public benefit of the colony. But such was the political atmosphere in Viriginia that the effect of this friendly gesture was apt to be slight.[40]

When the news of the disallowance of the Indian act reached Virginia the assembly was not in session. Indians had recently committed a number of murders in North Carolina, and the Iroquois were hovering on the frontier, threatening the Saponi at Christanna. It would have gone hard with the tributaries had they not been protected by the garrison of company servants, under the command of the old Indian trader, Captain Robert Hix. Could Fort Christanna safely be abandoned? The council thought not. It was also felt that to discontinue trade and close Griffin's school would endanger the friendly relations which had been established with the Indians of the southwest. The Indian Company was therefore requested to continue the work of maintaining the fortifications, the guard, and the hostages at Christanna, and it was urged to continue its trade. Spotswood declared that he would continue the schoolmaster's allowance. These arrangements were temporary, it being hoped, though doubtless with misgivings, that the assembly would work out a permanent solution of the problem.[41]

As the freeholders of Virginia chose their representatives in 1718, there was strong agitation against permitting Fort

[40] *C.O.5/1318*, p. 477; *C.O.5/1364*, p. 523; *Acts of Privy Coun., Col.*, II, 721.

[41] *Letters*, II, 263; Ex. Jour. Coun., III, 456, 483.

Christanna to become a "country charge." The Indian Company, it was argued, would continue to make use of it, and thus the repeal of the Indian act would merely shift the burden from company to country. Since no duty might now be imposed without waiting for the assent of the crown, (for did not all duties affect the trade of Great Britain?), the expense would have to be met by increasing the public levy. The considerable funds now in the treasury would soon disappear if the "court party" got into power.[42]

The opposition had its way. The burgesses voted to repay the £100 which the Indian Company had advanced toward building the magazine and the cost of maintaining the hostages and guards which it had borne since its dissolution in November 1717. They refused, however, any allowance for the expenses of the company prior to that time, the magazine excepted, or for the building and repairing of Fort Christanna at any time, declaring that keeping up and guarding the fort did not make for the security of the country, and was of no public benefit. But the work on the fortifications after November 1717, having been carried on at the request of the council, that body felt obliged to pay for it out of the two shillings a hogshead. Thus the company was reimbursed for that which it spent after its dissolution upon the faith of the government, some £334 in all, but not for any of its outlay upon works of a public nature during its legal existence as recommended by the order in council which abolished the company, the £100 contributed to the magazine alone excepted. How much injustice was done the company it is difficult to say. Perry, Byrd, and Hyde had told the board of trade that the company had been at little charge that did not immediately relate to trade, and thought that its members had been amply repaid "by the great profits they made." According to Hyde, the stock of the company had risen fifty per cent. Spotswood, however, had declared that the company's outlays had been so great that if it were reimbursed it

[42] *C.O.5/1318*, pp. 411, 412.

would doubtless "be very easy what becomes of the Law or the Trade either."[43]

Toward the solution of the frontier problem the burgesses did nothing. They declined to regulate the Indian trade upon the ground that they were not acquainted with any abuses in it. Holding that the Catawba hostages had been obtained to safeguard those trading to that nation, they voted that these be returned in such a manner as to preserve friendly relations, unless those engaged in the Indian trade saw fit to provide for their maintenance. They must have realized the high improbability of unorganized traders doing so. The burgesses further informed the governor that since the Saponi had been the only tributary nation to comply with its treaty, they considered his colonization project for the defense of the frontier a failure. It was therefore unreasonable to retain the fortifications at Christanna, and they hoped the Saponi would be content with the protection enjoyed by the other tributaries. "The Tributary Indians," wrote the irate governor to the board of trade, "who, in Complyance of a Treaty, removed from a place of Safety to that ffort, to serve as a Barrier to the Inhabitants, are voted to be entitled to no other protection than the other Tributaries (who refused to perform their Engagements,) and that for this extraordinary Reason . . . because they were the only nation of Tributarys who have comply'd w'th their Treaty." Spotswood realized that he was beaten. Unprotected by the fort, the work of enlightenment could not proceed at Christanna, and Griffin was recalled. The schoolmaster's labors among the Indians were not at an end, for he now took up the work of teaching the Boyle scholars at William and Mary. But other measures had to be devised for the protection of the frontier.[44]

The bonds between Virginia and the Indians of the southwest, while weakened by these developments were not entirely broken. The Catawba remained friendly, and the Indi-

[43] *Letters*, II, 237, 281, 282; *Jour. Burg.*, 1712-1726, pp. 200-343, *passim*; *Ex. Jour. Coun.*, IV, 43, 44; *B. T. Jour.*, 1715-1718, pp. 241-243.

[44] *Jour. Burg.*, 1712-1726, pp. 186, 207, 212, 213; *Letters*, II, 282; Jones, p. 15.

an company continued its trade for another four years, finally discontinuing it because it proved unprofitable. This cessation of trade brought to Virginia delegations from the Chickasaw and Cherokee. The former, at war with the French, wished to obtain guns and ammunition. They were not able, they said, to secure these from South Carolina because of the lack of pack horses. Both nations were anxious to enter into amicable relations with Virginia, and had trade been opened up with them it seems probable that their allegiance would have been secured. As it was, governor and council, while anxious not to let the Indians think that trade was to be discontinued altogether, had to tell them that the unsettled state of the country made trade at that time difficult, but that when any Virginians ventured into their country they should be directed to trade with them. In the meantime these nations were given permission, if they thought it worth their while, to come to Christanna to trade for the arms they desired. That they ever did so is doubtful, and an excellent opportunity of extending English influence in the southwest seems to have been lost, due to the unsatisfactory state of the trade of Virginia.[45]

That the Virginia Indian Company, as constituted by the act of 1714, would have made a permanent success in the southwestern trade cannot positively be stated, but it must readily be seen that by the repeal of that act the company was seriously hampered in its operations. The fluctuations of British imports of skins and furs from Virginia would seem to be explicable by peace and war in Europe and America rather than by the organization of the trade itself. At the turn of the century the trade was flourishing. With the outbreak of the War of the Spanish Succession violent fluctuations set in, some years being very good, others very poor. In 1713, 1714, and 1715 the trade was consistently low, due doubtless to the troubled conditions attending the Tuscarora War. After 1707 the interference of South Carolina was also encountered, but it seems probable that this annoyed

[45] *Ex. Jour. Coun.*, III, 507, 554, 555; IV, 1, 2.

rather than checked the Virginia traders. From 1718 to 1722, under the management of the Virginia Indian Company, the trade was consistently good. But since conditions were favorable, and the figures for Virginia and Maryland together, the only ones available, are no better than for Virginia alone during the better years of the war, it seems impossible to give the company so very much credit for the revival of the fur trade.[46] The true significance of the Virginia Indian Company is not to be sought in custom house statistics. It was a trading company, but it was more. It stands for an attempt to put relations between red man and white upon a basis of order and justice. The expense of this was to be borne by those who drew financial gain from the Indian. Contributions could hardly be levied from independent traders, nor could their activities be effectively supervised. The company was launched as a solution, only to be wrecked upon the rock of British antipathy to monopoly.

The repeal of the Indian act left the relations between Virginia and the northern Indians in a critical condition. Unsupported by a garrison at Christanna, the Saponi were more likely to prove a prey than a barrier to their traditional enemies, the Iroquois. Located in the Mohawk Valley, the Five Nations came into closest relationship with New York. Trade with them was confined to Albany, where there was stationed a standing body of commissioners of Indian affairs. Here negotiations upon the part of the British government were conducted with them, and here they received the annual presents which the crown deemed it prudent to give. For the friendship of the Iroquois was the keystone in the arch of defense which the twelve colonies had formed against the French and their savage allies. This friendship, or at least its converse, their hostility to the French, dated from the time of Champlain's ill-advised attack upon them in 1609. Their resentment of a single encounter, however, would hardly

[46] *C.O.5/1317*, pp. 364, 365. For the figures for the years 1718 to 1724 I am indebted to W. N. Franklin, *Indian Trade of Colonial Virginia*, Princeton, N.J., 1928.

have led to continued hostility to the French for a century and a half had not self-interest dictated that policy. The Iroquois had extended their influence into the far interior, where their intrepid war parties had made the inland tribes submissive to their will. Their own hunting grounds having become depleted, they subsisted largely by their profits as middlemen between the Indians of the interior and the English on the Hudson. The French, by extending their settlements from the St. Lawrence westward to the Great Lakes, were in a position to deal with the western Indians directly, and in such trade the Iroquois would have no part. Their interest therefore lay with the English in New York, and the French were unable to induce them to attack this province. However, like other Indian tribes, they failed to see in their alliance with one English colony the obligation of friendliness to all, an attitude for which colonial particularism was responsible. This put the French, with their unified administration, at a great advantage. Unable to induce the Five Nations to attack New York, they might nevertheless hope to embroil them with the British by hounding them upon the plantations to the south. Iroquois influence in this direction was well established by Spotswood's time. The Delaware and Conestoga of Pennsylvania were tributary to them, and we have already noted their relationship with the Tuscarora.[47]

In 1712 and 1713 the Iroquois had been active in aiding the Tuscarora, in robbing Virginia traders, and in committing a number of minor depredations which had kept the frontier in a state of uneasiness. Jealousy of Virginia's fur trade, no less than their traditional enmity to such Siouan peoples as the Catawba and Saponi, made the Iroquois dangerous foes of the régime at Christanna.[48] After their attack upon the

[47] Charles Howard McIlwain, *ed.*, *An Abridgment of the Indian Affairs by Peter Wraxall* (Cambridge, 1915), pp. xxxviii, *ff.*, lii, *n.*; *Minutes of the Provincial Council of Pennsylvania* (16 vols., Philadelphia, 1852-1855; hereinafter cited as *Pa. Col. Recs.*), III, 204, 205.

[48] *Documents relative to the Colonial History of the State of New York*, ed. by E. B. O'Callaghan (11 vols., Albany, 1853-1858; hereinafter cited as

Catawba there in 1717, Spotswood took up in earnest the task of working out with the provincial governments to the north a more satisfactory regulation of Indian affairs. Captain Christopher Smith was sent to New York, and arrived at Albany just as Governor Hunter was concluding a conference with the Five Nations. They admitted the attack at Christanna but claimed that they did not know that the Catawba were in friendship with the English, and were unaware of the proximity of Fort Christanna. Other offenses against Virginia they denied. To Smith's proposal that they send deputies back with him to Virginia to renew the "covenant chain" made in 1685 between the Iroquois and Lord Howard of Effingham, they replied that Albany had always been the place of their negotiations, and proposed that the governor of Virginia send agents to them the following summer. The Iroquois promised, however, that no more of their people should go out fighting "that way." Stopping on his return at Philadelphia Smith sought an understanding with the Indians of Pennsylvania, but was told that it was neither "necessary or usefull" for any persons to treat with Indians except the government to which they belonged. Only recently appointed, Governor Keith felt it necessary to defer to the particularism of his council. His personal sympathy for closer integration cannot be doubted.[49]

When Smith's report was considered in council, annoyance was expressed at the insistence of the Five Nations that agents be sent to treat with them at Albany. It was resolved that the constant excursions of the Five Nations along the frontiers made it necessary that they and their confederates be confined to the west of the mountains and the north of the Potomac. To this end the council approved a proposal of Spotswood's for making a settlement and erecting a fort at the recently discovered pass over the mountains and for ad-

---

N. Y. Col. Docs.), v, 492; *Letters*, II, 251, 252; *Pa. Col. Recs.*, III, 84; *B. T. Jour.*, 1718-1722, p. 181.

[49] *Ex. Jour. Coun.*, III, 446; *Letters*, II, 252; *N.Y. Col. Docs.*, v. 489-493; *Pa. Col. Recs.*, III, 21-23.

dressing the crown that this fort and Albany be alternately the place for delivering presents to the Five Nations and renewing alliances with them. The proposed fort being more accessible to the agents of Virginia and the neighboring colonies than Albany, better understanding would be promoted.[50]

Hoping to settle the Indian relations of New York, Pennsylvania, Maryland, and Virginia upon a more satisfactory basis, Spotswood in the fall of 1717 set out for Philadelphia, expecting to confer there with the governors of the other three provinces. Now that Britain was at peace with France conditions seemed favorable, for the colonial executives were agreed that the Iroquois could best be brought to terms while the English were not "under the necessity of Courting their Friendship." The New York assembly being in session, Hunter was unable to come, and Governor Hart of Maryland was compelled by sickness in his family to return home. Spotswood and Keith therefore proceeded to New York to confer with Hunter. Since it was too late in the year for a conference with the Five Nations, all that could be done was to leave with Hunter two preliminary articles of peace drawn up by Spotswood, which the Iroquois were to accept before a definitive treaty was concluded.[51]

The assembly of 1718 proved no more interested in Albany than in Christanna. Spotswood's lurid portrayal of a frontier crisis was heard with indifference, and when the governor sought to shame them into action by referring to his own past services the burgesses drew him from one pompous utterance to the next, and then demolished him with barbs of sarcasm. Nor did the council believe that danger was imminent, the Indians having given some satisfaction for the breach of their former treaty, and a promise to observe its terms in the future. When acts of hostility were committed it would be time enough to consider further measures. Spotswood blamed the failure of the assembly to act upon the

[50] *Ex. Jour. Coun.*, III, 450-452.

[51] *Letters*, II, 256, 258, 261, 262; *Ex. Jour. Coun.*, III, 457; *Pa. Col. Recs.*, III, 30.

"factious party" in the council. The opposition to his plans was certainly due in large measure to the tense political situation.[52]

The following summer, when Keith warned Spotswood of an impending attack upon Christanna, the council's sole advice was to call out the militia. More constructive was the attempt to promote a better understanding with the Nottoway and Meherrin. The Iroquoian tributaries were at odds both with the English and with the Saponi, and supported as they were by the Five Nations and the Tuscarora their disaffection was a serious menace to peace.[53]

In July 1719 Governor Hunter left New York for England. Realizing the paramount importance to the English of the friendship of the Iroquois, he may have humored them overmuch. His complacence at their attacks upon other Indians arose from the conviction that this warlike confederacy might otherwise turn upon the English. It was a party of Mohawk sent out by him against the Yamasee without European officers which had made the attack on Christanna in 1717. Such a policy scarcely accorded with Spotswood's conception of the "white man's burden." Yet Hunter, while urging upon Spotswood "the inconvenience of insisting on punctilios with those Indians" and the propriety of sending deputies from Virginia to Albany, recognized the intercolonial nature of the Indian problem.[54]

Peter Schuyler, upon whom the government of New York devolved after Hunter's departure, represented a different point of view. Long a commissioner of Indian affairs at Albany, and interested in the trade there, it was natural that he should wish to keep the Iroquois within the orbit of New York. Spotswood was soon protesting against his encouraging "those Savages in their haughty Demands of having all the King's Governours on this Continent dance many hundred

[52] *Jour. Burg.*, 1712-1726, pp. 174-213, *passim; Ex. Jour. Coun.*, III, 478, 479.

[53] *Ibid.*, pp. 498-521, *passim.*

[54] *N. Y. Col. Docs.*, V, 548, 549; *B. T. Jour.*, 1718-1722, pp. 181, 182.

of miles to Albany to treat there upon every Caprice of theirs." The ascendancy of the Five Nations was destroying "that Ballance of Power which we Christians ought to preserve among our neighbouring Heathen," while English prestige with both Indians and French was being undermined by the supine treatment accorded the arrogant Iroquois. Painting legislative indifference in bellicose colors, Spotswood informed Schuyler that the Virginia assembly had refused to send commissioners to Albany, and that if the Iroquois persisted in their outrages they would be met by eight or nine hundred men from the Virginia frontier, to say nothing of reinforcements from the tidewater counties, "and when once the Blow is struck, and We are involved in a Ware with the five Nations, I leave you to consider whether his Majesty will allow your province to stand Newter and carry on your Trade with them." He knew full well the serious consequences which war with the Five Nations would entail. "I for my part, shall do my utmost to put off the evil Day. . . . But, You are to understand that in an affair of this Nature, a Governour of Virginia has to steer between Scylla and Charybdis, either an Indian or a Civil War, for the famous Insurrection in this Colony called Bacon's Rebellion, was occasioned purely by the Governour and Council refusing to let the People go out against the Indians, who at that time annoyed the Frontiers, and it seems as if the same Humour was again rising in Virginia."[55] In his zeal to bring about a settlement of the Indian problem Spotswood had exaggerated in Virginia the danger from the Iroquois, and now overstated to New York the Virginia ardor to resist it. With the settling of the disputes between governor and council in 1720 the assembly indeed readdressed itself to the Indian problem, but the situation was nevertheless more the reverse than the parallel of that of 1676.

The board of trade, having received Spotswood's account of the situation, conferred with Hunter and his successor,

[55] *Letters*, II, 333, 334; Spotswood to Schuyler, Jan. 25, 1720, *Pa. Col. Recs.*, III, 82-89.

William Burnet, son of the bishop-historian. It then wrote to Spotswood that in view of the increase of the power of the French and of their activities to win the Iroquois over to their interest, the Five Nations should not be governed with a high hand, and Albany having generally been the appointed place for negotiating with them, "We would recommend to you to wave the Ceremonial provided the essential Part can be obtained." It therefore recommended that after Burnet's arrival commissioners be sent to Albany from Virginia, accompanied by some of the tributaries. These were to describe the location of their settlements, so that the Iroquois might avoid molesting them.[56]

Spotswood was willing to go to Albany, but the settlement which he proposed to make differed from that suggested by Hunter and approved by the board. It was not enough that the Iroquois should pledge themselves to refrain from molesting the English and certain designated villages of tributaries. They must be excluded from the Virginia frontier altogether. The preliminary articles left with Hunter in 1717 had accordingly specified that they should not proceed south of the Potomac or east of the Blue Ridge without permission from the governor of New York, while the Virginia tributaries were not to pass these bounds without the permission of their government. The assembly which met in 1720 shared this opinion, and the two houses jointly informed the governor that they could neither advise nor enable him to proceed to Albany until the preliminaries had been assented to. Spotswood undertook to convince the board of trade of the reasonableness of this attitude.[57] Keith had agreed with him from the first, and Burnet was soon won over. Thanks to the united efforts of the three governors, by October 1721 the preliminary articles of 1717 had been accepted in substance by all parties concerned except Maryland. That province was content with renewing the covenant of 1685 with five Iro-

[56] B. T. to Spotswood, July 14, 1720, *C.O.5/1365*, pp. 219-221.

[57] *Jour. Burg.*, 1712-1726, p. 301; Spotswood to B. T., March 6, 1721, *C.O.5/1319*, p. 98.

quois deputies and, while asking to be included in any treaties which might be made, took no active part in effecting a new settlement at Albany.[58] These deputies had been sent to negotiate with the three governments to the south. Though apparently without power to conclude a definitive treaty they presented a belt in token of their friendship to Virginia, and blandly requested permission to exterminate the Totero. Their mission scarcely contributed to the cause of peace. Four of their number died before reaching home, and the survivor declared that the others had been poisoned by the Virginia tributaries. Fear of reprisals created another frontier scare in Virginia.[59]

Governor and council now decided that the time was ripe for sending commissioners to Albany, and when the assembly met in May 1722, the burgesses agreed with them. The governor was requested in a joint address to lead the Virginia commission in person. A thousand pounds was voted to defray the expenses of the journey, and to this was added a further three hundred to cover Spotswood's expenses in 1717, a sure sign that old rancors were dying out. The assembly also provided for the enforcement of the proposed treaty by imposing the penalty of death or servitude upon Indians caught violating its provisions. There were three commissioners in all, the governor, Nathaniel Harrison of the council, and William Robinson of the burgesses. They were accompanied by John Randolph who acted as secretary, and by the old Indian trader Robert Hix, whose knowledge of the northern Indians was deemed invaluable. Proceeding to New York on board a man-o'-war, this embassy appears to have been as well provided with good cheer as the famous transmontane expedition of 1716, for Spotswood's expense account included one box of citron water and other rich cordials, two chests of arrack, one pipe of choice Madeira, and "30 dozen ditto @ 3 bitts p. Bottle." The Virginians were joined

[58] *N. Y. Col. Docs.*, V, 637-640; *Pa. Col. Recs.*, III, 114-119, 208; *Archives of Maryland*, XXV, 361-369, 388.

[59] *Ex. Jour. Coun.*, III, 552-554, IV, 8, 9.

by Governor Keith and four members of the Pennsylvania council. The conference at Albany was thus perhaps more catholic in its scope than any previously held in America. Its purview was further extended by Burnet's invocation of the good offices of the Five Nations to dissuade certain New England Indians from hostile designs upon the English in those parts. The commissioners arrived at Albany on August 20, but the Indians being late, negotiations did not begin until August 27, and were prolonged until September 14.[60]

The Albany conference gave Spotswood the opportunity of trying out in practice the theory propounded so vigorously to Schuyler, that better relations with the Iroquois would result if these Indians were dealt with more firmly. None too pleased by the week's delay, he declared that it was an old story of the Five Nations that the covenant chain had grown rusty, and that commissioners should be sent from Virginia to brighten it or, as Burnet had put it to the board of trade, "to give them a fine present to refresh their Memorys." None of the treaties made with Virginia for fifty years past had long been observed by the Five Nations, and nothing but their agreeing to the preliminaries had induced him and the other Virginia commissioners to come to Albany to arrange a perpetual peace. The terms of these preliminaries had been acceded to by the Virginia tributaries. He told them of the act which had passed the Virginia assembly, and demanded that the preliminaries be reaffirmed by all the Indians present and signed by the sachems "before I will either propose or present you with anything further on the part of Virginia." With this the Iroquois complied, but expressed regret that Spotswood had brought none of the Virginia tributaries. However they declared they accepted what the governor offered on their behalf "in the same manner as if they were present, and tho'," they proceeded, "there is a Nation among you, the Toderechrones [Saponi] . . . against whom we have had so inveterate an enmity, that we thought it impossible it could

[60] *Ex. Jour. Coun.*, pp. 552, 553; *Jour. Burg.*, 1712-1726, pp. 319-354, *passim*; Hening, IV, 103-106; *C.O.5/1322*, p. 139.

be extinguished, but by total Exterpation of them, yet since you desire it we are willing to receive them into this Peace & to forgive all that is past." They expressed the hope, frankly enough, that Spotswood would see to it that the Virginia tributaries abided by the terms which he had made on their behalf. A detail suggests Spotswood's attitude. While Burnet addressed the River Indians as "Children" and was called by them "Father," both Keith and he styled the Iroquois "Brethren," and each in return was termed "Brother." Spotswood, however, addressed the Indians with the non-committal "Sachims & Warriors of ye 5 Nations." The astute Iroquois took notice of this in their reply, though they also termed Spotswood "Brother."

The total lack of subservience on the part of the Iroquois may have nettled Spotswood, for upon the other two occasions he addressed the Indians he assumed a more imperious tone. He stressed the law recently enacted in Virginia to enforce the treaty, dwelling upon the penalties to which they would be liable if they came to Virginia to treat with the tributaries in any manner save through the government, even though bearing a passport from the governor of New York.

The sachems, apparently quite cowed, declared that they were very well satisfied with the law, and when told that they would not be held accountable for their treatment of any Virginia tributaries encountered without passports out of bounds, said they would treat them as friends, so desirous were they of peace. They acknowledged that they had been guilty "of a great many bad actions," and thanked Spotswood for forgiving them. They even admitted the attack upon the Virginia traders in 1713, of which Spotswood had long accused them, and which they had hitherto firmly denied, a confession which the presence of Hix, a victim of this escapade, may have expedited. They promised to make reparation when they were able. They also agreed to return to Colonel George Mason's house on the Potomac all Virginia runaways their people should encounter. Pressed by Spotswood, the Iroquois declared themselves satisfied that their four deputies had died natural deaths, and that they had no complaint to make against Virginia. Certain skins were given to Spotswood, which he promptly transferred to Hix, as a small compensation for his loss. At the conclusion of his conference Spotswood removed a golden horse shoe from his breast and gave it to the speaker of the Iroquois "& bid the Interpreter tell him there was an inscription upon [it] which signified that it would help to pass over the mountains." This was to be carried by any Iroquois coming to Virginia with a pass. The presentation of Virginia's gifts then closed his negotiations. Keith at the same time renewed the peace between the Iroquois on behalf of Pennsylvania and her Indians. His speech to the Iroquois was dignified, yet in keeping with the mild policy which his province had ever pursued towards the Indians. No direct attempt was made to exclude the Iroquois from Pennsylvania. The difficulty of enforcing such an agreement would probably have been insurmountable, and while Keith believed that it was absolutely necessary to prevent the passage of the Five Nations through the Quaker colony he hoped that the Virginia act would accomplish this. The pact just concluded was rendered more effective by an agreement between the governments of New York and Virginia that not more than ten Indians at a time should be permitted to pass the stipulated bounds.[61]

Instead of returning directly to Virginia, Spotswood accompanied Keith back to Philadelphia, the two governors intending to hold a conference with the Pennsylvania Indians in order to secure the confirmation of the terms agreed upon the year before. But whether prompted by objection to the Draconian provisions of the Virginia law, by disrelish of Spotswood's proposals for the return of runaway slaves, or by mere particularism, the Pennsylvania council opposed the conference. Nevertheless Keith offered to attend Spotswood at Conestoga. The latter, knowing from bitter experience the bane of a disaffected council, had no desire to involve his

[61] *N. Y. Col. Docs.*, v, 655-681; *Pa. Col. Recs.*, III, 204, 205; *Ex. Jour. Coun.*, IV, 22-24; *C.O.5/1319*, p. 305 ff.

friend in difficulties of that nature. He therefore departed for Virginia. The Pennsylvania Indians were with the approval of the council warned of the provisions of the Virginia act, and told that a reward of one good gun and two blankets would be given them for every runaway slave delivered to Colonel Mason.[62]

Upon Spotswood's arrival in Virginia he found himself retired to private life. He made his report to governor and council, and was cordially thanked by Drysdale in the name of the board.[63] If words went for anything, his negotiations with the Five Nations had proven an unqualified success. So awed do the Iroquois appear to have been by his imperious manner and commanding presence that they conceded almost without demur even more than he demanded of them. Needless to say, however, if it was to succeed, the policy which he had inaugurated would need to be vigorously prosecuted. There is reason to believe that his easy-going successors failed to do this. Drysdale was warned by the board of trade of the disastrous results which would be entailed by a break with the Iroquois, and was cautioned not to use high-handed methods in dealing with them.[64] This advice he seems to have followed, and it is doubtful if the penalties of the act of 1722 were ever imposed.

Spotswood's Indian policy has little permanent significance from the practical point of view. Since tenure of office was insecure, and his successors were likely to be as indifferent to his schemes as were the generality of the inhabitants of Virginia, this was perhaps inevitable from the first. But it was toward a permanent solution of the frontier problem that he strove. The governor's chief difficulty lay in raising funds. The Virginia assembly, chary of projects of remote and uncertain benefit, preferred to meet emergencies as they arose without borrowing trouble from the future. The crown, its exchequer depleted by a quarter-century of warfare, was not

[62] *Pa. Col. Recs.*, III, 202-212.
[63] *Ex. Jour. Coun.*, IV, 22, 23.
[64] B. T. to Drysdale, June 19, 1723, *C.O.5/1365*, pp. 247-249.

disposed to be prodigal with the quit rents of the only colony whose lands yielded a surplus revenue. The S. P. G., while sufficiently interested in Spotswood's activities to admit him to its membership,[65] does not appear to have contributed to his work, despite his many urgent appeals. Spotswood was thus thrown upon his own resources, and he concluded that the Indian policy had best be financed by those to whom the Indians were a source of profit. The Indian Company was the result. With its dissolution his cherished schemes were doomed. Thenceforth his policy was confined to securing the frontier from attack, and he seems to have abandoned hope of civilizing the Indians.

Spotswood was not a visionary idealist. His views with regard to the treatment of the Indians were generally sound. His dealings with them were both firm and just. He repeatedly emphasized the necessity of keeping faith with them, and the scrupulousness with which he abided by this precept appears to have given the Indians complete confidence in him. He was farsighted enough to see, and enough of an empire-builder to desire, that the British population would expand to the westward, and realized that the Indians must give way before it. His treaties with the tributaries therefore contained provisions whereby this might be accomplished without injustice to them.

A word might be said as to Spotswood's motives. They were doubtless mixed. He may have thought that the conversion of the Indians would win his administration the support of the bishop of London and others in England who might favor this "pious" undertaking. Compton certainly was sympathetic. But in all his correspondence with Bishop Robinson, Spotswood seems to have been the enthusiast, urging a somewhat apathetic diocesan to greater efforts in a manner more calculated to give annoyance than to excite approbation. As we have seen, the governor held shares in the Virginia Indian Company, and was thus financially interested. His private fortune was never a matter of indifference to Spots-

[65] *Letters*, II, 255.

wood. Yet in this instance the desire to support a cherished enterprise, sadly in need of capital, doubtless prompted his investment. His paying Griffin's salary, at least, does not have the appearance of mere self-interest. We must seek worthier motives than these.

Spotswood belongs to that class of colonial officials, none too numerous at the beginning of the century, who saw that the English colonies in America had a great future before them. They would expand into the interior, and of this expansion a struggle for supremacy with New France would be an inevitable consequence. In this struggle the friendship of the Indians would be a great, perhaps a decisive, factor. Defense of some sort against the Indians was necessary and Spotswood, with an eye upon the future as well as the present, wished to replace the hand-to-mouth methods theretofore practised by a permanent policy. Kindly disposed toward all who did not thwart his somewhat imperious will, the governor sought to promote the temporal welfare of the Indians, nor can his numerous expressions of solicitude for the salvation of their souls be regarded as mere cant. The heyday of foreign missions had not yet come, and his was the zeal of the churchman rather than of the evangelical. Free from that obsession of the "noble savage" which lent a bizarre aspect to the work of humanitarians a century later, he realized full well that the Indian was a "weaker vessel." To Spotswood the interests of the Indian were always secondary to those of the English. Yet he saw in the white man's superior position not opportunity alone, but obligation. In place of exploitation today and extermination tomorrow he sought the assimilation of the native through order, justice, and enlightenment.

Chapter VI

THE PEOPLE OPPOSE

THE first five years of Spotswood's governorship revealed many of the qualities of an able administrator. He had a genius for order, reinforced by seventeen years of army life. Himself methodical, he was impatient of lack of system in others. Such a man inevitably found much to be desired in the public life of Virginia; that his efforts to remould it would prove fruitful sources of friction was no less inevitable. A faithful subordinate, he took the royal instructions for his lodestar, and his full and lucid correspondence kept the authorities in London well posted on the situation in Virginia. But he was no mere automaton. If he deemed the policies of his superiors ill advised, he did not hesitate to say so. And, as we have seen, he was capable of embarking upon comprehensive policies of his own with a mere "by your leave" to the authorities at home. His dealings were for the most part frank and straightforward, but his treatment of the revenue question in 1714 revealed a capacity for the devious.

It has already been stated that the royal revenue in Virginia was derived from two main sources, the duty of two shillings a hogshead and the quit rents. The former, at the disposal of governor and council, yielded about £3000 a year, while the standing expenses of the government amounted to about £3500. It had therefore been the policy of the crown to allow the payment of certain salaries out of the quit rents, and to make grants from time to time out of that fund to make up the deficiency in the two shillings a hogshead. Whatever balance was left was usually applied to the encouragement of various undertakings in the colony. But an exhausting war disposed the home government to seize upon every possible means of recouping the depleted exchequer. Accordingly, in 1712, Spotswood received a warrant for remitting home the sum of £3000. All the quit rent fund had been employed the previous year to buy pork for the Canada expedition, so only £600 could be sent at that time, the balance to be sent as future revenue came in. Spotswood protested, for to deprive the government of a reserve fund for use in emergency seemed especially ill advised in view of the troubled conditions in North Carolina,[1] and in this protest Nathaniel Blakiston, Virginia agent at London, joined him.[2]

Since the tobacco trade was depressed this new policy obliged the governor to seek some other fund to defray the standing expenses of government. This was the more necessary because the burgesses had refused to recognize as "country claims" any expenditures, howsoever necessary, which had not been authorized by act of assembly. Spotswood broached this matter to the burgesses in 1712, but it was so close to the end of the session that nothing was done.[3] In 1714, however, the suggestion was again made, and both houses united in an address to the crown, asking that the quit rents might be directed "back into their old Channel." Not only did they ask that the current deficit be made up, but also that the governor be given power with the advice and consent of the council, to expend the quit rents "for Answering any Sudden Emergencys where your Majestys Service might Suffer for want of a more timely Supply than Application at So great Distance will Admit Subject nevertheless to be duly

[1] *Letters*, I, 154-158. "I'm sure," he wrote to Blathwayt, "there was never greater Occasion since Bacon's Rebellion for leaving some money to answer the Exigencys of the Government."

[2] "I am under some concerne," he wrote to Ludwell, "to see our Grandees as some are so Regardless of ye Interst of Virginia as to be Constantly seeking that Country of ye . . . that was always appropriated to Defray ye Contingent Charges of ye Govermt your hive of Virginia brings a great deal of Hony to this Nation and costs them nothing; this illegal practice was never used till of late and is only to stop some . . . here." Blakiston to Ludwell, Jan. 18, 1711 [1712], *Va. Mag. Hist.*, IV, 20, 21. Blakiston's letters give ample evidence that he was a strong Whig, and the fact that this was a Tory innovation may have increased his ire against it.

[3] *Jour. Burg.*, 1712-1726, pp. 41, 42.

Accounted for as formerly to your Majesty."[4] The governor was requested to support the address with his own recommendation.[5] The assembly had asked nothing more than Spotswood had himself proposed in the most urgent terms, and there is no evidence that the governor expressed in Virginia the least opposition.[6] Yet in writing to the board of trade he vigorously attacked the proposal as an attempt to divest the crown of the whole revenue of quit rents, which would prevent future royal support of worthy undertakings in the colony.[7] The governor's action, suggestive of double dealing, is a striking example of his unwillingness to see a concession made at the request of the colonists which he would surely have welcomed had it come in response to a proposal of his own. An even less worthy motive may have prompted his action. A new king had just ascended the throne, and all royal officials had to be either recommissioned or superseded. Spotswood may have thought that a display of zeal for the royal interest would increase his chances of continuance in office.

Relations between governor and assembly from 1710 to 1714 were, on the whole, happy. There were, it is true, frequent disagreements, as was to be expected when an executive of Spotswood's parts encountered the colonial proclivity to let well enough alone. His conception of the necessary functions of government, like that of the authorities at home, ever tended to exceed that entertained by the colonial population. At times the governor gave sharp expression to his annoyance at legislative intractability, but experience seems to have convinced him that the wiser course lay in patience and conciliation. Thus the strictures with which the assembly was dissolved in January 1712 were not repeated in the fall of that year, though the provocation was nearly as great. He

[4] As a matter of fact, while not authorized by law so to do, governor and council had in times of unusual stress drawn upon the quit rents.

[5] *Jour. Burg.*, 1712-1726, pp. 109, 110.

[6] Spotswood referred the board of trade to his answer to the address of the assembly on the thirtieth page of the council journal as a proof of his opposition to the proposal. No such answer, however, is to be found in the printed journal of either house.

[7] *Letters*, II, 101, 102.

had his reward; during the remaining two years of its existence his second assembly proved remarkably tractable.

As already recorded, this concord enabled Spotswood to carry through sweeping reforms in frontier policy and trade regulation. In other matters, also, progress was made. In 1713 the burgesses assented to an act, similar to a council bill which they had rejected the previous year, specifying the improvements which were to be made upon newly patented lands.[8] They also facilitated the collection of vital statistics.[9]

Spotswood had called the attention of the assembly to the necessity of repairing the capitol and the advisability of assisting the infant town of Williamsburg to make certain needed improvements, such as "building a Market House, bettering the Landings, and Securing a few Publick Springs" which, he declared, "would not only Redound to the Credit of the Country when Strangers Resort hither, but would likewise be for the benefit of all those whose business calls them to the Assemblys And Generall Courts." It had already been necessary, he stated, to resurvey and mark out anew the bounds and streets of the town.[10] The assembly authorized John Clayton and John Holloway to make the necessary repairs

[8] *Infra*, pp. 138-140.

[9] The governor was instructed to cause an exact account to be kept of all births, deaths, and christenings in the colony, an abstract of which was to be sent home annually. It was no easy task, for the people, associating the compilation of such reports with the assessment of taxes, were reluctant to divulge the desired information. The act of 1661, providing for the registry of births, marriages, and deaths by ministers (Hening, II, 54), had long since fallen into desuetude. Failing to revive it by proclamation (*Ex. Jour. Coun.*, III, 303, 588, 589; *C.O.5/1316*, O. 129; *Jour. Burg.*, 1712-1726, pp. 64, 65) Spotswood now secured from the assembly a new act, providing that all births and deaths be notified to minister or clerk, by whom they were to be recorded, along with all christenings. Non-observance was punishable by a fine of two hundred pounds of tobacco, while the fees collectable by the recording officer were reduced from fifty pounds to three. Hening, IV, 42-45. This act doubtless fell short of complete effectiveness, but it enabled the governor the following year to transmit to the board of trade a fuller account than theretofore possible. This report for all twenty-five counties for the six months following April 20, 1714, was as follows: Births: free males, 379; females, 320; slave males, 121; females, 132. Burials: Free males, 116; females, 123; slave males, 28; females, 34. *C.O.5/1317*, pp. 262, 263.

[10] *Jour. Burg.*, 1712-1726, pp. 47, 48.

upon the capitol and other desired improvements, part of the expense of the latter being defrayed by the sale of city lots. They were also empowered to keep the accounts of the governor's house, provision being made for finishing that building.[11]

Acts for regulating ferries, the appointment of sheriffs, the dispatching of public expresses, and the apprehension of runaway seamen were also passed by the assembly of 1713, while the governor expressed satisfaction over the passage of a bill to limit the excessive number of horses. Substantial progress was made during this session, the harmonious spirit of which is reflected in the address of the assembly to the queen upon the conclusion of peace with France.[12]

When it reconvened in 1714 Spotswood outlined to the assembly the progress of his frontier policy and secured the passage of an act exempting the Palatines, whom he was settling at Germanna, from the payment of all levies for the period of seven years. Provision was also made for the erection of a magazine to hold the military stores of the colony. Another act regulated the vital question of the rates at which gold and silver coin should circulate in the colony.[13] The expired act for the security and defense of the country in times of danger was passed by both houses, but the governor's instructions concerning temporary laws compelled him to withhold his signature.[14]

[11] *Jour. Burg.*, 1712-1726, pp. 50-73, *passim.*

[12] *Ibid.*, pp. 52, 53.

[13] In all, seventeen acts were passed in 1714, though Hening mentions only five. *Jour. Burg.*, 1712-1726, pp. 116, 117; Hening, IV, 51-57.

[14] *Leg. Jour. Coun.*, I, 591. The whole question of the evasion of the veto power of the crown by the passage of temporary laws had been up for consideration before the privy council and the board of trade. Attorney-General Northey had declared at that time that while this matter could only be regulated in the proprietaries by act of parliament, the instructions of the royal governors already contained provision against the practice, and therefore it was only necessary to require the governors to observe them. *C.O.323/7*, K.35; *B. T. Jour.*, 1709-1715, pp. 540, 565. The act for the security and defense of the country was one to which nobody in the colony seems to have objected, and there is apparently no explanation for its passage for such short periods other than that it was the colonial counterpart of the mutiny act, used as a weapon to compel the governor to call frequent assemblies.

The tobacco act, passed the previous session, had gone into effect on November 10, 1714, a few days before the assembly convened. That so fundamental an alteration of the economic organization of the province could be effected without friction was hardly to be expected. The debtor class, ever an advocate of cheap money, was not apt to favor the change, and it is probable that the increase which the act effected in the value of fees and salaries did not meet with the uniform approval of the taxpayers. Yet this opposition was for the time being more than offset by the support which the new regulations received from the creditor and official classes, and from those who believed that the elimination of trash tobacco was essential to the economic prosperity of the province. Yet the opposition was rising, and was doubtless intensified by the drought which had damaged the corn and tobacco crops. It was therefore deemed necessary to pass an act excusing the poor from levies and permitting them to export the tobacco then on hand under the old conditions. At the same time, however, the new policy was strengthened by placing a penalty upon the exportation of hogsheads which had not been stamped by the tobacco agents. Another act, to prevent the malicious burning or destroying of the public storehouses of tobacco agents indicates that opposition of a violent nature to the new regulations was anticipated.

In using the patronage of the new office of tobacco agent to gain control of the house of burgesses, the governor had offered a serious affront to colonial liberties. Certain it is that there were those in Virginia who viewed with alarm the acquiescence of the assembly with the governor's wishes. The tobacco act of 1713 had been enacted for three years, and would thus be in force until November, 1717. Yet the assembly of 1714 passed another act continuing it, with little revision, for still another year, a move evidently prompted by fear that subsequent assemblies would not renew it.[15]

In November, John Cottrell of Northumberland was sent

[15] *C.O. 5/1386*, p. 87; *Leg. Jour. Coun.*, I, 591; *Letters*, II, 96.

for in custody of the messenger of the house "for Speaking Scandalous Words Reflecting upon this House and arraigning their proceedings and for Affronting and publickly abusing *George Eskridge*," the latter a burgess from Northumberland. He was found not guilty and discharged. At about the same time it was complained that George Marable "did . . . in a Debate in the House utter many undecent and Reflecting Speeches against Several Members of this House then present in breach of the Rules of the House." He was found guilty but "Declared that he intended no Reflection by any Words or Speeches by him uttered in that Debate." He was thereupon readmitted.[16] Feeling was evidently running high.

The representatives of the people no longer reflected the views of the constituencies which had elected them over two years before. Agitation for a new election was in the air. It was urged that a triennial act be passed or, failing this, that the provisions of the British statute ought to be observed. These proposals were rejected by the burgesses.[17] Such agitation was unnecessary, however, for the assembly was dissolved automatically six months after its first meeting in a new reign. Queen Anne had died on the first of August, and the assembly had met on the sixteenth of the following November. Its legal existence was thus bound to terminate in May, 1715, and it was dissolved in February.[18]

With widespread discontent prevailing in the early summer of 1715, Spotswood had little desire to measure his administration by the touchstone of popular approval. Yet call an assembly he must, for the attack of the Yamasee upon South Carolina[19] had created a crisis which the standing revenue could not meet. An election was therefore ordered.

The campaign, evidently a stormy one,[20] resulted in a po-

[16] *Jour. Burg.*, 1712-1726, pp. 91-93, 99.

[17] *Ibid.*, pp. 83, 84.

[18] *Ex. Jour. Coun.*, III, 395.

[19] *Supra*, p. 32 ff.

[20] As an aftermath of a lively election in Henrico, it was complained that Robert Bolling, late incumbent from that county, had "Assaulted beaten and very much wounded" Richard Cocke, one of the successful candidates. *Jour. Burg.*, 1712-1726, p. 125.

litical landslide. Only sixteen of the fifty-one burgesses retained their seats, and among this sixteen were numbered some of the governor's outstanding opponents, such as George Marable and Edwin Conway. The newcomers included such disaffected spirits as Gawin Corbin, whom Spotswood had removed from his post as naval officer of Rappahannock on a charge of forgery. Not all the changes in personnel were unfavorable to the governor's policies. William Cole and Cole Diggs, who were but now returned for Warwick, appear to have been two of his strongest supporters. Yet the election was an unmistakable indictment of the administration by the voting population of Virginia.

In his opening speech the governor set forth the urgent necessity for aiding South Carolina. Timely assistance, he declared, might be rendered with comparative ease, and would certainly enhance Virginia's prestige among her sister colonies. He also urged reorganization of the militia and provision for an adequate standing revenue, projects intimately connected with the problem of defense.[21] Spotswood desired quick despatch, so that he might dismiss the assembly and return to the frontier. The burgesses, however, had other ideas of the business to be transacted. They declined to consider the revenue question until the crown had answered the address of the previous session upon that score, and to gain time they asked the governor for further information upon the question of militia reform and the demands of South Carolina for assistance.[22]

In the meantime, the house took up the problem of organization. Peter Beverley, speaker of three previous assemblies,[23] had apparently been defeated in Gloucester, since he was elected by William and Mary College. The right of the College, as then organized, to be represented was contested, and decided in the negative. Beverley thus lost his seat.[24] Even

[21] *Jour. Burg.*, 1712-1726, pp. 121-123.

[22] *Ibid.*, pp. 128, 129, 131.

[23] 1703-1705, 1710-1712, and 1712-1714.

[24] *Ibid.*, pp. 127, 138. Beverley was excluded from the house ten days after the beginning of the session, and the fact that Marable was chosen to succeed him

before this, Daniel McCarty had been elected speaker, Beverley being demoted to the chairmanship of the committee for public claims. The chairmanship of the committee of elections and privileges went to Corbin, but the committee of greatest importance, that for propositions and grievances, was headed by John Clayton, the recently appointed attorney-general.

Two days after they had been declared duly elected, the right of William Cole and Cole Diggs to represent Warwick was challenged by William Harwood, a former incumbent. They had promised their constituents that, if elected, they would serve without salary.[25] The law against bribery was comprehensive, forbidding gifts or promises of gifts not only to individuals but to "any county, town or corporation."[26] Since the salaries of burgesses were paid by county levy, a bribe had in effect been offered to the county. When, therefore, the burgesses resolved that the representatives from Warwick were not duly elected, their action was correct, even though it may have been inspired by the fact that Cole and Diggs were supporters of the governor.[27] Writs were issued for a new election, Cole and Diggs were once more returned, and "having made this time no ante-election promises we may be sure, were allowed to take their seats."[28]

Thus far the house had proceeded with moderation. In the process of receiving propositions and grievances, however, it was discovered that some from New Kent had not been certified by the county courts, as the law required. The county court clerk, one Thornton, was at the door of the house, which suggested a prearranged affair. His evidence that four of the justices had refused to certify the proposi-

---

as chairman of the committee for claims indicates the increasingly radical spirit of the burgesses as the session wore on.

[25] *Jour. Burg.*, 1712-1726, pp. 126, 128, 153.

[26] Hening, III, 243.

[27] Cole was one of the tobacco agents. *Cal. Va. State Paps.*, I, 175, 176. Diggs was later appointed to the council upon Spotswood's recommendation, (*Letters*, II, 304) and subsequently rose to the presidency.

[28] *Jour. Burg.*, 1712-1726, pp. 141, xxxiii.

tions and grievances in question provoked the burgesses to take the decisive step of ordering that they be sent for in custody of the messenger of the house. A similar course was taken with three justices of Charles City charged with like offenses, while the justices of Richmond County were ordered prosecuted by the attorney-general for neglecting to meet to certify claims.[29] Regardless of their technical defects, these propositions, grievances, and claims were promptly referred to the appropriate committees. The burgesses had thus launched an attack upon the county courts which, appointed as they were by governor and council, doubtless favored the new policies.

The Charles City justices were examined at the bar of the house and discharged without paying fees.[30] Walker and Littlepage of New Kent were also examined, and the house resolved that they "make an Humble Acknowledgment of their Error. . . . And then Receive a Reprimand from Mr. *Speaker*." Walker made his acknowledgment, received his reprimand, and was discharged, paying fees. Littlepage proved obdurate and was ordered continued in the custody of the messenger. Three days later the house received the news that Littlepage, together with his fellow justice Butts, had escaped, and the speaker was ordered to issue a warrant to pursue and retake them. Both justices refused to surrender themselves, denying the authority of the burgesses. The house then called upon the governor to take steps to bring the offenders "to Answer their Repeated Contempts and Misdemeanours before this House." Spotswood's reply was short, but significant. "My concern for the Honour of the House of Burgesses Shall always be equal to theirs for the Honour of their Country, and the Executive power Shall Vindicate the Representatives of ye People Conformable to the Support they agree to afford it."[31]

The burgesses were not to be rebuffed. They promptly

[29] *Ibid.*, pp. 124, 125, 129.
[30] *Ibid.*, p. 135.
[31] *Ibid.*, pp. 130-142, *passim.*

sent another message reiterating their request and reasserting their privileges in terms which, though more pressing, did not transgress good usage. This time Spotswood left no room for misconceptions as to his attitude. "I am Sorry," he replied, "to find your utmost Concern to be about what you call the Rights and Priviledges of your House, while you Seem to Reserve none for the Distressed Condition of your Neighbours, and testify the greatest Indifference for the Safety and Honour of your Country." While willing to aid the house in maintaining its just rights, the governor begged to be excused from assisting it in any invasion upon the prerogative, or in an attempt to recover all its "Ancient Priviledges," for among these were such executive functions as the appointment of justices. The house had an officer authorized to bring before it persons whom it wished to examine, and to keep in custody those found guilty of a breach of its privileges. In the present case, however, by presuming to put justices on trial for judgments which they had given upon the bench, the house was attempting to erect itself into a court of judicature. In this he could not assist them. "And Seeing your proceedings make the Load of Government Sit already heavily Enough upon my Shoulders, I have the more reason to decline taking up any other Burdens, in this perilous Juncture of Affairs, than Such as Regard the Present Safety of the Country."[32]

As Spotswood implied, measures for the relief of South Carolina were not progressing very rapidly in the house. The burgesses were more interested in the repeal of the tobacco act. Grievances and propositions from twenty-two counties demanding either partial or entire repeal gave them a good starting point, and a repealing act was ordered brought in which should at the same time make "Publick Tobacco payments good and convenient."[33] From this point on the house demonstrated marked singleness of purpose. All proposals to modify the act so as to remove its more objectionable features while retaining the general scheme of regulation

[32] *Jour. Burg.*, 1712-1726, pp. 142-145.
[33] *Ibid.*, pp. 132, 133.

which it established were promptly rejected, as were also all those advocating temporary measures of relief from its provisions. In fact, as if to heighten popular discontent, propositions and grievances upon practically all other matters were rejected. The burgesses would be satisfied with nothing short of outright repeal. They indeed resolved to "endeavour" to raise money to enable the governor to perform the treaty made for the assistance of South Carolina, and exempted all volunteers going to the aid of the southern province from the payment of levies for the current year.[34] But the measure to raise money for the relief of South Carolina by an export duty of a shilling a hogshead on tobacco was tacked as a rider to the bill repealing the tobacco act and all other acts relating to it.[35] It was inconceivable that the high-spirited governor would submit to so flagrant a piece of coercion, even had his instructions permitted his assent to so heterogeneous a measure. That Spotswood would under any circumstances have sanctioned the repeal of the tobacco act is highly improbable, but the action of the assembly made it impossible for him to do so gracefully. There was now but slight prospect that an accommodation could be reached.

At this point the burgesses received the governor's answer to their second request for the apprehension of Littlepage and Butts, and promptly replied with a message of vindication, declaring their sincerity in all efforts for the relief of Carolina. Convinced that Virginia could not afford such aid unless her people were relieved "of those Burthens which they Complain Lye So uneasy on them and which was Represented to us as the General Grievance of this Country, We have made Provision for both in one Bill without which we are not of ability to afford any Such Supplys as are required." The functions in which Littlepage and Butts had been remiss were not judicial but ministerial. In other words, they considered it the business of the justices to receive and cause to be certified all propositions, grievances, and claims presented to them, without the discretion to reject any. Fail-

[34] *Jour. Burg.*, 1712-1726, pp. 139, 140.
[35] *Ibid.*, pp. 141-143.

ure on their part so to do was a matter cognizable by the burgesses in assembly.[36]

On the following day, August 23, the house rejected after a single reading a bill which had passed the council remedying "certain Inconveniencys" in the tobacco act. The council then took up the cudgels. The house had passed a resolution asserting its undoubted right to hear and redress grievances. This, the council pointed out, seemed to impute to the burgesses a power which could be exercised only by both houses with the concurrence of the governor. It desired the burgesses either to recede from their resolve or explain it. The house had considered, without referring them to the council, grievances addressed to the general assembly. It was hoped that this departure from the custom of communicating grievances first to the council would not be made a precedent.[37]

On August 24, the council in executive session considered the question of the grievances presented to the assembly. It was declared that, contrary to law,[38] several seditious and scandalous papers had been drawn up and signed by people called together in a tumultuous manner, instead of at the county courts. Some of these, though signed by only a few obscure persons, had been certified as general county grievances. Other irregularities were enumerated. To prevent the recurrence of these practices, a proclamation was issued, charging the justices to observe the act and certify only those grievances signed at the time and place prescribed by law, and to punish those assembling to draw up grievances in any other manner.[39] Two weeks later the council declared that a number of persons, lacking both the legal knowledge and the integrity requisite for such a calling, were practising as attorneys in the county courts. These pretended attorneys not only fostered many unnecessary disputes among the ignorant, but also exercised a sinister influence upon public affairs

[36] *Jour. Burg.*, 1712-1726, pp. 147, 148.

[37] *Ibid.*, pp. 148, 149; *Leg. Jour. Coun.*, II, 600. Blair, Ludwell, Smith, Cocke, Harrison, Porteus, Lewis, and Page were present at the time of the council's action, the governor being absent.

[38] See Hening, II, 482.

[39] *Ex. Jour. Coun.*, III, 409; *C.O.5/1317*, pp. 301-303.

by persuading the people of their competence in affairs of state, and by drawing up and obtaining signatures to scandalous and seditious papers under the title of grievances. It was therefore ordered that no person should thenceforth practise as an attorney in any court within the colony unless approved by governor and council.[40]

Meanwhile a motion that leave be given to bring in a bill amending the tobacco act was lost in the house.[41] Next day, August 25, in a message to the council the burgesses denied any pretension to redress grievances independently of the other branches of the legislature, but asserted their right to receive those not specifically addressed to governor and council. To preserve a good correspondence between the two houses, however, they were willing to transmit to the council for its perusal any propositions and grievances which it should see fit to require.[42]

On August 26, the burgesses complained to the governor of the removal of James City county court from Jamestown to Williamsburg, and proposed that a number of inhabitants who had offered at their own cost to erect the necessary buildings at a more convenient place be permitted so to do. This question of local politics had reached an acute stage, and the message produced an explosion. "I know," Spotswood declared, "by what Malignant person that Grievance was drawn up and in what unlawful manner it was got Signed and after ffive years Residence upon the borders of *James City* County, I think it hard that I may not be allowed to be as good a Judge as *Mr. Marable's* Rable of a proper Place for the

[40] *Ex. Jour. Coun,* III, 411. The following December it was resolved in council that those desiring to practice as attorneys should furnish proof of their knowledge of both English and colonial law, that they should take the oaths of loyalty required of other officers, that they should give evidence that in their former practice their conduct had been characterized by a respectful attitude towards the government and the courts, and that they should be neither promoters of strife nor encouragers of lawsuits. It was referred to Attorney-General John Clayton, John Holloway, and Robert Beverley, or to any two of them to prepare a scheme of rules for examining the ability and regulating the practices of attorneys, as conformable to the rules and customs of England as the circumstances of the country would permit. *Ex. Jour. Coun.,* III, 420.

[41] *Jour. Burg.,* 1712-1726, p. 149.

[42] *Ibid.,* pp. 149, 150.

Court house. To remove a County Court upon the Application of its Justices (as I have done) is expressly according to the Law of this Colony, and I am not inclinable to do extraordinary Acts merely to gratify the humour of Some persons who make it their greatest Meritt with the people to oppose whatever may be for the interest and Dignity of this his Majestys Government."[43]

The following day a bill to regulate the militia was lost upon the third reading,[44] and the house, after considering the recent proclamation, resolved "That those Persons who have Informed the Honourable the Lt. Governor that the People have been called together in a Riotous manner to Sign any of the Papers presented to this House as Grievances this Session are evil Disposed persons and Disturbers of and Enemys to the Peace and Tranquility of this Country."[45] A message from the governor, received at that juncture, was hardly calculated to pour oil on the troubled waters. "The Surest Information I can have of your Resolutions and Endeavours is, from the Bills you Send the Council, but I can therein no more Discover any Measures taken for the Security of your ffrontiers, than any Supply granted for the Support of your Neighbours, unless you will reckon £450: which you tack'd to a Bill that you were Sensible would never pass the Council or me." He went on to declare that there was "Scarce a Country of its figure in the Christian World" less burdened with taxes than Virginia. "If you your Selves Sincerely believe that it is reduced to the last Degree of Poverty, I wonder the more, that you Should Report [sic] Propositions for lessening the charge of Assemblys, That you should expel Gentlemen out of your House for only offering to Serve their Countys upon their own expence,[46] and that while each day of your Siting is So costly to your Country, you Should Spend time So fruitlesly." Spotswood was not surprised, he said, at the "extraordinary Stress" which the

[43] *Jour. Burg.*, 1712-1726, pp. 151, 152.
[44] *Ibid.*, p. 152.
[45] *Jour. Burg.*, 1712-1726, p. 152.
[46] A reference to the case of Cole and Diggs.

burgesses laid upon the grievances which they had received, "Since I know them to have been originally framed and drawn up by many persons among you, and perhaps their bearing So near a Relation to your House, may incline you to Judge it a Breach of your Priviledges, That Some Justices in the Courts held for Certifying Grievances have declared them to be false and Seditious, and given them Some obstruction in their Passage." The governor proceeded to resurvey the question of the certification of grievances by the county courts, declaring that in the past justices had exercised discretion in this matter,[47] "And if in this Case you will Reckon them only Ministerial Officers, and Divesting them of their Judicial capacity expect they must Certify all Remonstrances whether true or false, lawful or Seditious; and in what manner Soever they be presented, then I cannot See to what end the Laws for presentation of Grievances have been made, or of what Signification the Justices Attestations are."[48]

On August 30 the motion was again made and the question put that leave be given to bring in a bill to amend the tobacco act, only to be defeated.[49] The composite bill repealing the tobacco act and raising the appropriation for the relief of South Carolina had been rejected ten days before by the council upon the first reading, with the declaration "that the Tacking things of a different nature to a Money-Bill is an Encroachment on the priviledge of the Council."[50] The burgesses made no attempt to frame another repeal measure, while they continued to reject all proposals for modification. By retaining all the objectionable features of the tobacco act the house evidently hoped to discredit the new policy, and perhaps the administration. The following day a bill "for Disabling persons holding certain Places of profit in this Colony from being Members of the house of Burgesses" passed the house.[51] The "Places of profit" in question were

[47] From this statement of fact the burgesses apparently dissented. *Jour. Burg.*, 1712-1726, p. 160.

[48] *Ibid.*, pp. 152, 153.

[49] *Ibid.*, p. 156.

[50] *Leg. Jour. Coun.*, II, 599, 600.

[51] *Jour. Burg.*, 1712-1726, p. 158.

evidently those of the tobacco agents, and in opposing a dangerous extension of patronage the burgesses were certainly in the right. The measure was lost in the council.[52]

All hope of reaching an agreement upon the main points at issue having disappeared, the few remaining days of the session were devoted to political pyrotechnics. On September 2 the burgesses adopted a series of resolutions in response to the governor's message of August 27. They held the governor obligated to defend the frontiers until December, 1716, with the funds placed at his disposal by the legislature in 1714. In self-vindication they attributed the *impasse* over the South Carolina appropriation to the governor's unwillingness to remove the "Extraordinary Imposition upon Tobacco for the use of the Tobacco Agents which is more Grievous than any Publick Tax," and the delays in their proceedings to his "Denying to Assist this House in their Just Rights and Priviledges." In conclusion they resolved "That the Message from the Lt. Governor of the 27th: *August* last contains in it undeserved and Scandalous Reflections upon the Persons and Proceedings of this House of Burgesses."[53]

This was too much for the council. The men of substance and position who sat at its board were at one with the governor in supporting the new reforms, and it was little to their liking to see the executive, of which they constituted so essential a part, browbeaten by the Virginia democracy. The council therefore unanimously declared that in passing resolves so disrespectful to the lieutenant governor, several of the burgesses had offered a high indignity to the king. It also asserted that those who should justify or approve these ignominious resolves were unfit to serve the crown in any place of trust or profit, a move doubtless intended to prevent the disaffection from spreading among the official class.

This action was taken in executive session.[54] As the upper house of assembly, the council sent the burgesses a message taking up the resolutions *seriatim* and setting in clear light the

[52] *Leg. Jour. Coun.*, II, 603.
[53] *Jour. Burg.*, 1712-1726, pp. 159, 160.
[54] *Ex. Jour. Coun.*, III, 411.

extravagances of statement. While careful to avoid any expression of approval of the harsh language Spotswood had applied to the lower house, the council gave his policy as complete an endorsement as he could well have wished. It clearly refuted the absurd allegation that the defense of the frontier devolved solely upon the governor, and showed itself strongly in favor of continuing the tobacco act, though in a somewhat modified form. The last resolve of the house, it declared, was "Contrived in Such haughty and indeed Scurrilous terms, and So unbecoming the respect due to his Majestys Representative, and the Gratitude the Country owes to Colonel *Spotswood* for his Vigilant and just Government, and his zeal both for his Majestys and the Countrys Service, that we are mightily Surprized at it, as Savouring more of passion than Deliberation."[55]

Had Spotswood been content to let the matter close with this whole-hearted vindication of his conduct by the men who had not only been the closest observers of his administration but were also the most influential inhabitants of the province, it is by no means improbable that the excesses of the house would have been followed by a reaction of opinion in the colony wholly favorable to the governor. Indeed it is quite likely, as the council had implied in its message, that upon second thought many of the burgesses would have regretted their rashness. Unhappily, the events of the session seem to have deprived Spotswood of that moderation which he had shown to the assembly with such happy results three years before. After the message of the council had been delivered, he summoned the house to the council chamber where, after giving his assent to three acts,[56] he brought the stormy session to a climacteric finish with "one of the most imperious messages ever sent to a colonial assembly,"[57] This speech, which

[55] *Jour. Burg.*, 1712-1726, pp. 165, 166.

[56] These provided for the encouragement of the Carolina volunteers, the building of a chapel in Henrico parish, and the raising of the public levy. A triennial act had been halted by the failure of the two houses to reach an agreement regarding amendments. Other acts hostile to the administration, such as one compelling the Indian Company to defray the entire cost of Indian relations, were also initiated in the house.

[57] Osgood, *Eighteenth Cent.*, II, 236.

was addressed, not in the customary manner to both houses, but merely to the burgesses, occupies four pages of the printed journal.[58] It is a masterpiece of haughty invective. Not content to subject the conduct of the burgesses to the most scathing condemnation, the governor lashed their constituents as well. "The Giddy Resolves of the illiterate Vulgar in their Drunken Conventions," he declared, "you hold for the most Sacred Dictates to your proceedings," thus not only embittering his hearers but offending the people whom they represented. The governor gave a clue to the identity of his principal opponents in the house by hurling defiance at "even a *Conway*, a *Corbin*, or a *Marable*" to show that he had received from the former assembly any larger appropriation than was necessary to defray the expenses actually incurred in the defense of the frontier. His philippic delivered, the governor dissolved the assembly after a short session of barely five weeks, singularly barren of important legislation, but far-reaching in its effect upon the subsequent course of events. The dispute between Spotswood and certain elements in the colony had become an open and ugly quarrel. Thereafter those who crossed swords with the governor were not to lack supporters.[59]

The session ended, Spotswood seized an opportunity to turn the attack of the burgesses upon the justices of the peace to the disadvantage of the former. It had been the custom for the county courts to levy the salaries of the burgesses, a practice now discovered to be without legal basis. The burgesses had insisted that the function of the judges in connection with grievances was not judicial but merely ministerial. Having thus been called so strictly to account for exceeding

[58] *Jour. Burg.*, 1712-1726, pp. 166-170.

[59] The board of trade wrote to Spotswood that though the assembly was composed of mean and ignorant persons who did not comply with that which might reasonably be expected of them, it feared that a speech so full of sharp expressions might so incense both them and their electors that it would be a considerable time before they could be "brought to Temper again." It hoped, however, that by the governor's prudent management no future assemblies would deserve such a reprimand. B. T. to Spotswood, June 1, 1716. *C.O.5/1364*, pp. 380, 381.

their supposed powers, could the county justices with prudence exercise so evident a legislative function as the levying of taxes? Spotswood had these considerations printed and circulated among the justices. He also wrote a circular letter to the councillors, telling them that he intended to bring this question before the general court. When the matter came before the councillors in executive session, they begged to be excused from expressing their opinion of an issue likely to come before them as judges of the general court. The attorney-general was called in. He declared that a careful perusal of the laws did not reveal any power in the county courts to lay a levy upon the inhabitants for paying the burgesses their allowances.[60]

In the spring of 1716 a paper was sent to the board of trade embodying accusations against Spotswood in the form of fifteen queries. The accusers failed to sign their names. It was a terrific and sweeping indictment, portraying the man as harsh as a plundering proconsul of Rome. He had no regard for law, forcing customs officials to extort illegal fees and placing foreigners in courts of judicature. He was a mercenary creature, seeking his own ends at public expense, building forts upon the frontier at public charge to protect his private interests and refusing to permit the king's subjects to take up land while engrossing great tracts himself. Under him there was little justice. Not only Englishmen, but Indians and slaves suffered from his tyranny. He aroused sedition and rebellion by fostering disregard for the existing forms of government. He was greedy of power, driving from office those who ventured to oppose his will and seeking by the creation of a standing militia to establish a military dictatorship.[61]

The indictment was sent to the governor who replied in a long and able defense, pointing out that some of the accu-

[60] *C.O.5/1318*, pp. 185, 707; *Ex. Jour. Coun.*, III, 413. Whether the matter came up in general court, and if so what decision was arrived at, is not known, the general court records for the entire period under consideration being unfortunately lost.

[61] *C.O.5/1317*, pp. 95, 96.

sations were too vague to be capable of an answer, declaring others to be false, and justifying the course which he had pursued in connection with the rest.[62] To show that the country was not disaffected to his administration, he sent the board an address presented to him by the grand jury at the October general court of 1716 begging him to resume his place upon the general court bench, from which he had for some time absented himself because of differences with the other judges. The grand jury was assured, it said, that the governor would have the goodness to pass over the occasion for his withdrawal. This would give great satisfaction to the people he governed, who wished for nothing more than that the king would continue him long in his office.[63] It must be borne in mind, however, that the governor was able to influence the selection of grand jurymen. That they were now voicing the sentiments of the colony in general is improbable.

Difficult as Spotswood's task had proven during the first five years of his administration, it would have been far more difficult had he not been able to depend on the close cooperation of the council. Not that the governor had succeeded in dominating this body. Accustomed to play no small part in the public life of the colony, the men who composed it were perfectly capable of independent action. If they acted with the governor it was out of sympathy with the policies which he was trying to promote. On several important questions, however, the governor found himself opposed by certain members of the council, and this opposition was destined to grow until, reenforced by personal animosity, it threatened to disrupt the administration.

[62] *Letters*, II, 189-218. Attorney-General John Clayton, in order to vindicate both himself and the governor from one of the accusations, wrote an account of the case of Frances Wilson, the only woman who had been brought to trial during Spotswood's administration for murdering a slave. Clayton had prosecuted the case in the belief that no subject had the power of life and death over his slave. Frances Wilson took the contrary view that according to law she ought not to be molested for killing her slave. The jury were apparently of the same opinion, for although there was no doubt as to the facts of the case the defendant was acquitted. *C.O.5/1318*, pp. 189-191.

[63] Address of grand jury to Spotswood, October General Court, 1716. *Ibid.*, p. 205.

Chapter VII

THE LAND SYSTEM

AT THE dawn of the eighteenth century, an unbroken settlement of a hundred years notwithstanding, the taking up of free land was still an important factor in the social and economic life of Virginia.[1] Moreover, since land was subject to a perpetual quit rent, old holdings as well as new were affected by the land system. The London Company had reserved a quit rent of two shillings for every hundred acres granted to settlers, and this practice was continued when Virginia became a royal province. But specie being scarce, tobacco came to be accepted in lieu of the money payment at the rate of a penny a pound.[2]

It was the policy of the crown to promote the occupation of waste land. The practice of obtaining large grants for speculative purposes was, however, discouraged. For such grants kept actual settlers off the land, and it was found impracticable to collect quit rents from them. Non-payment of quit rents did not constitute a ground for forfeiture, and arrears could be levied only by distraint. If the land were unimproved there was nothing to distrain, and the position of the patentee was impregnable.

[1] In 1711 the quit rent account (that for 1710) placed the patented land at 2,450,998 acres. *C.O.5/1316*, O.100. The total was doubtless greater than this, due to "concealed" land, i.e., land surreptitiously omitted from the rent rolls. During the first eight years of Spotswood's administration, 344,181 acres of new land was granted, and in 1718 the governor estimated the land held immediately of the crown in Virginia at "near three millions of acres." During the last four years, land was disposed of in even greater quantities. *C.O.5/1318*, pp. 467-491; *Letters*, II, 265. These figures do not include the "Northern Neck," the five counties lying between the Rappahannock and the Potomac, the land of which had been granted to proprietors who paid a nominal quit rent of £6.13.4 per annum to the crown.

[2] Beverley W. Bond, Jr., *The Quit Rent System in the American Colonies* (New Haven, 1919), pp. 221, 224, 225.

That each colonist might have a modest holding, every settler arriving in the colony was entitled to a tract of fifty acres. In practice, however, the royal will was evaded. "Importation" or "head" rights (the terms are reciprocal) were assigned to others in return for a money payment, and more than one head right was often obtained for the importation of a single person. Where the immigrant was an indentured servant not only did he obtain his right when he had served his time,[3] but the shipmaster, the merchant who disposed of his services, and the planter who purchased them all obtained head rights.[4] A speculator thus had little difficulty in buying up a number of rights. The large grants thus obtained seem at times to have been increased by actual peculation. Philip Ludwell originally held 2000 acres by forty head rights, but by adding a cipher to each figure in his patent he obtained 20,000.[5] Where a member of the council who later became deputy auditor was capable of such malfeasance, the task of reforming the land system was apt to prove difficult. An act of 1705 curbed the clandestine multiplication of head rights by confining the privilege to the person imported, but facilitated the taking up of large tracts by authorizing the receiver-general to issue certificates entitling the bearer to fifty acres. A consideration of five shillings current money was to be paid for each of these "treasury" rights.[6]

Since the objection to large estates rested not so much upon the concentration of wealth in a few hands as upon the probability that these tracts would remain unutilized, a remedy was sought in regulations enjoining certain minimum improvements, failure to make which would invalidate pat-

[3] See Orkney's instructions, *Va. Mag. Hist.*, XXI, 232.

[4] *Letters*, II, 15.

[5] Bond, p. 228.

[6] Hening, III, 304, 305. This was a change in precept rather than in practice, for it had long been the custom of the secretary to accept money payments varying from one to five shillings in lieu of head rights. Percy Scott Flippin, *The Royal Government in Virginia* (New York, 1919), p. 215. In 1699 governor and council had set the rate at fifty acres a crown, and according to Spotswood the circulation of treasury rights dated from that time. *Ex. Jour. Coun.*, I, 457; *Letters*, II, 177.

ents. Instructions to this end given to Governors Nott and Hunter aroused vigorous protest, as might be expected. The royal authorities therefore ordered that for the future land be granted upon the conditions prevalent previous to the instructions to Hunter. But what they gave with one hand they took away with the other, for they insisted that "regard be had to the profitable and unprofitable acres,"[7] and that every patentee be required to cultivate and improve "in the best and most effectual manner" three acres out of every fifty.[8]

Dissatisfied with the new regulations, Virginians now hesitated to take out patents. Grievances from the counties voiced the popular discontent, and the burgesses petitioned Spotswood to allow patents to pass under the old provisions. The governor sought to allay the fear of the people that they were to be deprived of ancient privileges, and promised to refer to the crown the case of those who had already taken up land and made their surveys, and upon whom the instructions therefore imposed *ex post facto* conditions. At the same time he declared that the crown had never intended to pass grants which the patentee was unable to cultivate, and that the obligation to cultivate three acres out of every fifty was more conformable to former usage than the granting of land without restriction. He therefore prohibited grants of more than 400 acres unless the patentee appeared able to improve his tract according to law.[9] He reported "much struggle, both with the Council and Burgesses," but the colony finally submitted with tolerably good grace.[10] Dissatisfaction with the

[7] That is to say the bad land was to be granted with the good, otherwise when the good land was taken up the bad would be left unpatented and pay no quit rents even though used for pasturing and other purposes by the inhabitants. In his proclamation of December 8, 1710, Spotswood required surveyors to lay out tracts so that the breadth was at least one-third of the width, unless hindered by rivers, creeks, impassible swamps, or the bounds of other patents. No land was to be left because of poorer quality. *C.O.5/1316*, O.76.

[8] *C.O.5/1363*, pp. 39-43, *C.O.5/1316* O.52; *Va. Mag. Hist.*, XXI, 233.

[9] *Letters*, I, 61, 62; *C.O.5/1316*, O.76.

[10] *Letters*, I, 19, 39, 40; *Jour. Burg.*, 1702-1712, pp. 265, 292, 293. It was at this time that Spotswood made his proposal to the board of the trade that the

act of 1705[11] enabled the governor to induce the assembly to enact in 1710 an entirely new land law, in which several important reforms were incorporated. All future patents were to be entered upon the records in the secretary's office, but the omission of this form in earlier patents was not to invalidate them. Failure to seat and plant or the non-payment of quit rents for three consecutive years constituted a ground for forfeiture, together with the loss of the rights paid for the land. Forfeiture, however, did not take place automatically, but only if some other party petitioned for the land, and was averted if at the trial it could be shown that the improvements had been completed, either during the first three years or subsequently. Owners of contiguous high land were given the prior right to take up unpatented swamp and marsh land. Similarly, while a second party might take up land held in excess of the patent, the holder had the prior right to take up the surplus and, failing this, the choice as to what part of his patent he surrendered.[12] An excess of five acres in the hundred was allowed "for the variation of instruments." Provision was made for quadrennial processionings, three processionings being deemed sufficient to establish the bounds for all time.[13] Spotswood had found it necessary to make concessions to vested interests in order to pass the bill through an assembly of landowners representing constituents all of whom were freeholders. Nevertheless the provision permitting another to take out a patent for excess land and that invalidating a patent for non-payment of quit rents or failure to improve marked a real advance. The act also definitely placed the right of granting escheated land in the hands of the gover-

---

frontier settlements be extended by granting land on one side of the James upon the old conditions. *Infra*, p. 238.

[11] This act had been disallowed in 1707 (*B. T. Jour.*, 1704-1709, p. 355), but the colonial government had not been notified to that effect.

[12] Qualified though it was, this provision was calculated to discourage "concealed" land and, as Spotswood pointed out to Blathwayt, laid a foundation for obtaining a complete rent roll. *Letters*, I, 69. The 1711 quit rent account received the addition of nearly 10,000 acres of "concealed" land. *Ibid.*, p. 90.

[13] Hening, III, 523-532.

nor.[14] Since the act of 1710 specified no terms of seating and planting[15] that matter now rested, as Spotswood contended that it should, upon the basis of the royal instructions.[16] The governor was willing to let the matter rest here, for he felt that the granting of land, ostensibly a matter entirely within the province of the crown, ought not to be regulated by act of assembly. Paradoxically, however, this encroachment upon the royal prerogative was encouraged from England, Lord Dartmouth directing Spotswood to secure the enactment into law of the royal instructions concerning land grants. With some misgivings that this would arouse once more the apprehensions which he had just succeeded in quieting,[17] the governor obtained from the council in 1712 a bill setting forth the conditions of seating and planting, only to have it rejected by the burgesses.[18] There were evidently those in England who felt that an act of assembly was apt to have more weight in Virginia than the royal instructions!

Since no orders came from England with regard to those who had taken up land upon the strength of the act of 1705, numbers of these persons continued to hold tracts without patenting them, and therefore without the obligation to pay quit rents, in the hope that they would be exempted from

[14] The granting of lapsed or escheated land by the general court was objected to by the governor. This practice was based upon the act of 1705, and since the council was satisfied that the crown had repealed this act the governor was given his way. In cases of lapse or escheat the general court was to pass upon the fact, but the power of regranting was to rest in the governor. *Ex. Jour. Coun.*, III, 255, 256.

[15] At Spotswood's suggestion, a law of 1666 which became operative upon the repeal of that of 1705 and which provided uniform conditions for seating and planting irrespective of the size of the patent, was repealed by the crown. *Letters*, I, 24; Hening, II, 244; *C.O.5/1363*, pp. 249-252; *Cal. State Paps., Col.*, 1710-1711, p. 436.

[16] *Letters*, I, 61. The words of the charter of 1679 were too ambiguous to form a very strong basis for opposition.

[17] *Ibid.*, pp. 109-112; *B. T. Jour.*, 1709-1715, p. 260.

[18] *Leg. Jour. Coun.*, I, 546; *Jour. Burg.*, 1712-1726, p. 29. During the same session a law was passed providing that land could not lapse from minors for non-improvement or non-payment of quit rents until three years after their majority. Although this act did not meet with his approval, Spotswood signed it to humor the burgesses, passing to the crown the problem of veto. Hening, IV, 31, 32; *Letters*, II, 12, 13.

the terms of the recent instructions. Spotswood therefore issued a proclamation in August 1713 requiring all those who had surveyed land since the death of Governor Nott to secure patents by the following April. Those unable to cultivate upon the new terms had the privilege of assigning their entries to others or of withdrawing their rights from the secretary's office. If they did not wish to take up other land the receiver-general was to redeem the rights in money. Titles to escheated lands held without grant were to be secured before December 25, and thereafter those taking up escheated lands were to make a new survey.[19] This proclamation had immediate effect. Within a month Spotswood reported that over a hundred patents for new land had been bespoken, while those who had held escheated land for many years now applied for grants.[20]

Since the board of trade was unwilling to make exceptions to the terms laid down in the governor's instructions, Spotswood informed the burgesses in 1713 that the members of the council and others with pretensions to large tracts of land favored the enactment of the conditions of seating and planting in a bill similar to that sent them by the council the previous session.[21] Accordingly a measure as conformable to the wishes of the crown as could well be expected was brought in and passed. It reaffirmed parts of the act of 1710 and of Spotswood's proclamations, provided for the survey of patents by commissioned and sworn surveyors only,[22] and al-

[19] *Ex. Jour. Coun.*, III, 348, 349. The former practice of granting patents for escheated lands in the general terms of the old grants was said to occasion disputes over boundary lines and, by understating the acreage, to deprive the crown of composition and quit rents.

[20] *Letters*, II, 35, 36.

[21] *Jour. Burg.*, 1712-1726, p. 65.

[22] That is to say, by the county surveyors or their deputies. County surveyors were theoretically appointed by the surveyor-general, who was an appointee of William and Mary College. In practice, however, they were nominated by the trustees of the college and approved by governor and council, who at times assumed the power of appointment and removal without consulting the trustees. Jones, *Present State of Virginia*, p. 61; *Ex. Jour. Coun.*, III, 319, 340, 462, 463, 477. Flippin (*Royal Government in Virginia*, p. 218) points out in this connection that the governor and several councillors were among the visitors and trustees of the college and its president was a councillor.

lowed to those who had taken up land before the proclamation of December 8, 1710, five years in which to make improvements. Holders of land formerly patented were not obliged to make further improvements, but forfeiture for non-payment of three years' quit rents was made operative upon old lands as well as new.[23] The most notable innovation, however, was the substitution for the uniform requirements for improvement, conditions adapted to variations in the quality of the land. "Plantable" land was to be seated by the cultivation of three acres out of every fifty, or by the draining of three acres of marsh land; "barren" land by pasturing upon a like quantity within three years of the passing of the grant three head of cattle or six sheep or goats, which were to remain upon it until three acres out of every fifty were cultivated. If a tract of land were taken up, no part of which was fit for cultivation, the patentee was to pasture cattle upon it as for other "barren" land, and also build upon it within three years a good dwelling house "after the manner of *Virginia*," at least sixteen by twenty feet in size. Mine and quarry land was to be improved by employing upon it for three consecutive years "one good able hand" for every hundred acres. Improvements made in any part of a tract applied to the tract as a whole, and where improvements were partially completed, they were to keep a proportionate part of the grant from lapsing. When improvements were completed, evidence to that effect was to

[23] Spotswood intended that this should be the purport of the act of 1710, but the general sentiment of the colony interpreted that provision otherwise. Realizing that an appeal to the courts would be almost certain to go against the crown, the governor had perforce to get the provision reenacted in more specific terms. *Letters*, II, 81. Nevertheless, in 1715 the question whether this provision applied to land patented before its enactment was again raised in the house of burgesses and a bill was introduced and passed to explain it. The nature of such explanation may readily be guessed from the temper of the house at that time. The council, however, rejected the bill. *Jour. Burg.*, 1712-1726, pp. 155-158; *Leg. Jour. Coun.*, II, 605. The effectiveness of this provision was greatly reduced by the retention of the provision of the act of 1710 which made forfeiture not automatic, but contingent upon some other party suing out a patent for the land. Needless to say, however, the crown had nothing to gain by confiscation, and the object of the act was merely to induce proprietors, through fear of confiscation, to give a true account of the land they held, and pay quit rents accordingly. *Letters*, II, 266, 267.

be presented to the county courts, where it was to be recorded. Thus, in a rudimentary way, provision was made for the taking up of land for purposes other than agriculture, lack of which provision constituted the principal defect of the homestead act of our national period.[24] The operation of the act was suspended until December 1, 1714, that the crown might have opportunity to disallow it before it went into operation, but while it was not quite what the British authorities desired, they doubtless concluded that it was all that there was any reason to expect, and in 1716 the act was confirmed.[25]

In 1712 Spotswood gave his attention to the method of obtaining "importation rights." It was ordered in council that all outstanding importation rights be examined at the April 1713 general court. Those duly obtained were to be registered in the secretary's office, the rest canceled. In future county court clerks were to return semi-annually to the secretary's office a list of all persons making oath to their importation, with the date of their arrival. The practice of granting rights for those entering the Northern Neck was discontinued. There was now a prospect of preventing frauds, since no importation right would be honored which had not been recorded, and checking the list would halt the practice of securing a number of rights for a single importation, which upon the repeal of the act of 1705 had sprung up anew.[26] The examination of the outstanding rights was delegated to the receiver-general and the deputy auditor. No rights were to be allowed for importations before 1692, none before 1706 except to free immigrants, and none since 1706 except to the person imported. Entries made upon the basis of rights found to be void were to stand good till the next April general

[24] Cf. F. L. Paxson, *History of the American Frontier, 1763-1893* (Boston, 1924), p. 551.

[25] Hening, IV, 37-42; *C.O.5/1317*, pp. 503, 504. William Byrd appeared before the board of trade in behalf of this act. *B. T. Jour.*, 1715-1718, p. 137.

[26] *Ex. Jour. Coun.*, III, 305, 306, 330, 331; *C.O.5/1316*, O.139; *C.O.5/1363*, p. 485; *Letters*, II, 14, 15, 21, 22. The act of 1705 being repealed, the charter of Charles II constituted the sole basis for taking up land upon importation rights. Apparently treasury rights were now once more without legal authorization, other than the executive order of governor and council.

court, to allow time for the substitution of bona fide rights.[27]

Spotswood was enjoined by his instructions to see to it that quit rents were publicly sold every year at the county courts by "inch of candle,"[28] but he found that this custom had been discontinued for some years past, the quit rent tobacco being disposed of by the deputy auditor and the receiver-general by public sale at the general court. The council was unanimously agreed that this method should be continued, and the governor was won over. The board of trade remaining unconvinced, Spotswood submitted documents in support of his position, among them a letter from William Byrd in which the receiver-general declared that sale at the county courts was found to reduce the revenue because the buyers were few, and could easily agree to beat down the price. Sheriffs were not over-nice in judging the value of the bills of exchange which they received, and since he was held responsible for all, Byrd contended that is was only fair that he be obliged to take only those which he considered good.[29] The board of trade then laid the matter before the lord treasurer, but apparently no further action was taken.[30]

The duty of collecting the quit rents fell to the lot of the sheriffs, under warrants from the governor in council. They frequently delegated the actual collection to deputies of their own choosing, who were under neither oath nor other particular obligation for the scrupulous execution of their trust. Questionable practices thus crept in. In April 1711, therefore, under-sheriffs were required by proclamation to make oath at the county courts that their accounts contained all the quit rents which they had received and a complete rent roll of all the lands that they had been able to discover. These oaths were to be recorded upon the rent rolls by the county court clerk, and were to be produced by the high sheriff to the audi-

[27] *Ex. Jour. Coun.*, III, 336, 344, 345.

[28] *Va. Mag. Hist.* XXI, 356. See the note upon "inch of candle," *Letters*, I, 7.

[29] *Cal. State Paps., Col.*, 1710-1711, p. 242; *C.O.5/1316*, O.102; *Letters*, I, 7, 8, 87. Spotswood was not long in discovering that the current method of selling the quit rent tobacco also had its abuses. *Letters*, II, 178.

[30] *B. T. Jour.*, 1709-1715, p. 313; *Cal. State Paps., Col.*, 1711-1712, p. 162.

tor before he was permitted to pass his accounts. The following year the high sheriff was further required to give an account upon oath to the auditor of the quit rent money which he had received.[31]

Spotswood thought that the task of quit rent collection might profitably be transferred from the sheriffs who were handicapped by their short terms and the pressure of other matters to the surveyors, permanent officials with ample opportunity to discover what each man in the county held. But such an innovation was likely to provoke opposition and should therefore come from a higher authority than the governor. Spotswood was willing that Blathwayt, to whom he communicated the plan, should "have the hon'r of making the proposals." Later he renewed the suggestion to the board of trade. This method, he wrote, was "Disliked upon two Accounts very extraordinary, first, because it would Introduce a Greater Exactness than is consistent w'th the popular Notions of Liberty, and, secondly, because it would Create so great a dependance of these Officers on the Government."[32]

The sheriffs' returns, "uncouth medleys of rough, unmethodized Papers," were the only rent rolls which the officers of the revenue[33] pretended to keep. The quit rents were collected by different persons nearly every year, and since only the name of the proprietor, which might change from time to time, and not that of the original patentee, was recorded, nothing like a workable rent roll existed. The officers of the revenue, whose labors were multiplied by Spotswood's flair for efficiency, made little effort to secure one. In fact, if we may believe the governor, they did their utmost to prevent its being procured. They eventually consented, however, that the clerk of the council should enter their general accounts in a book to be kept at the council office, that the governor might consult it. The latter delayed proposing new reforms for a time in the hope that he would shortly

[31] *Ex. Jour. Coun.*, III, 261, 319, 320; *C.O.5/1316*, O.96.
[32] *Letters*, II, 162, 268.
[33] That is, the deputy auditor and the receiver-general.

be aided by Francis Nicholson, who was coming to America to investigate the revenues of the various colonies. But the death of the queen terminated Nicholson's commission, and Spotswood was thrown upon his own resources. The measures which had been taken appear nevertheless to have had gratifying results, and Spotswood anticipated further improvement when a few years' peace had raised the price of tobacco. Nor did he wait for this slow process to have its fruition, but by the passage of the tobacco act of 1713 endeavored to ensure the payment of public dues in high-grade tobacco, and at the same time to raise the price of the commodity as a whole.[34]

The passage of the tobacco act revolutionized the collection of the quit rents. Reorganization was delayed for a time while Spotswood sought permission from the lord treasurer to receive pieces of eight in payment of the revenue at current rates.[35] According to the regulations eventually proposed by the governor and adopted with some modifications by the council, each sheriff was to receive in person the quit rents for his county only at the time and place appointed by the county court for paying the levies. Foreign coin current in Virginia was to be accepted at rates somewhat lower than those established by colonial law,[36] while tobacco notes of any agent in the colony were to be received provided they were for the kind of tobacco grown in that county.[37] The sheriff was to deliver upon oath the same notes which he received. He was to accept only such bills of exchange as he would endorse. Five per cent was to be allowed the sheriff for the

[34] *Letters*, II, 20, 21, 61, 62, 177-179. Spotswood endeavored to impress Blathwayt with the beneficial effect which the tobacco act would have upon the revenues, and to get him to secure for it the approval of the lord treasurer.

[35] *Ex. Jour. Coun.*, III, 373. This had been authorized by Charles II, but never put into effect.

[36] It was natural that there should be a discount, the surprising thing being that this was not uniform. Foreign coins rated with the currency of Mexico were to be received at a shade under the current rate. Those rated with Peru were subject to a discount of about ten per cent. *Ex. Jour. Coun.*, III, 389, 390; Hening, III, 503.

[37] A provision designed to prevent Oronoco from being received in "sweet-scented" counties.

quit rents which he collected. A discount of five per cent was to be allowed to those who paid their quit rents before March 31, which was increased to eight per cent if they paid them directly to the receiver-general.[38] The sheriffs were to meet the auditor and receiver-general at Williamsburg in April to pass their accounts, and were to bring rent rolls in duplicate.[39] The accounts of the rents paid directly to the receiver-general were to be passed at the same time. Both were to be signed jointly by auditor and sheriff. One copy of the rent roll was then to be posted upon the county courthouse door, that concealed land might be detected and that those who had paid their rents might see whether the sheriff had given them due credit. On the first day of the April general court, the receiver-general was to deliver upon oath to the governor a list of all the agents' notes received for quit rents. The auditor and receiver-general were then to receive bids in writing, to be entered in the list opposite the tobacco bid for, and on the tenth day of the general court the highest offers were to be accepted.[40]

Though Spotswood induced the majority of the council to assent to the new scheme it encountered considerable opposition, of which the officers of the revenue were the guiding spirits. Spotswood proposed that objections be submitted in writing, which he would then answer and refer to the authorities in England. Byrd alone acted upon this proposal and he, though the governor declared he opposed the whole, confined his criticism to the additional discount of three per cent allowed to those who paid the quit rents directly to him. This, he said, was a hardship to the sheriffs since it reduced their income, and also to the receiver-general, since it increased his duties without additional compensation. If few

[38] This was shortly changed to one-twelfth to facilitate computation. *Ex. Jour. Coun.*, III, 396.

[39] The rent rolls were to be in accordance with a form which the governor had had printed, specifying the proprietors, the original patentees, the acreage, and the medium in which the rent was paid, there being columns for money or bills, and for Oronoco and sweetscented tobacco.

[40] *Ibid.*, pp. 385, 389, 390.

were to avail themselves of this provision the saving to the revenue, amounting only to two per cent, would be so slight that the crown might well waive it; but if, as he thought more likely, a considerable number would do so, injustice would be done to sheriff and receiver-general. The latter contingency, however, was just what Spotswood desired. The former system involved, he declared, "the grossest Mismanagements and most fraudulent Collections that ever was known in a Revenue," and this he offered to prove if contradicted. The root of these abuses lay in the collection by the sheriffs and by the "baser sort of men" who acted as their deputies. By securing direct payment to the receiver-general he hoped to save in some instances not two per cent, but one hundred. "I have no hopes," he added however, "and the receiv'r Gen'l need have no Fear y't the People of ye whole Colony will ever be perswaded to come and pay him their Q't rents, unless, indeed, he should be order'd to take a progress once a Year through the several Countys."[41] If the sheriff were still paid pro rata for the quit rents which he collected, the governor professed inability to see that injustice was done him.[42] If it were the duty of the receiver-general to record only the total receipts for each county,[43] then the new regulations admittedly occasioned him more work, but if in accordance with the royal instructions he was to keep detailed accounts by reference to which it could be seen from whom and for how much land quit rents were due, no further labor was involved.[44]

The reforms which the governor was attempting to initiate were in marked contrast to the mode of procedure theretofore

[41] For 1714 ten, and for 1715 fourteen per cent of the quit rent revenue was paid directly to the receiver-general. *C.O.5/1317*, pp. 184, 185; *Blathwayt's Virginia Papers*, MSS. 1675-1717. Thereafter the accounts do not specify such payments.

[42] The governor asserted that the office of sheriff was sought by the gentlemen of the country, but his efforts to secure the passage of a law compelling an appointee to accept office seem to indicate that such was not always the case.

[43] This would appear to have been the former practice, and was doubtless the basis of the receiver-general's opposition.

[44] *Letters*, II, 81-87.

customary. The public and private accounts of the receiver-general were not kept separate, and such accounts of the revenue as existed consisted of bundles of papers, which usually specified only the gross totals of the various branches of the revenue. Spotswood had contended from the first that the accounts should be entered into books kept for that particular purpose, which should specify the source of each item. The governor complained that he was unable to lay any accounts of the revenue before the assembly, since there were no books fit for that purpose, and the officers of the revenue would not prepare transcripts. Ample opportunity was offered for fraud in the sale of treasury rights, since the receiver-general could issue them at will, and was only obliged to give an account of his total receipts. Since treasury rights circulated as currency without any time limit, it was impossible to check the number issued with the number presented for land grants.[45]

That the fiscal affairs of Virginia stood sadly in need of reform cannot be doubted. At times, however, the governor was meticulous to the point of pettiness. He complained that twopence per acre had been received as composition for escheated land instead of two pounds of tobacco as the charter of Charles II required. He also criticized the receiver-general for taking current money at the rate of nineteen pennyweight to the crown,[46] while the exchange with England was between sixteen and seventeen.[47] Byrd admitted that he had received some small advantage from the use of Spanish coins but rejoined, with some justice, that he had frequently advanced sums without interest to supply the deficit in the revenue, amounting at one time to nearly £2000. He estimated that he was thus out of pocket nearly £70, while his gains from the exchange on Spanish money were not quite £10.[48]

Shortly after the enactment of the new regulations for the

[45] *Letters*, II, 176, 177.
[46] Presumably in payment for treasury rights.
[47] *Ibid.*, II, 179, 182.
[48] *C.O.5/1317*, pp. 507-509.

collection of the revenue Byrd departed for England, leaving Nathaniel Harrison to act as his deputy. The brunt of the opposition to the governor therefore devolved upon the deputy auditor, Philip Ludwell. Lacking the brilliance and personal magnetism of Byrd, Ludwell was equally an opponent of reform, and if less ingenuous was not less active in his resistance. He advised others, so said the governor, not to accede to the new regulations, since they rested upon no law but merely upon the authority of governor and council, and set the example of refusing, in paying his quit rents, to give the name of the original patentee of his lands.[49] The petition of the assembly to the crown that the quit rents might be placed upon the same footing as the two shillings per hogshead was ascribed by Spotswood to Ludwell and Byrd, and the lack of proper accounts to lay before the assembly upon that occasion brought matters to a head. Spotswood sent Ludwell a copy of the governor's twenty-ninth instruction, requiring the accounts of the revenue to be kept in books specifying every particular sum raised or disposed of, and demanded his answer whether he would forthwith comply with it. Ludwell replied that he could make no alteration in the method of keeping accounts without instruction from the auditor-general.[50] Thereupon, on May 24, 1716, Spotswood suspended him, drawing up a statement of the situation which, together with his charges against Ludwell, he sent to the board of trade and to the treasury board.[51] He accused the deputy auditor of conniving at abuses in the revenue, of obstructing all attempts at reform, and of courting the favor of the people by posing as their protector against the aggressions of the governor. Ludwell had refused to express an opinion upon the question of

[49] *Letters,* II, 184, 185. Spotswood told Blathwayt that but for the opposition of the officers of the revenue, he could in a short time have obtained an exact rent roll of all lands held of the crown.

[50] "Thereby," declared Spotswood, "endeavouring to set up the Authority of the Auditor General in Competition with that of his Majesty, which it is certain the said Auditor General would not offer at himself, nor countenance in his Deputy." *Ibid.*, p. 184.

[51] This is to be found in *Letters,* II, 176-187.

encouraging the direct payment of quit rents to the receiver-general because of his close relationship to Byrd, and was thus by his own admission unfit to hold the office of auditor as long as Byrd occupied that of receiver-general. These accusations he submitted to Ludwell for his answers, but the latter declined to "enter into a paper War" with an "unequal Adversary," and declared he would send his defense directly to the board of trade unless Spotswood would permit the dispute between them to be decided by the council. His instructions giving the council no cognizance of such matters, and six of the ten councillors being related to Ludwell, Spotswood was naturally unwilling to do this.[52]

In the expectation that the authorities in England would sustain him by confirming the removal of Ludwell, Spotswood proposed to Blathwayt that either Peter Beverley or John Robinson be appointed in his place. Neither of these men belonged to the family clique in the council and Spotswood considered them qualified in other respects.[53] Ludwell's removal was confirmed, but he was succeeded by his nephew, John Grymes, later one of the governor's most active opponents in the house of burgesses, an appointment little to Spotswood's taste. Meanwhile, Byrd's commission had expired. He was then in England, seeking reappointment, but James Roscowe shortly afterwards became receiver-general. Active opposition to the governor's reforms on the part of the officers of the revenue thereupon ceased.[54]

More serious was the opposition of the people. Whatever the defects of the system which Spotswood found in Virginia, it apparently had the virtue of securing prompt payment of the quit rents for land upon the rent rolls. Concealed land there doubtless was, and rents were frequently paid in tobacco which fetched but a low price. But the acreage of the various counties upon which rent was paid for the years 1710, 1711,

[52] *Letters*, II, 171; *Va. Mag. Hist.*, XXI, 118, 119.

[53] *Letters*, II, 162.

[54] See patent to James Roscowe, April 21, 1716, and deputation to John Grymes, July 2, 1716. *Treas.*, *64/90*, pp. 100-102.

and 1713 is relatively uniform, showing that upward trend which was to be expected from new patents and the occasional discovery of concealed land. The passage of the tobacco act, from which so much was expected by way of quit rent reform, threw everything into confusion. The new regulations provoked widespread popular opposition, and crops were bad. What actually happened is a matter for speculation since Spotswood, desirous of putting the new reforms in their best light, made no reference to the matter in his correspondence. But the accounts indicate a general attempt to checkmate the governor by refusing to pay quit rents. Less than forty-four per cent for 1714 could be collected on time, and although the following years brought some improvement and back rents were collected in part, the quit rents were by 1717 hopelessly in arrears.[55] This, the governor said, had been fostered by rumors that the crown had repealed the act which made three years' non-payment a ground for forfeiture.[56]

It was evidently Spotswood's desire to dispel this illusion by enforcing the penalty, but here he encountered the opposition of the council, which was only willing to order that the sheriffs demand the arrears, and in case of refusal that they record the reason given. Moreover the councillors, so said the governor, having done their utmost to get the assembly to repeal the land act of 1713, decided in their capacity as judges of the general court, apparently at the April session in 1717, that forfeiture for three years' non-payment of quit rents applied only to lands patented after its passage.[57] Since this decision was contrary to the express provision of the act, it constituted a case of judicial review rather than judicial interpretation. The general court being the final court of appeal in all cases involving less than £300, its decision was in practice final. Even with respect to land patented after 1713 the law seems to have been a dead letter. In 1718 Chichley Corbin Thacker, clerk of the secretary's office, certified that having

[55] See Appendix III.
[56] *Ex. Jour. Coun.*, III, 447.
[57] *Letters*, II, 266.

carefully searched the records of land grants since December 1710, he had not found, nor could he remember, any patent granted for land which had lapsed because of non-payment of quit rents.[58] In 1718 Spotswood was charged by the burgesses with having perverted many of their laws, notably the land act of 1710, by extending this provision to lands patented previous to its passage.[59] But as Spotswood pointed out to the board of trade, there was no occasion for his doing this, the act of 1713 having applied the provision to all lands held from the crown.[60] The board of trade referred the matter to Richard West, whose opinion that all patents regardless of date were within the purview of the act of 1713 upheld Spotswood's contention.[61]

The repeal of the tobacco act of 1713 necessitated a new code of regulations for the collection of the quit rents. The system in vogue before its passage was thereupon revived with a few alterations. The quit rent tobacco was to be sold at auction at Williamsburg. The sheriffs were to account for the medium in which payment was made, whether bills of exchange, Spanish silver,[62] or tobacco, and were to make out their rent rolls in accordance with a set form. They were to be allowed some ten and some fourteen per cent for the trouble of collecting, the larger allowance being for those counties where the poverty of the people or the inaccessibility of navigable streams made collection difficult.[63] If quit rents were paid directly to the receiver-general the sheriffs were to receive the same allowance as if they had collected them, since they would in either case be at the trouble of demanding them.[64] Sheriffs were to make good the highest rent rolls ever

[58] *C.O.5/1318*, p. 699.

[59] *Jour. Burg.*, 1712-1726, pp. 230, 231.

[60] *C.O.5/1318*, pp. 582-584.

[61] *B. T. Jour.*, 1718-1722, pp. 64, 65; *C.O.5/1365*, p. 199; *C.O.5/1318*, p. 723.

[62] This was to be received at the rate of 17½ pennyweight to 5*s*. *Ex. Jour. Coun.*, III, 458.

[63] Some twelve years later, when settlement had proceeded still further from navigable rivers, the sheriffs of the frontier counties were allowed as much as forty per cent. *Ibid.*, IV, 198.

[64] Thus one of the points contended for by Byrd was conceded.

returned from their respective counties. If they could not collect it all, the balance was to come from their own pockets.[65] This last regulation elicited a protest from the sheriff of Nansemond, a county notorious for remissness in paying public dues. The auditor had refused to receive from him the money he had actually collected until he would give bond for paying the arrears, much of which, he declared, he had no prospect of obtaining, "all which will tend very Much to the Impoverishing & great Dimunition of the Estate of your pet'r." He was thereupon permitted to account for what he had received, and was furnished with the rent roll of 1713 together with a list of the patents since granted, and ordered to levy the arrears by distress if the owners had no tobacco, he being held accountable for the value of the goods distrained. The officers of the revenue were ordered to notify the sheriffs that if they did not complete their rent rolls, and pay the money due for the quit rents by October 20, directions would be given for suing their bonds. Allowances to sheriffs for detecting "concealed" land were now restricted to land patented "3 Years before the year 1713," for which no quit rents had thitherto been paid.[66] The office of sheriff was becoming no sinecure.

These strong measures were not without result. Some back rents were collected. The acreage upon which quit rents were paid on time showed a marked increase, though neither in 1717 nor in 1718 did it equal that of 1710, despite the fact that some 350,000 acres had since been patented. The last three years of the administration, however, showed a return to normality, though even then arrears were more common than at its beginning. That all back rents for the period 1714 to 1718 were ever collected seems doubtful.[67]

While Spotswood's attempt to reform the quit rent system thus recoiled in part upon his own head, he doubtless succeded

[65] *Ex. Jour. Coun.*, III, 458, 465.

[66] Petition of Thomas Jordan, Jr., to governor and council (erroneously endorsed 1710), *Colonial Papers*, 1703-1710, MSS. preserved in Virginia State Library; *Ex. Jour. Coun.*, III, 468, 478.

[67] The lack of accounts for 1719 leaves this point uncertain.

in the long run in bringing things to a better order. The widespread default for the years 1714 to 1718 was offset by progress along other lines. Payment in tobacco, a clumsy medium, was largely eliminated. When tobacco was well below its nominal value of a penny a pound it naturally was the medium tendered, apparently universally so from 1710 to 1713. But with the return of peace and high prices money would be paid by those who could get it. Sterling and bills of exchange upon England were scarce, and the government therefore began to accept Spanish money at current rates.[68] The result was instantaneous. During none of the remaining years of the administration was as much as forty per cent of the quit rent revenue received in tobacco, and for three of these years the amount was negligible. Great indeed must have been the relief to the machinery of collection, and it was increased by the fact that from 1714 to 1717 the tobacco payments were made in agents' notes. These fetched at Williamsburg a price half as high again as the nominal eight shillings and fourpence a hundred.[69] Thus while it was possible to collect on time quit rents for 1714 from less than half the acreage, the cash value of the receipts was approximately the same as the year before. The just distribution of the credit for this situation between Spotswood and the Treaty of Utrecht is a matter for speculation. The honors are probably not uneven. At all events, the repeal of the tobacco act not only reduced the sheriffs once more to the necessity of handling the commodity itself; it brought a decline in one year of five shillings and sixpence per hundred in the price fetched by quit rent tobacco and a decrease, somewhat longer deferred, in the proportion of money payments.[70] Nevertheless by 1722 the quit rent accounts showed a favorable balance of nearly £8000 sterling.[71]

Meanwhile, the issuance of treasury rights had been set

[68] *Letters*, II, 67-69.

[69] Doubtless partly due to the accepting of Spanish money in payment. This would, of course, be represented in the accounts by its corresponding sterling value.

[70] See Appendix III.

[71] *C.O.5/1319*, p. 145.

upon a sound footing. The notes theretofore struck off by hand by the receiver-general were all called in, and printed certificates were issued in their place. These certificates, of various denominations, were to be numbered and issued in definite quantities by order of the government, and signed by both officers of the revenue. The clerk of the secretary's office was to record the numbers of the rights for which land was granted. The new rights were to be distributed by the surveyors, who were to give bond for the rights they received, and were allowed a commission of five per cent. They were to be exchanged for old rights free of charge, or sold at the former rate of five shillings sterling or nineteen pennyweight Spanish money for each right to take up fifty acres. In January 1717, 1000 rights, to the value of £500, were issued, but these being barely enough to cancel the old rights, in April 250 more were ordered to issue. Later a further issue of 1000 rights was authorized.[72]

In announcing these reforms to the board of trade, Spotswood declared that several hundred more old rights were redeemed than had ever been accounted for, and many were still in circulation. "I can't determine w'ch of the Rec'r Gen'lls are in fault, only that there has been no other person concerned therein, except Mr. Byrd and his Father."[73] The insinuation was hardly just. That rights were counterfeited was one of the indictments brought against the old system, and the extra notes may have come into existence in this manner.

When the general assembly convened in 1720, governor, council, and burgesses cooperated in the regulation of the land system to an extent unknown in Virginia for the past six years. The burgesses were well disposed to the administration, and a reconciliation had taken place between Spotswood and the insurgent group in the council. But more than this, the attitude of the governor had softened. It may be that he was convinced of the futility of contending for the interests of the

[72] *C.O.5/1318*, pp. 292, 293; *Ex. Jour. Coun.*, III, 434, 435, 437, 441; IV, 4. Single, double, and triple rights were issued.

[73] *Letters*, II, 271.

crown in the teeth of the all but unanimous opposition of the colony.[74] Perchance his years of residence in the colony had given him a greater appreciation of and sympathy for the interests of the colonial landowner which indeed, now that he had taken up extensive tracts in the colony, had come to be his own. At all events, the two acts relative to the land system which were passed during the session were calculated to ease the lot of the colonists rather than to forward the interests of the crown.

One of these acts supplemented that of 1713 by enumerating additional kinds of improvements the making of which would keep land from lapsing. Every three acres well cleared and fenced, and used for a pasture for three years, was sufficient to save fifty acres.[75] The erection of houses, water mills, or other works, and the planting of trees and hedges, together with any other kinds of improvements not mentioned in the act of 1713 were to keep land from lapsing at the rate of fifty acres for every £10 current money expended in making them. The value of the improvements was to be appraised by two disinterested persons appointed at the request of the proprietor by the county court. Where the possessor of one tract took up adjoining tracts and obtained one patent for the whole, improvements on any of these tracts were to apply to the whole.[76] Provision was made for the recovery of lapsed lands from non-residents, a process which had been practically impossible under the act of 1713.[77] No new principles were involved in this measure. It merely adapted those already laid down to the more diversified conditions of life which were coming into existence in Virginia, and appears to have encountered no opposition in England.

[74] *Letters*, II, 267-269.

[75] No specified number of cattle was required as in the act of 1713, nor was this provision restricted to "barren" land.

[76] As will be seen in a later chapter, it was only by virtue of this act that Spotswood was able to keep parts of his extensive holdings from lapsing, as they would have done by the terms of the act of 1713, or by those of the royal instructions.

[77] Hening, IV, 81-83.

The second act made extensive changes in the quit rent system. Each sheriff was to appoint places where at set times before February 20 annually he would receive the quit rents, either in current money or tobacco at the usual rate. People might pay their quit rents in money either to the sheriff or receiver-general at any place or time before February 20. The appointed places in the settled areas were to be within ten miles of the residences of the inhabitants, but in the frontier districts the latter might be required to carry their tobacco further. Sheriffs were to be responsible for quit rents on all land where sufficient distress could be obtained. If the proprietor lived in another county provision was made for collection by distraint there. Concealed lands, and the lands of absentee proprietors for which no distress was to be obtained, were to pay double all arrears, in the case of the former one-half being given to the informer. But the clause in the act which denotes a striking change of attitude on Spotswood's part is that which provided that no land should be forfeited for non-payment of quit rents, provisions in the patent or other laws to the contrary notwithstanding.[78] Thus a regulation which the governor had labored to secure and maintain was discarded after it had proved an empty form. For what could the law avail when the courts refused to enforce it? The new act was popular in the colony. Both Spotswood and his successor, Drysdale, recommended its confirmation to the board of trade, while the council instructed the solicitor for Virginia to use his influence in its favor.[79] But in England it met with opposition. Both Richard West and Horace Walpole,[80] while approving the system of collection for which it provided, opposed the repeal of the provision making lands forfeited for non-payment of quit rents, "especially," added the latter, "since of late great art and industry seem to be us'd in taking

[78] Hening, IV, 79, 80.

[79] Spotswood to Board of Trade, June 11, 1722. *C.O.5/1319*, p. 131; Drysdale to Board of Trade, Dec. 20, 1722. *Ibid.*, pp. 164, 165; *Ex. Jour. Coun.*, IV, 27.

[80] Walpole had succeeded Blathwayt as auditor-general.

up Lands in such a manner as to avoid the Payments of any Quit Rents at all."[81] Both officers thought the act unfit for confirmation. Therefore, although at one time disposed to favor it,[82] the board of trade finally recommended and secured the disallowance of the act. Walpole's objections were forwarded to Governor Drysdale, that he might secure the passage of another act more in conformity with the interests of the crown.[83] It is no matter for surprise that Spotswood's successor failed so to do.

The story of the land system under Spotswood mirrors the course of political events. The preliminary sparring when the colonists were testing the mettle of the new governor; the tractable second assembly; the subsequent legislative recalcitrance;[84] the friendly council which later became hostile; the ultimate partial capitulation of the governor to colonial interests—all these are reflected here. But we have run ahead of our chronology, and must now return several years to consider other sources of friction between governor and council.

[81] *C.O.5/1319*, pp. 65-67, 185-191. Doubtless a reference to the exemption from quit rents and rights sought for the newly erected counties of Spotsylvania and Brunswick, in the former of which the holdings of Spotswood were located.

[82] *B. T. Jour.*, 1718-1722, p. 379.

[83] *C.O.391/32*, p. 134; *C.O.5/1365*, pp. 249, 250. *Acts of Privy Coun., Col.*, III, 54, 55. Thus, since it contained a suspending clause, the act which Professor Bond considers the climax of Spotswood's reforms in the quit rent system (*Quit Rent System*, p. 224) never went into effect.

[84] A negative image. Spotswood could obtain scant legislation in 1715 and 1718 in support of his land policy.

Chapter VIII

GOVERNOR AND COUNCIL

THE gentry of colonial Virginia composed an influential class. Old-world titles were little known among them (in Spotswood's time there was one innocuous baronet, Sir William Skipwith) their places being taken by commissions in the colonial militia, supplemented in the case of those who held certain offices under the crown by the dignified suffix of Esquire. As sheriffs, as vestrymen, as justices of the peace, and in innumerable other capacities[1] they influenced the public life of the Old Dominion. Most influential of all were "the Honourable the Council."[2]

The twelve men who sat at the council board were apt to embrace the pick of the wealth and ability of the province. Appointed by the crown, usually upon the nomination of the governor, they held office during the royal pleasure, though in practice their tenure was permanent. The governor could not suspend a councillor without the consent of his colleagues, which virtually meant that he had no power of removal at all, such was the sense of solidarity in the council. For "the Violence of neither *Whig* nor *Tory*"[3] was known in Virginia, and factional strife did not go the length, as it did in some other colonies, of compassing the expulsion of rivals from the council. That different points of view were represented at the council board augured well for the healthy development of the colony.

[1] His instructions enjoined the governor to take care in the choice of councillors and other chief officers, judges, justices, and sheriffs that his appointees were of good estates and abilities, and "not Necessitous People, or much in debt." *Va. Mag. Hist.*, XXI, 5.

[2] Jones, *Present State of Virginia*, pp. 62, 63.

[3] *Ibid.*, p. 47. None the less the fortunes of parties in England were closely watched by Virginians seeking office under the crown. *Ludwell Papers*, MSS., I, 1-10.

The council acted in a threefold capacity. As an executive body it cooperated with the governor, its functions frequently transcending the merely advisory. It also served as the upper house of the general assembly. Councillors were *ipso facto* members of the general court, the supreme judicial body of the colony. Even so determined and independent an executive as Spotswood found it necessary to work in close cooperation with his council; while under weaker governors that body rose to a dominating position. And during intervals when no governor was resident in Virginia the executive power devolved upon the senior councillor, who was known as the president. This may account in part for the importance which councillors attached to questions of seniority. It was after such an interregnum, four years in length, that Spotswood arrived in Virginia.

The choicest political plums in Virginia were the offices of secretary, receiver-general, and deputy auditor. Edmund Jennings, president of the council, had been secretary since 1702, when he had won the office over two other candidates, one of them William Byrd.[4] In 1705 Byrd received the office of receiver-general, vacated by the death of his father.[5] In 1710 Philip Ludwell was scheming to get the office of secretary away from Jennings. Prompted by Nathaniel Blakiston, Virginia agent in London, Ludwell sought to ingratiate himself with the new governor, and Spotswood's first night on Virginia soil was spent as Ludwell's guest at Green Spring. Jennings, who may have realized what was going on, also proffered his good offices to the governor, "advancing to him some schemes of Poloticks how he was to manage ye Councill, but" wrote Blakiston, "they were soe preposterous that Coll. Spotswood must have him in much contempt for his wild notions."[6] Since Jennings seems to have relied upon the favor of the Duchess of Marlborough, the eclipse of that lady in the graces of Queen

[4] Representation of Board of Trade to Coun., Dec. 22, 1701; *Blathwayt's Colonial Papers, Virginia*, 1664-1712, MS.

[5] Byrd to Wm. Lowndes, May 9, 1705. *Ibid.*

[6] *Va. Mag. Hist.*, IV, 17, 18, V, 45-47; *Letters*, I, 1.

Anne might have simplified Ludwell's problem, had not the tumult raised by the trial of Dr. Sacheverell ("I think it had been happy for England," wrote Stephen Fouace to Ludwell, "if that man had never been born") swept from office the Whig ministers upon whose influence the would-be secretary was counting.[7] Jennings kept the secretaryship, and upon the death of Dudley Diggs in 1711 Ludwell was able to console himself with the deputy auditorship, which, if a less desirable post, was obtainable by the simpler expedient of outbidding all rivals, for Auditor-General William Blathwayt did not appoint his deputies with a disinterested view to the public weal. The support, however, of both Blakiston and Spotswood may have furthered Ludwell's candidacy.[8]

In 1711 Jennings left for England, disregarding Spotswood's suggestion that he commission Ludwell as his deputy in the secretary's office. Spotswood thereupon recommended to the board of trade that Dr. William Cocke, the Williamsburg physician, supersede him. Cocke's candidacy was supported by Blakiston, who incurred the ire of Jennings for not procuring merely a deputation for Cocke. Presumably Jennings felt equally resentful towards the governor. Cocke assumed office in 1712. William Byrd was one of his bondsmen.[9] Since Spotswood desired to have as many royal officials as possible in the council, and Cocke's residence at Williamsburg made his attendance possible at all times, he secured a councillorship for the new secretary.[10] With Jennings in the rôle of Ishmael, and the rest of the council working with the governor, the situation was far different from what it became a few years later.

There was no dearth of aspirants to places at the council board, but candidates to the governor's taste were far to seek. The case of William Bassett illustrates the pains which the

[7] Stephen Fouace to Philip Ludwell, August 10 and 14, 1710, *Ludwell Papers*, I, 5-10.

[8] *Ibid.*, II, No. 10; *Va. Mag. Hist.*, IV, 15-17, 19; *Letters*, I, 71.

[9] *Va. Mag. Hist.*, IV, 18, 21; *Cal. State Paps.*, *Col.*, 1711-1712, pp. 202, 276; *Ex. Jour. Coun.*, III, 317, 481.

[10] *Letters*, I, 7; II, 17; *B. T. Jour.*, 1709-1715, p. 426.

governor would take to secure an ideal appointment. Formerly a member of the council, Bassett had resigned ostensibly because of ill health, actually (so he confessed to Spotswood) to avoid the necessity of working with a governor "with whom he could not live in that ease and quiett he so much desires." Spotswood overcame his prejudices and secured his reappointment. Contrary to custom, Bassett was not restored to his former ranking, but was placed at the foot of the council roll. Resenting this slight, Bassett refused to serve. Both Spotswood and Orkney appealed to the board of trade to have him satisfied, but the authorities proved inexplicably obdurate, and no change was made. Spotswood thought he saw the hand of Jennings in this, though Jennings' rank was not affected. When the governor's commission was reissued, ranking him from the time of his second appointment, Bassett bowed to the inevitable and took his seat.[11]

In the selection of councillors the nominees of the lieutenant governor were usually appointed. Orkney was indeed consulted by the board of trade, but his recommendations were usually followed only in so far as they coincided with those of his subordinate. His recommendation of Archibald Blair in 1713 was ignored[12] as that of Edward Hill by the bishop of London had been in 1711.[13] Instead of Blair, the board proposed Edmund Berkeley, apparently upon the basis of the list of eligible candidates drawn up by Spotswood.[14] Berkeley's appointment raised once more the question of seniority. The governor had the power, when the number of councillors in the colony fell below nine, to make temporary appointments which were usually confirmed in England, thus becoming permanent. Between the date of the royal warrant appointing Berkeley and the time of its delivery, Nathaniel Harrison and

[11] Bassett to Ludwell, Sept. 22, 1713, *Ludwell Papers,* II, No. 13; *Letters,* I, 63, 64, 154; II, 38-41; *B. T. Jour.,* 1709-1715, p. 406; *Acts of Privy Coun., Col.,* II, 824, 825; Orkney to B. T., July 22, 1713, *C.O.5/1316,* O. 148; *Ex. Jour. Coun.,* III, 417.

[12] *C.O.5/1316,* O. 148; *B. T. Jour.,* 1709-1715, p. 459.

[13] *C.O.5/1316,* O. 86; *B. T. Jour.,* 1709-1715, p. 284.

[14] *Ibid.,* p. 459.

Mann Page were elevated to the council by Spotswood. Berkeley contended that his membership should be reckoned from the date of the warrant, giving him precedence over Harrison and Page. Spotswood and the rest of the council took the contrary view. Berkeley protested to the authorities in England, declaring that he had been deliberately prevented from presenting his warrant before Harrison and Page were sworn. It was also bruited in England that this incident had occasioned a dispute between governor and council. Both Spotswood and the council vindicated themselves in letters to England and their attitude was sustained.[15]

George Chalmers has stated in a well-known passage that Spotswood "was received by the Virginians with acclamations, because he had brought them liberty," since "the Queen gave, unsolicited to the provincials, the invaluable benefit of the *habeas corpus* act."[16] We are told by a more recent writer, however, that "it is doubtful if this so-called extension of the writ of habeas corpus really gave the Virginians much more than they already possessed," for the colonists had long enjoyed the right of habeas corpus by virtue of their heritage of the common law.[17] Although the assembly formally thanked the queen in an address,[18] the incident appears to have aroused little further comment in the province. But another provision in the royal instructions designed to the same end, namely the prevention of long imprisonments without trial, was destined to occasion a dispute which all but brought Spotswood's administration to a premature close. The major criminal cases in Virginia were tried before the general court, which met but twice a year, in April and October. The crown now instructed

[15] *Ex. Jour. Coun.*, III, 367, 382-384, 386; Spotswood to Popple, Nov. 26, 1714, *C.O.5/1317*, pp. 197, 198; Council to B. T., Nov. 25, 1714, *ibid.*, p. 205; Blakiston to Ludwell, July 18, 1714, *Va. Mag. Hist.*, IV, 22, 23; *B. T. Jour.*, 1715-1718, p. 2.

[16] George Chalmers, *Introduction to the History of the Revolt of the American Colonies* (2 vols., Boston 1845), I, 395. See also *Va. Mag. Hist.*, XXI, 119, 120.

[17] A. H. Carpenter, "Habeas Corpus in the Colonies," *Am. Hist. Rev.*, VIII, 18, 24-26.

[18] *Jour. Burg.*, 1702-1712, pp. 282, 283.

the governor to appoint two annual courts of oyer and terminer, in June and December.[19] The establishment of regulations for the new court was evidently considered a matter of prime importance, for it was delayed until all members of the council were present.[20]

Spotswood took the precaution of having the assembly of 1710 declare the right of the crown to erect in the province courts other than the general court.[21] The governor's power to appoint court of oyer and terminer was therefore clear. Two points of dispute, however, arose between governor and council. One was relatively unimportant. The council thought that the court ought to meet whether there were cases on the docket or not, which the governor considered a needless burden upon the revenue. This dispute was compromised without difficulty.[22] The question of the personnel of the new courts was a very much more weighty matter. The councillors considered themselves *ipso facto* judges of the court of oyer and terminer, the governor having no power to appoint others to that position. Spotswood considered himself empowered to appoint whomsoever he pleased. The councillors were not likely to view with equanimity the prospect of losing the exclusive right to exercise the supreme judicial power of the province, and a conflict was inevitable. To attempt to meet, single handed, the opposition of the council would have been foolhardy, and Spotswood sought to win the lower house to his side of the controversy by appointing, in December 1712, the speaker and two other members of the house of burgesses with the council upon a commission of oyer and terminer. The council protested, and the matter was referred to the board of trade.

The first members of his council with whom the governor was to have serious trouble were the officers of the revenue. Spotswood seems to have been on the best of terms with Byrd

[19] *Va. Mag. Hist.*, XXI, 121.
[20] *Ex. Jour. Coun.*, III, 250, 255.
[21] Hening, III, 489; *Letters*, I, 50.
[22] *Ex. Jour. Coun.*, III, 313, 314, 341, 342.

and Ludwell during the first three years of his administration, but when the governor took up the problem of quit rent reform friction speedily arose. The more technical aspects of the issue have been considered elsewhere.[23] We are here concerned with personal repercussions and their political consequences.

Briefly, the case was this. The royal quit rents were collected by a system anything but efficient, over which the receiver-general and the deputy auditor exercised but nominal supervision. Their offices were thus to a large extent sinecures. To Spotswood, thrifty Caledonian that he was, such a state of affairs was intolerable. He proposed a series of reforms, looking toward a more effective system in which receiver-general and auditor were active factors.

William Byrd was a man of parts. A liberal education, broad intellectual interests, and above all an inimitable literary style, differentiate him clearly from the ordinary run of colonial gentlemen. Nimble of wit, and blessed with excellent connections both in Virginia and England, he was no mean adversary. In 1705, when he hoped to succeed William Byrd I in the combined offices of receiver-general and deputy auditor, Byrd had pointed to his father's record with proper filial pride, and had blandly described the fiscal machinery of Virginia as a smoothly operating system in which there was no opportunity for fraud even though both the chief offices were held by one man.[24] As we have seen, he secured the receiver-generalship only, and now he faced the unwelcome prospect of an accretion of work which promised to transform that office from a sinecure to a post of drudgery. He admitted that reform was necessary, but his pride was touched when he saw that the governor's proposals implied a severe censure both of himself and of his father. He prepared for resistance. Early in 1714, having received permission from the British authorities to go to England,[25] Byrd left his office in the hands of Nathaniel

[23] *Supra*, pp. 141-148.

[24] Byrd to Wm. Lowndes, May 9, 1705, *Blathwayt's Colonial Papers, Virginia*, 1664-1712.

[25] *C.O.5/1364*, pp. 24, 25; *B. T. Jour.*, 1709-1715, p. 505.

Harrison. He was not to return to Virginia for five years. His journey may have been occasioned, as his request implied, solely by private business.[26] On the other hand, he may have desired to predispose the board of trade in favor of his attitude upon the Virginia revenue question, and other schemes of public import seem to have been germinating in his active brain. As yet, however, no personal break had occurred between him and the governor.

That trouble was ahead both Byrd and Spotswood must plainly have discerned, and the governor, with a soldier's foresight, began to reconnoiter the position of his opponents. He quickly saw that in the event of an open break, Byrd and Ludwell could count upon the support of those councillors who were allied to them by blood or marriage. These numbered four, and thus with their own votes, the officers of the revenue could hope to control the voice of the council. Prudence demanded that the governor see to it that this advantage was not increased. When therefore, the winter of 1713-1714 proved fatal to three councillors, Spotswood took care that his appointees, Nathaniel Harrison, Mann Page, and Robert Porteus,[27] were not "related to one particular Family, to which the greatest part of the present Council are already nearly allyed." Spotswood explained to the board of trade that his principal objection to the family alliance was their position upon the bench of the general court, where if a case arose affecting one of them none of the rest could sit and justice would miscarry for lack of judges.[28] But that the governor was also thinking of administrative matters cannot be doubted.

For a time after Byrd's departure Spotswood concentrated his attack upon Ludwell, a less skilful tactician (he himself

[26] Byrd had married Lucy Parke, daughter of the governor of the Leeward Islands who had been murdered in Antigua in 1710, and he had business in England in connection with the estate of his father-in-law.

[27] Harrison and Page were confirmed, but Spotswood later changed his opinion of Porteus, and he was left off the council when the governor's commission was reissued at the accession of George I.

[28] *Letters*, II, 54, 55.

has testified to his "want of a more polite education and conversation"), who was soon placed in a position where he had to choose between coming into the governor's plans and refusing point-blank to be guided by the royal instructions. He chose the latter course, softening his action with the declaration that he could not adopt a new system of accounting without the authorization of his superior, Blathwayt. The governor nevertheless suspended him, and sent to England as strong a case as possible for his removal. Stressing the deputy auditor's alleged maladministration, he declared that by Ludwell's own admission his close relationship to Byrd disqualified him for acting as a check upon the receiver-general. Neither Spotswood's accusation nor the defense which Ludwell wrote in reply[29] had much to do with the course of events, for before their arrival Blathwayt had removed Ludwell from office. The auditor-general was not actuated by the abstract merits of the dispute between governor and deputy auditor. He seems to have considered it a personal and family quarrel, and pictured Spotswood as desiring to concentrate the management of the revenue into his own hands.[30] He doubtless wished to cut short the controversy. The governor's triumph was not complete, for Blathwayt named as Ludwell's successor his nephew John Grymes, later one of Spotswood's most inveterate opponents in the house of burgesses.[31]

As Blathwayt had suggested, antagonism between Spotswood and Ludwell had not been confined to public finance. Since the days of the London Company there had been at Jamestown a 3000-acre gubernatorial demesne. During his administration, Sir William Berkeley had received a grant in his own right of 1000 acres contiguous to the governor's tract, and had secured a long-time lease for a part of the latter. His father having married Berkeley's widow, Ludwell was now

[29] *Ludwell Paps.*, II, nos. 36, 37.

[30] Blathwayt to Popple, Aug. 27, 1716, *C.O.5/1364*, pp. 520, 521.

[31] Spotswood had proposed the names of Peter Beverley and John Robinson. *Letters*, II, 162.

proprietor of Green Spring, as this estate was called. The capital having been moved to Williamsburg, the land at Jamestown was of little use to the governor. Ludwell owned fifty acres near the governor's mansion at Williamsburg, and Spotswood applied to England for permission to exchange for this an equal amount of the governor's lands at Jamestown, an arrangement which seems to have been mutually satisfactory.[32] But in processioning these lands in accordance with the act of 1713, it was found that the governor's tract had shrunk to about 2400 acres. It was bounded by definite natural landmarks on all sides but that adjoining Green Spring. Therefore, while there may be justice in the claim that the erosion of thirty years had disposed of 100 acres, Spotswood was not unreasonable in concluding that there had been systematic encroachments upon the governor's lands from that side. Ludwell's third processioning, which would have made his title good, was only halted by a caveat, issued at the instance of the governor.

The inevitable trial upon the spot was not a model of legal procedure. According to Ludwell, Spotswood browbeat the witnesses until they were terrified out of their wits, and when he found it was about to return an adverse decision hectored the panel for a "Chickahominy Jury" and an ignorant, obstinate set of fellows. And if we may believe Spotswood, Ludwell retorted "with more rudeness & ill-manners than I believe any Governor ever was treated."[33] Despite his strenuous tactics, Spotswood did not obtain the desired verdict, and the case was appealed to the general court, a full account being sent to the board of trade. "I shall only add this observation," wrote Spotswood to that body, "that since the Lands now in dispute came into the hands of Mr. Ludwell's Father, that Family have never suffered any Governor to be at ease after he once begun to enquire into their Title, as y'r Lo'ps . . . will find that all the Clamours rais'd against Colo. Jeffreys, L'd Effingham,

[32] *B. T. Jour.*, 1709-1715, p. 495; *C.O.5/1316*, O. 150; *C.O.5/1364*, pp. 19-21.

[33] Byrd, *Writings*, intro., pp. lxv-lxviii.

S'r Edmund Andrews and Colo. Nicholson have been fomented and Carryed on either by the Father or the Son."[34]

After Ludwell's removal from office, Spotswood seems to have dropped the case, and Byrd intimated to the former auditor that the governor was attempting a rapprochement with him. Micajah Perry had essayed the rôle of peacemaker,[35] but the proffered mediation from Leadenhall Street found little favor with the governor. "I have yet seen no other Overtures towards an Accomodation," he wrote to Blakiston, "but what is dictated to me by Mr. Perry, the Sum of which is, that I should own myself wrong in that suspension and the Law Suit; And, in short, little better than asking pardon for accusing falsely two such honest Gen'n, and endeavouring to take away Collo. Ludwell's freehold without any pretence of Right."[36] The merchant's proposal was ignored, and Spotswood strengthened his position in England by winning Orkney to his side. He wrote to the earl (the story is a trifle bizarre) that Byrd and Ludwell had done him more damage than they could repair even if they were to obtain him the government of Virginia for life, for by writing malicious and treacherous letters to his late brother they had so convinced the latter of the unworthiness of his heir that in sheer resentment he had married and gotten a son.[37] Spotswood was thus deprived of a vast inheritance.[38] He also imputed to the revenue officers the

[34] *C.O.5/1317*, pp. 447-452; *Letters*, II, 155-157. Not long afterwards Spotswood incurred the ill will of John Custis, who claimed that the governor had practically ruined some of his land by indiscriminately cutting down trees for firewood. Custis to Ludwell, April 18, 1717, *Ludwell Paps.*, II, no. 72.

[35] *Ludwell Paps.*, II, no. 41; *Va. Mag. Hist.*, III, 351.

[36] *Letters*, II, 243.

[37] Spotswood repeated the story to Popple, placing the value of the estate which he had lost at £20,000. *Ibid.*, p. 187.

[38] Spotswood was not alone in imputing the dispute, in part at least, to private differences. Byrd had told Orkney that the origin of the dispute had been "owing to the Women." This Spotswood denied, interpreting it to mean that Mrs. Byrd and Mrs. Ludwell had been at odds with Mrs. Russell, "who manages the affairs of my family, and is the only Woman in the Country I can be said to have any Relation to." *Ibid.*, pp. 242, 243. A perusal of the controversy which led to the removal of Nicholson a dozen years before, reveals the possibility that Byrd's allegation is capable of a less savory construction.

authorship of the anonymous articles against him which had been sent to the board of trade.[39] Byrd, to whom the letter was read in part by Orkney, scouted both accusations. He wrote to Ludwell that the governor was "as exorbitant in doing himself too much honour as he is in doing us too much wrong." In such positive terms had he stated his case against the two that Orkney was almost persuaded of its entire truth. Byrd begged the titular governor to suspend his judgment until more proof should be submitted than the mere word of an adversary.[40]

During all this time, Byrd was in England. He may have been called there by private interests but none the less found time to engage actively in public affairs. It was due in some measure to his hearty support of the assembly's address on that score that the crown decided for the future to leave the quit rent balance in the colony.[41] But governor and council were not definitely authorized to expend the quit rents without warrant from the treasury. This was more comformable to the attitude of Spotswood than to that of the assembly.[42]

Byrd also interested himself in the repeal of the Indian and tobacco acts. With the former he might well be disgruntled upon personal grounds. He of all the old Indian traders had not been invited to subscribe to the Indian Company, and while

[39] *Supra*, p. 131.

[40] *Va. Mag. Hist.*, III, 349-351.

[41] Byrd, *Writings*, intro., pp. lx, lxi.

[42] A considerable diversion of the quit-rent money to England was occasioned in 1717 by the granting of an annuity of £500 for 31 years, to one Henry Rainsford, Esq., who seems to have been a resident of London, and in 1721 nearly £5500 was granted to John Hamilton, Lord Belhaven, recently appointed governor of Barbadoes, who was drowned two months later on the way to his post. *Ex. Jour. Coun.*, III, 462; *C.O.5/1319*, p. 245; *Dictionary of National Biography*, XXIV, pp. 198, 199. Thus, counting the earlier warrant for £3000, some £10,000 of the quit-rent revenue was diverted from Virginia while Spotswood was governor. The income which the crown derived from certain of the colonies was obviously becoming entangled in the net of corruption which was enmeshing British political life. Ten years after his removal from office Spotswood told Byrd of the anxiety of the ministry lest the House of Commons enquire into the disposal of funds raised in America to support colonial civil lists, particularly the four and a half per cent duty on sugar, producing an annual revenue of nearly £20,000, which "moulders away between the Ministers' Fingers, no body knows how, like the Quitrents of Virginia." Byrd, *Writings*, p. 365.

he declared himself to be satisfied with Spotswood's rather insipid explanation that this was because Byrd was about to leave for England, he could scarcely have relished exclusion from a lucrative trade which he, and his father before him, had enjoyed for so many years. As to the tobacco act Byrd seems for a while to have been beset with genuine uncertainty. Some measure to revive the tobacco trade and outlaw its more glaring abuses was plainly necessary. His fellow councillors in Virginia had high hopes that the act would accomplish these ends. Perhaps Byrd in England had a better opportunity to discover the effect of the act upon the trade. On the other hand he was not likely to forget that the tobacco notes were the foundation of Spotswood's new quit rent policy. But whatever his motives, by 1716 Byrd had arrayed himself definitely against both the Indian and tobacco acts. This was not calculated to restore him to the governor's favor. "Whatever grace you may find," he wrote to Ludwell in 1717, "it seems I am not like to come off so. . . . For I have had a hand in procuring the Solicitor Gen^lls^ opinion, and the Council of Trade's report in prejudice of the 2 Laws. This will never be forgiven, but I would venture any resentment rather than suffer that Country to grone under such hardships as it does by that means."[43]

In the meantime, Byrd had ceased to be receiver-general. His commission was about to expire, and he was endeavoring to have it renewed. Whether he succeeded is not known. His account of the affair is to be found in a letter written in October 1716 to John Custis. He had sold his office for £500 to James Roscowe, the first person whom he found willing to pay his price. This he had done not because he feared removal, but because the governor's policy had rendered the position of the receiver-general intolerable. Under the "pious pretence" of advancing the royal interests, Spotswood was in a position to "heap insupportable trouble upon that officer," so that the latter "must either be a slave to his humour, must fawn upon him, jump over a stick whenever he was bid, or else he must

[43] *Va. Mag. Hist.*, III, 351, 352.

have so much trouble loaded on him as to make his place uneasy. In short, such a man must be either the governor's dog or his ass; neither of which stations suit in the least with my constitution." Now he was in a position to oppose Spotswood's policies unhandicapped by that deference which a patent officer of the crown was expected to show the governor.[44]

The dispute between Spotswood and the officers of the revenue does not appear to have affected the relations between him and the other councillors. There had naturally been points of difference. Spotswood had objected to the council's passing an act of assembly in their capacity as upper house of the legislature because it was for the benefit of the colony, and then in executive session advising the governor to veto it because it was contrary to the interests of the crown.[45] He claimed that since the councillors were only members of the upper house by virtue of their place in the governor's council, their oath to uphold the interests of the crown was equally binding upon them in both capacities. Governor and council had also differed over the newly authorized courts of oyer and terminer. But the matter was referred to England, and the calmness with which the council abided the decision indicates either that they were confident of success or else that the matter had not yet assumed great importance in their eyes. The council, it would seem, was shaken from its complacence in October, 1716 by a letter from the board of trade, declaring that it saw no reason why the council should insist upon being sole judges of the courts of oyer and terminer. The governor was empowered by his commission to appoint what persons he pleased as judges. Even though councillors were constituted by act of assembly sole judges of the general court, this would not prevent the governor from appointing by his commission a particular court of oyer and terminer unless expressly forbidden by the act.[46]

[44] G. W. P. Custis, *Recollections of George Washington*, Lossing, ed., pp. 29, 30.

[45] Their action in 1714 on the *Act for the Security and Defense of the Country* is a case in point. *Ex. Jour. Coun.*, III, 393.

[46] This, it will be remembered, Spotswood had taken particular care that the act should not forbid.

The board also held the council to be mistaken in asserting that in England gentlemen were never added to commissions of oyer and terminer except in the circuits.[47] It came out that Spotswood had not sent the representation of the council to the board of trade, but had stated their objections in a letter of his own. This he caused to be read in council, but the councillors were not satisfied, and those who had signed the representation desired the governor to transmit a copy of it to the board of trade "that their Lord Ships may have the whole matter under their consideration."[48] Spotswood complied.

The disaffection grew. By the following spring it had gained such headway that eight of the council sent to the board of trade a representation reflecting anything but cordiality toward the governor. That their course was unusual they admitted, but explained that they were at the mercy of the governor, who could lay the blame of everything that went amiss upon the council, and take to himself the praise for all that was well done. Their attitude upon the courts of oyer and terminer had been misrepresented. They did not dispute the royal prerogative, but maintained that, the power of the crown notwithstanding, the governor ought not to act contrary to the laws, charters, and ancient usages of the colony without express instructions.[49] The claim of the council to be the sole judges of life and member was not based on custom alone, but upon the charter of Charles II and the laws of the colony which expressly confined that jurisdiction to the general court. They passed on to other grievances. Spotswood had accused Ludwell of originating the assembly's address with a design to deprive the crown of its quit rents. This was a reflection upon the council, for if Ludwell deserved suspension for originating the address, did not his fellow councillors merit the same penalty for approving it? By representing the former methods of collecting the revenue as dark and confused, the governor

[47] B. T. to Spotswood, June 1, 1716, *C.O.5/1364*, pp. 376, 377.

[48] *Ex. Jour. Coun.*, III, 431.

[49] In other words, councillors should be appointed to the new courts, since the instructions did not direct otherwise.

had vilified president[50] and council, and he was unjust in assuming to himself the entire credit for the recent reforms. Spotswood had laid his difficulties with the late assembly to the factious tampering of some of the council, whereas that body had taken much pains to heal the differences occasioned by the inflaming speeches and messages which the governor had formulated without the council's advice. They had always paid the utmost deference to the governor, and had complied with his desires as far as possible, but had they assented to all the new measures which he had proposed and urged upon them, very bad consequences would doubtless have resulted. They begged that none of the council be suspended without a chance to answer the accusations against them. They were writing, they declared, with the desire to maintain a good understanding with the lieutenant governor, and without any attempt to accuse any person, desiring merely to clear their reputations and prevent further misunderstanding. This document bore the signatures of Robert Carter, James Blair, Philip Ludwell, John Smith, John Lewis, William Bassett, Nathaniel Harrison and Edmund Berkeley.[51]

Some criminal cases arose after the close of the April general court in 1717, and Spotswood appointed a commission of oyer and terminer composed of five councillors and four other gentlemen. This he did, he informed the board of trade, to "remove that wrong Notion, w'ch has been carefully infused into the people here, that his Ma'ty has not the same power of constituting Judges here as in England."[52] But with the exception of Jennings the council proved obdurate, and Byrd was gratified to learn that "that mean Sycophant Colo. Heartless" had been the only councillor to sit on "yt Linsey woolsey Commission."[53]

By August, the governor seems to have been aware of the council's memorial to the board of trade, and he commented

[50] It is to be noted that Jennings, president from 1706 to 1710, did not sign the message.

[51] *C.O.5/1318*, pp. 239-243.

[52] *Letters*, II, 259, 260.

[53] Byrd to Ludwell, Sept. 24, 1717. *Ludwell Paps.*, II, no. 55.

darkly to the board upon the practice of confiding "Secret Remonstrances of the Affairs of Government, without any knowledge to private Agents, to be use of [sic] for concealed Designs."[54] If by his reference to "private Agents" Spotswood meant that Byrd would be entrusted with the task of pleading the cause of the council in England, his surmise was entirely correct. Byrd entered upon the task with alacrity. "I am glad to find," he wrote, "that the Councill is fairly ingaged with the Lieut-Governour. They have a good cause & I hope I shall be able to procure justice to be done to them."[55]

In the fall of 1717 Byrd was memorializing the board of trade, recapitulating the arguments already brought forward by the council, and pointing out the overweening power which would be given the governor were he permitted to exercise the prerogatives which he now claimed. Governors were not exempt from such human frailties as the love of money, resentment against those who ventured to oppose their designs, partiality to their creatures and favorites, and many other passions to which men in power are subject. If the governor were permitted to name, without the advice of anybody, judges for a particular time and perhaps for a particular purpose, would he not be able to condemn the innocent and acquit the guilty? The governor's actions were contrary to his instruction to erect no new judicature without the consent of the council, and even if an instruction could repeal an act of assembly, which he believed no good lawyer would maintain, such instruction should run counter to the act in express terms, and not merely by implication.[56] The governor was not empowered to appoint so much as a justice of the peace without the consent of the council. Councillors were appointed by the king, and the royal instructions insisted that they be men of ability and of good estate. It was from these men that impartial justice could best be expected.[57]

[54] *Letters*, II, 260.

[55] Byrd, *Writings*, intro., p. lxx.

[56] This was a bolder attempt at a strict construction of the royal prerogative than the council had ventured to make.

[57] *C.O.5/1318*, pp. 249-252, 257.

Here Byrd was on somewhat dangerous ground. He was enough of a lawyer to realize the legal ignorance of most of the council, and admitted to Ludwell the absurdity of having such men decide "matters of Law which they did not understand." He had, in fact, formulated the plan of a supreme court of trained lawyers in Virginia, "but that diminished nothing belonging to the Council, except their trouble, for they were to continue by my scheme the Supreme Court of Chancery, for which they were to retain their salaries of £350 a year." The salaries of the judges would keep more of the quit rent money in the colonies, and colonial gentlemen would be encouraged "to breed up their Sons to the study of the Law." Byrd had revealed his plan to Lord Chief Justice Parker, who approved it. But this project accorded ill with the position of the council in their dispute with the governor, and the matter was hushed up. Several councillors seem to have known of it, but fortunately for Byrd Spotswood was none the wiser.[58]

Byrd encountered a "very unexpected Rubb" in the reluctance of the board of trade to receive representations from the plantations through any but the accredited colonial agents. "Now I own this Rule is very usefull to save them abundance of trouble: but may be very pernicious to the Plantations, especially to Virginia, that has no agent except Col. Blakeston who is in truth the Lieut: Governor's Solicitor, and not the Country's."[59] Byrd had succeeded in inducing the board to permit him to appear in his capacity as a councillor, "but without departing from their General Rule. Thus you see how necessary it will be for the Country to have an agent residing here, or else I don't understand how their wrongs will ever be righted."[60]

The board of trade referred the oyer and terminer question

[58] *Ludwell Paps.*, II, no. 55.

[59] Blakiston, however, seems to have done his utmost to keep in the good graces of both parties to the controversy. *Ibid.*, *passim*.

[60] Byrd to Ludwell, Oct. 28, 1717, *Va. Mag. Hist.*, III, 352, 353.

to Attorney-General Northey, whose report, dated December 24, 1717, was entirely favorable to Spotswood's position in so far as the law was concerned. In erecting governor and council as a court in Virginia the charter did not bar the crown from erecting other courts, nor was the trial of criminals in courts other than the general court contrary to Virginia law. The power to erect courts of oyer and terminer thus rested in the crown, and the governor might appoint commissions either with or exclusive of the council. The attorney-general proposed, however, that to prevent abuses and to quiet the minds of the people the governor be restrained from issuing special commissions of oyer and terminer except in cases of extraordinary emergency.[61] This opinion was sent to Spotswood, the board of trade declaring that it still entertained the views which it had already expressed upon the subject. It cautioned the governor to exercise discreetly the power thus lodged in his hands, which seemed only proper for use on rare occasions.[62]

This turn of events was naturally unwelcome to Byrd, who sought to bridle the governor with a harder curb than a mere word of caution. He now took the only course still open to him. He petitioned the crown that the governor be constrained to make the judges of the general court the judges of oyer and terminer except upon extraordinary occasions.[63] But the board of trade was not to be moved from its position. In a representation, dated March 3, 1718, it opposed Byrd's petition. No complaint had yet been made that the governor abused his power. He had always chosen the majority of the judges from the council. The petition came, not from the people of Virginia who would be the sufferers from the abuse of power which Byrd contemplated, but from the persons who sought to engross the privilege of being sole judges in all criminal cases. The board therefore hoped that the matter

[61] *C.O.5/1318*, pp. 297-301.
[62] B. T. to Spotswood, Jan. 29, 1718, *C.O.5/1365*, pp. 40, 41.
[63] *C.O.5/1318*, pp. 321-325, 337; *Acts of Privy Coun., Col.*, II, 731.

would be left as it was, the governor retaining the power conferred upon him by his commission.[64] This representation closed the affair, so far as the board was concerned.

In course of time the text of the council's memorial to the board of trade came into the governor's hands. On March 12, at the conclusion of the day's business, he desired the five subscribers then present in council to explain what new measures had thus been pressed upon them.[65] Nonplussed, the councillors desired that their answer might be delayed until the general court, when all those who had signed the letter would be present. The governor said that he would not press them, but thought an hour sufficient time for them to give some instances of what they had alleged, though if they did not think fit to answer then, they might have what further time they pleased. He then went through the mummery of sitting in the council chamber for an hour, awaiting a reply which he knew full well the councillors did not intend to give.[66]

On March 20, Spotswood wrote a long letter to the board of trade. He began it with a thorough and able summary of his case upon the oyer and terminer controversy which, while affording the clearest statement of the governor's position, did not affect the decision of the matter, which had been settled before it reached England. He then took up the other points touched upon in the memorial of the council, his most startling assertion being that the councillors had formulated the demand that the quit rents be placed at their disposal as a preliminary step to voting themselves salaries of £100 each. The governor's letter deepens the impression received from this dispute, that the real struggle was not over the courts of oyer and terminer, or any other specific point of difference. The issue was whether the governor or his council should be paramount in the public affairs of Virginia.[67]

[64] *C.O.5/1365*, pp. 52-57.

[65] *Supra*, p. 172.

[66] *Ex. Jour. Coun.*, III, 464, 465; *C.O.5/1318*, pp. 371-388. Besides the governor, Jennings, Blair, Ludwell, Smith, Lewis, and Bassett were present.

[67] *C.O.5/1318*, pp. 371-388.

Upon receiving the opinions of the board of trade and the attorney-general upon the courts of oyer and terminer, Spotswood in May 1718 laid them before the council asking whether, in view of the board's caution to him to make discreet use of his power, the June and December courts of oyer and terminer should be discontinued. The council replied that the king's instructions ought to be followed when there were any criminals to be tried.[68] Turning to those councillors who had disputed his appointive power, the governor asked if they now agreed that the governor had the power of constituting judges of those courts with or exclusive of the council. To this the councillors returned the somewhat ambiguous reply that they acquiesced in the determination of the board of trade.[69] It appears likely that no court of oyer and terminer was held in June. The following December, however, a prisoner was in the public jail awaiting trial. The governor thereupon announced that he intended to appoint a commission of oyer and terminer with none but councillors upon it. Since, however, he understood that it was commonly reported that by acquiescing the preceding April to the decision of the board of trade the council did not intend to yield the right which it claimed of exclusive jurisdiction in criminal cases, or to recognize the power of the governor to appoint others except upon extraordinary occasions, he insisted that the councillors acquiesce in the opinion of Attorney-General Northey, that their appointment might not be construed to confer upon them the power which the crown had vested in the governor. Jennings and Page declared they had never disputed the governor's power, and readily acquiesced, while the five insurgent councillors present, Blair, Ludwell, Smith, Bassett, and Harrison, replied, as non-

[68] This reply of the council was recorded in the transcript of the council minutes sent to England, but not in the journal which remained in Virginia. *Ex. Jour. Coun.*, III, 470, IV, xxxv.

[69] *Ibid.*, III, 470. Two days later a commission of oyer and terminer was ordered to issue for the trial of a Negro in Nansemond County. It was composed of county justices. *Ibid.*, p. 472. Spotswood had urged as precedents for the appointing of persons other than councillors to commissions of oyer and terminer the numerous courts so appointed for the trial of Negroes. This argument was evidently beside the point.

committally as before, that since the determination of the board of trade appeared to be grounded upon Northey's opinion, they supposed that in submitting to the one they acquiesced in the other.[70]

With this Spotswood was ill content, and a year later he again took the offensive, albeit with caution. Having reason to believe that Diggs and Beverley had been made councillors, although their credentials had not arrived, Spotswood appointed them with the council upon a commission of oyer and terminer. Five councillors promptly withdrew from the bench and presented a remonstrance to the governor in public court, and a crowd having collected, Ludwell declared in the hearing of all that the governor's power of naming judges other than the council in cases of life and death was of dangerous consequence to the lives and liberties of free subjects.[71]

Spotswood had won a victory which was worse than defeat. His legal right to appoint whomsoever he pleased to the courts of oyer and terminer had been upheld. But it would be hazardous to exercise this power, to secure which he had estranged the most influential men in the colony. The prerogative had been vindicated in theory; there had been no commensurate increase in the power and influence of the governor.[72]

In the meantime another assembly had been elected, had met, had been prorogued, had met again, and had been dissolved. The election of 1718 made eighteen changes in the membership of the house. John Custis, returned from William

[70] *Ex. Jour. Coun.*, III, 493-495.

[71] Spotswood to B. T., March 5, 1720. *C.O.5/1318*, pp. 735, 736.

[72] The council succeeded in persuading Spotswood's successor that the courts of oyer and terminer ought always to be held upon the appointed days whether there were criminals to be tried or not, in order that late commitments should be taken care of. Since he thus conceded a point which Spotswood had gained with comparatively little trouble, there is little probability that Drysdale ventured to appoint any but councillors upon these commissions. *Ex. Jour. Coun.*, IV, 41, 42; Drysdale to B. T., June 23, 1723, *C.O.5/1319*, p. 232. Indeed, the distinction between general court and court of oyer and terminer seems rapidly to have disappeared. From being merely a court of jail delivery the latter came to handle civil cases, disputes over land titles being repeatedly referred to it once Spotswood's influence was removed. *Ex. Jour. Coun.*, *passim*.

and Mary College, was permitted to retain his seat.[73] Daniel McCarty was rechosen speaker, George Eskridge was chosen chairman of the committee for elections and privileges, and Henry Harrison of that for public claims, while the committee for propositions and grievances was headed by the irreconcilable Corbin.[74] The governor's opponents were still in the ascendancy.

With the return of peace to Europe the tobacco industry was now restored to prosperity. Whether this had been because of Spotswood's policy or in spite of it was a purely academic question, since the tobacco act had been disallowed. The revival of the tobacco trade had increased the demand for Negro labor. It had also augmented the purchasing power of the planter. Consequently, the duty on liquors and slaves had piled up in the treasury the greatest balance in the history of the colony.[75] The disposal of this surplus and the provision for negotiations with the Iroquois at Albany were the two matters recommended by Spotswood in his opening address to the assembly,[76] while shortly afterwards he urged that it reimburse the defunct Virginia Indian Company for expenses incurred for the public weal.

No great question of public policy was at issue in 1718. The appropriations which the governor was asking might easily have been met. Spotswood was seeking neither to promote nor to uphold any basically unpopular policies. Yet throughout the session the burgesses maintained an attitude of ill-disguised hostility. In 1715 the governor had sown the wind. He was now reaping the whirlwind. The issue was personal. Conscious that the majority of the council bore to Spotswood an animosity not less than their own, the burgesses proceeded to lengths of audacity which even the stormy session of 1715 had not known. On the other hand, the governor bore himself with considerable restraint. The lessons of the past few years,

[73] *Jour. Burg.*, 1712-1726, pp. viii, ix.
[74] *Ibid.*, pp. 173, 175, 176.
[75] In November 1718 the balance was £17,995.16.3. *Ibid.*, p. 228.
[76] *Ibid.*, pp. 174, 175.

backed by the warnings of the board of trade, had not been lost on him. His aggressive, combative personality was becoming tempered with political wisdom.

He was given ample scope for the exercise of self-control. The house shifted the responsibility for the negotiations with the Five Nations upon the council, while the council declined to move until some overt act was committed. The governor's expectations of repayment for journeys undertaken to secure the frontier were disappointed in the most insulting manner.[77] Upon Indian affairs the burgesses acted as contrary to Spotswood's desires as the letter of the law would permit, and practically sounded the knell of projects which the governor had fostered for the past five years.[78]

The large surplus gave unwonted prominence to the treasurer of Virginia. It was customary for the speaker to hold this office, to which he was appointed by act of assembly. No appointment had been made in 1715, so Peter Beverley, now no longer a member of the house, remained the incumbent. Beverley was well disposed toward the governor, and the dominant party in the house naturally desired to transfer the colony's funds to one of its way of thinking. The way of securing this end closest in accord with precedent was the passage of an act appointing McCarty treasurer. The burgesses might well doubt, however, that the governor would give his assent. Yet in a country where capital was scarce it was vitally important that the surplus be put in circulation. A bill was therefore passed authorizing the treasurer to put out at interest for one year a sum not exceeding £4000 at four per cent. He was to be allowed one-half the interest, but was to loan the money at his own risk. Provision was also made for paying another £4000 to Archibald Blair. Blair was to give security and might loan out any part of the sum under the same terms as the speaker.[79] The council approved the measure without amendment.[80] It had not escaped the governor's notice that

[77] *Supra*, p. 101.
[78] *Supra*, pp. 94-96.
[79] *Jour. Burg.*, 1712-1726, p. 200.
[80] *Ibid.*, p. 214.

while the treasurer was permitted to loan money for one year only, no time limit was set upon the fund entrusted to Blair. He was empowered, but not enjoined, to loan it out, and might therefore retain it for his own use without interest until it was recalled by act of assembly. Archibald Blair, his brother the commissary, and Philip Ludwell were partners "in one of the most considerable Trading Stores in this Country." The knot of relations in the council might refuse to assent to any measure recalling the money, thus permitting Blair to retain it, interest free, as long as he pleased. Spotswood therefore resolved to veto the measure,[81] and it was never presented for his signature. However, an appropriation for scholarships at William and Mary College reduced the surplus by £1000.[82]

At the time of the repeal of the tobacco and Indian acts an additional instruction had been sent to the royal governors not to assent to any bill affecting the trade of Great Britain without a suspending clause.[83] The colonists seemed thus deprived of the power to raise money by import or export duties without abiding the delay necessary to secure the royal approval. In times of emergency this might prove more than inconvenient. The burgesses therefore framed an address to the crown, asking that this instruction be withdrawn.[84] They also thanked the king for his "great Care of the Trade of our Mother Country," in other words for repealing the Indian and tobacco acts, and asked that the power of the governor in appointing judges of oyer and terminer be restrained.[85] The address was hardly one to be presented through the regular channel, by way of the governor and the Virginia agent in London. Spotswood would scarcely have dared to

[81] *Letters*, II, 278, 279.

[82] Hening, IV, 74.

[83] *Supra*, p. 57.

[84] This demand Spotswood opposed in a letter to the board of trade, saying that the instruction was necessary to save a governor from the importunities of the people. "For my own part," he continued, "I could wish the passing of Laws were more restrained, for I am perswaded the present Council here would gladly lay hold of any Opportunity to promote popular Bills, to traduce me among the people if I refused my Assent without Express Authority for my so doing." *Letters*, II, 286.

[85] *Jour. Burg.*, 1712-1726, pp. 207, 208.

withhold it, but a document so hostile to the governor would receive scant support from Blakiston. What the opposition wanted was an advocate in London who would work for their interests and against those of the governor. William Byrd was therefore appointed agent for the burgesses. He was desired to secure favorable consideration for the address and, if the late proceedings of the burgesses were misrepresented, to "have regard to their Honour."[86]

Officers' fees stood sadly in need of regulation. Acts to that end had expired, and opportunity was thus given for extortion. Realizing that the fear of popular resentment might deter the governor from vetoing the regulatory measure now introduced, his opponents attached to it a rider that county courts should appoint their own clerks, a displaced clerk having the right of appeal to the general court. The power to appoint county court clerks had been granted by royal patent to the secretary of Virginia, now Spotswood's loyal supporter, Dr. William Cocke. This measure would therefore have lessened the prerogative, weakened the political influence of the governor's party, and increased the power of the general court, where the opposition had a clear majority. But the governor was not to be drawn into the trap. He gave his opponents to understand that the bill in that form would never receive his signature, and that the responsibility for its failure would devolve exclusively upon them. The offensive clause was withdrawn, and the bill passed.[87]

Besides the bill for disposing of the treasury surplus, another for preventing abuses in the post office passed both houses without being presented to the governor for his assent. Acting under authority of an act of parliament the postmaster-general of America had in the fall of 1717 established a fortnightly post between Philadelphia and Williamsburg. The cry was thereupon raised that parliament could not levy a tax (so the postal rates were characterized) in the colonies.

[86] *Jour. Burg.*, 1712-1726, pp. 194, 210, 216.
[87] *Letters*, II, 279, 280; Hening, IV, 59-74.

The proposed act of assembly imposed impossible conditions upon the postal system, and was designed to prevent its operation. While Spotswood did not have to veto this measure his opposition certainly prevented its enactment.[88]

The session had commenced on April 23. On May 30, there being no immediate prospect that measures would be taken to forward the governor's Indian policy, the house adjourned and was subsequently prorogued.[89] It reconvened on November 11. Omitting the customary opening address, Spotswood notified the burgesses that he had nothing immediately to lay before them and desired them to proceed on the propositions and grievances from the counties. Few had been presented, however, such was the general prosperity of the country. It thus appeared that little of importance was to take place. A number of the burgesses went home "and others believing their presence unnecessary, were gone to take the Diversion of a horse Race near the Town."[90] It seems likely that these absentees were those well disposed towards the governor, for the attendance of his opponents was needed to promote a plan which they had secretly been formulating. On November 20, Nicholas Meriwether presented to the house an address to the king and some instructions to "*William Byrd* Esqr Agent for the Colony of *Virginia*." The address to the crown was taken into immediate consideration, and adopted.[91] It stated that having considered "severall Attempts of Your Lieutenant

[88] *Letters*, II, pp. 280, 281, 288. This was reported by the board of trade to the postmaster-general in England, and a copy of the reply from the general post-office, approving his conduct, was forwarded to the governor. *B. T. Jour.*, 1718-1722, pp. 65, 77; *C.O.5/1318*, p. 631; *C.O.5/1365*, pp. 142, 200.

[89] This occasioned another skirmish between Spotswood and his council over the prerogative. The council questioned the governor's power to prorogue an assembly during an adjournment. The point was submitted to the board of trade by whom it was referred to Richard West, who as usual supported the governor's contention. *Ex. Jour. Coun.*, III, 480; *Letters*, II, 288-290; *C.O.323/7*, I, 154; *B. T. Jour.*, 1719-1722, p. 73.

[90] *C.O.5/1318*, p. 580.

[91] The address, though much of a unit, was voted upon paragraph by paragraph. The first paragraph was adopted 22 to 14, the second 19 to 14, and the third 19 to 13. This is the first instance during Spotswood's administration of the recording of a division.

Governor towards the Subversion of the Constitution of our Government, the depriving us of our ancient Rights & priviledges and many hardships which he daily exercises upon your Majestys good Subjects of this Colony" they thought it their duty to lay these facts before the throne. They therefore hoped that the crown would receive some particulars from William Byrd, "whom we have desired to appear in behalf of your oppressed Subjects of this Colony" this being the only way they had of making known their grievances. They attributed their troubles to their being governed by a lieutenant governor, while the governor-in-chief resided in London.[92]

The proposed instructions were fourteen in number. The first was to the effect that Byrd should present the address, lay before the crown the accusations of the burgesses against the governor, and do the utmost in his power to secure Spotswood's removal. The following eleven set forth the counts against the governor, the thirteenth desired Byrd "to represent to His Majesty the Inconveniences that attend this Plantation's being governed by a Lieutenant while the Governor in Chief resides in *England*, and if possible to obtain Redress therein," while the last was to the effect that he should seek an instruction obliging the governor to consent to any appropriation voted by the burgesses for the payment of an agent. Of the eleven counts against the governor, seven were rejected by the house.[93] Three were adopted as they stood,[94]

[92] *Jour. Burg.*, 1712-1726, pp. 228, 229.

[93] These accused him of insisting upon the right of patronage, and presenting and inducting ministers contrary to law and to Sir Edward Northey's opinion, of appointing a known Quaker naval officer, of neglecting the militia, of refusing to pass laws which had passed both houses and which were contrary to no known instruction and did not concern trade, of appointing new judges to try free subjects for their lives without the consent of the council, of condemning a person unheard, and of discouraging the lawyers of those who incurred his displeasure, so that it was difficult to secure any to undertake a case against him.

[94] These were to the effect that Spotswood had lavished money upon the governor's house to a greater extent than the law warranted, that he had endeavored to deter the county justices from paying the burgesses' salaries settled by law, and that he had browbeaten the house.

while another was softened in its wording.[95] The first instruction was adopted with the omission of the reference to the governor's removal. Byrd required no such prompting. The thirteenth was rejected. The last was incorporated into the final document with but slight change. A motion for an additional instruction to Byrd not to represent against the governor any matter not contained in the instructions was lost.[96] The case against Spotswood was palpably weak. Most of the rejected accusations were either frivolous, untrue, or against actions of the governor in accordance with instructions from the British authorities. Of those that remained, three concerned the interpretation of laws, while the fourth, that the governor had "by provoking Speeches & Messages abused the House of Burgesses, and thrown undeserved Reflections upon them," would better have been made in 1715. In 1718 it was Spotswood, rather than the house, who had occasion to complain of provoking messages. Such a case was apt to have little weight with the board of trade, particularly when presented by an agent not duly accredited.[97]

Spotswood flatly accused his opponents of trickery in forcing the measures against him through a "thin house." The burgesses retorted in kind. An attempt by Spotswood to straighten out the question of the accounts of the governor's house, by this time hopelessly entangled with the political controversy, was met by the burgesses' refusal to take action until the pleasure of the crown was known. The book of claims was also a bone of contention. Spotswood refused to sanction the rejection of expenses for the capture and trial of pirates. Neither would he assent to the allowance of £300 to William Byrd as agent. He agreed to pass the book of claims in all other particulars. The burgesses refused to alter the book, and when the governor gave his assent only to

[95] The governor was here accused of perverting the land laws so as to make retroactive the penalty of forfeiture for non-payment of quit rents.

[96] *Jour. Burg.*, 1712-1726, pp. 230, 231.

[97] Spotswood offered to transmit the address and accusations through Blakiston, but the burgesses were not likely thus to dispense with the services of Byrd. *Ibid.*, p. 237.

those items which he had previously approved they declined to proportion the levy. They were in no mood to increase the governor's control of the public purse by permitting him to exercise a "discriminative veto."[98]

On December 1 the session ended. It had resulted in the passage of three acts.[99] One offered rewards for Thatch and his pirate crew, dead or alive.[100] A second met the problem of getting the balance in the treasury back into circulation by empowering the treasurer to put £10,000 out at interest. The third raised a public levy for the payment of the claims of the previous session. The governor seemed to be in a buoyant mood. With a sporting gesture he offered to wager the "Cataline Crew of Male Contents" a thousand pounds that the crown would decide the dispute in his favor. "I take this to be an happy Crisis," he told the burgesses in his final address, "when the Country will be no longer imposed upon by malicious Whisperers, Clandestine Informers, and Anonymous Libellers of Government; for none could have been more Eager than my present Accusers to lay open every Act of Male Administration, and it cannot be doubted but that they have now drawn up the Total of my Charge."[101]

His bold front notwithstanding, Spotswood was shrewd enough to realize that he was face to face with a crisis. If ever the authorities in England became convinced that he had alienated the people he was apt to be removed. It would not suffice to demonstrate that he had acted in his office as a loyal and energetic servant of the crown; his administration stood in need of popular endorsement. Accordingly, during the year 1719, he sent the board a formidable array of papers, giving evidence of a remarkable demonstration upon the governor's behalf. Twenty-one counties[102] sent addresses,

[98] *Jour. Burg.*, 1712-1726, pp. xl, 232-241.

[99] A bill declaring who shall not bear office passed both houses. A similar act having been disallowed by the crown (*supra*, pp. 65, 66), Spotswood had a clear case for withholding his approval. *Jour. Burg.*, 1712-1726, pp. 225, 227.

[100] *Infra*, pp. 217-219.

[101] *Jour. Burg.*, 1712-1726, pp. 239, 242-244.

[102] All but Isle of Wight, Lancaster, Princess Anne, and Surry.

signed by justices, officers, vestries, clergy, principal inhabitants and freeholders, expressing surprise at and dissent from the proceedings of the burgesses, endorsing Spotswood's administration, and praying for its long continuance.[103] It is improbable that these addresses had their spontaneous rise in the affection of Virginia for her governor. The counties were aided in framing their addresses by a pamphlet of four printed pages, entitled "Some Remarkable Proceedings in the Assembly of Virginia, Anno 1718,"[104] which was doubtless published by Spotswood. But so ready a response from the people of the province indicates either that a strong minority had all along favored the governor, or else that by 1719 the tide of opposition was receding. Spotswood also received addresses from the clergy in convention[105] and the masters of William and Mary College,[106] while the governor and council of Maryland wrote him a letter of thanks for compassing the destruction of Thatch and his crew,[107] and several North Carolina skippers addressed him to the same effect.[108] The addresses indicated, so William Robertson informed the board of trade, that a greater number of burgesses dissented from the charges against the governor than had voted for them in the house.[109]

Meanwhile the address which the burgesses had sent to the crown in the spring of 1718 had been passed upon by the board of trade. The board was determined to tolerate no longer agents with credentials so irregular as those of William Byrd,[110] but that gentleman had succeeded in getting the address into the hands of Secretary of State James Craggs, by whom, on November 20, 1718, it was referred to the board. On April 10, 1719, the latter reported. The address had been presented in a very extraordinary manner, contrary

[103] *C.O.5/1318*, pp. 647-662, 798-808.
[104] *Ibid.*, pp. 621-624.
[105] *Historical Collections relating to the American Colonial Church*, William Stevens Perry, ed. (5 vols., Hartford, 1870-1878), I, pp. 108, 109.
[106] *C.O.5/1318*, pp. 664, 665.
[107] *B. T. Jour.*, 1718-1722, p. 172.
[108] *C.O.5/1318*, p. 663.
[109] *Ibid.*, pp. 827-829.
[110] *B. T. Jour.*, 1718-1722, p. 10.

to the royal instructions, which allowed separate addresses only when the governor refused to transmit them or when the burgesses had occasion to complain against the governor. In this case no application had been made to the governor, and the complaints were not against him, but against the powers vested in him by the crown. With more vehemence than logic the board expressed astonishment at the proposal that the instruction requiring a suspending clause in all acts affecting the trade of Great Britain be revoked, since it could never be supposed that the plantations had the power of making laws prejudicial to the trade of Great Britain. As to the request that the council be the sole judges of oyer and terminer, the board was informed that the council, the chief promoters of this claim of power for themselves, had since acquiesced in Sir Edward Northey's opinion upon that score.[111]

Thus the first appeal to Caesar came to naught. The second was thwarted by the refusal of the board of trade (which made clear its attitude to Craggs) to recognize Byrd, the agent to whose charge it had been committed. "We take notice," wrote the board to Spotswood in June 1719, "of the Complaints that you mention the Assembly have lately exhibited against You; All that we can say at present (no Body having yet apply'd on that Subject) is that You may depend upon all the Countenance & Support that We can give you which We think You have deserved."[112]

[111] B. T. to Craggs, April 10, 1719, *C.O.5/1365*, pp. 187-191.

[112] B. T. to Spotswood, June 26, 1719, *Ibid.*, p. 203. The first and largest batch of addresses to the governor had been read by the board three days before the date of this letter, and doubtless had something to do with its favorable tone. *C.O.5/1318*, p. 666.

Chapter IX

THE CHURCH

THE nature of Virginia's agricultural development seriously hampered the growth of organized religion. The closely knit township which did so much to promote the influence of the New England clergyman was here replaced by the sprawling plantation system. With parishes measuring anything up to sixty miles in length, regular attendance at public worship was not to be expected. And where participation faltered, interest flagged also.[1]

The salary of a clergyman was fixed by law at 16,000 pounds of tobacco, nominally the equivalent of £80 currency. When the market was good the minister in the best "sweetscented" parish might realize twice this sum, but the incumbent of one of the poorer parishes was fortunate during times of depression if his tobacco fetched half its theoretical price.[2] The clergyman was apt to be underpaid, and where he addressed himself conscientiously to his mission he was sure to be overworked. It was therefore difficult to supply the pulpits of Virginia with men of proper parts, difficult in fact to supply them at all.

Parish matters were regulated in Virginia by the vestries. Elected in the first instance by the voters, they were self-perpetuating bodies[3] which might or might not reflect the wishes of their respective parishes.[4] The twelve vestrymen

[1] No attempt is made in the present work to give an adequate picture of the Church in Spotswood's day. The reader is referred to T. J. Wertenbaker, "The Attempt to Reform the Church of Colonial Virginia," *Sewanee Review*, XXV (1917), 257-282.

[2] Perry, I, 329, 330.

[3] Hening, II, 44, 45.

[4] The parish of Accomac was at odds with its vestry throughout Spotswood's administration, and grievances from the counties indicate popular discontent with the actions of vestries elsewhere. *Jour. Burg.*, *passim*.

were none the less apt to be the most influential men of the parish, and their power was great. The vestries claimed the right of choosing their own minister, and preferred to reserve also that of ridding themselves of him at will. Indeed, the character of certain clerics makes perfectly understandable the disrelish of their parishioners for being tied to them for life. Nor were the vestries solely responsible for the precarious tenure of the clergy. It is a minister who tells us that some of his brethren were "of too vagrant a temper never fixing their resolutions on the discharge of their Office over one flock." "The custom here of Ministers so frequently changing their Parishes," declared the Rev. Alexander Forbes, "not for laudable or necessary ends, is very offensive, and always interpreted by the People to proceed from levity or avarice."[5] This impermanence was an abuse. "They [the clergy] are to their several vestries in the nature of hired servants," wrote Blair, "agreed with from year to year, and dismissed if they please without any crime proved or so much as alleged against them. . . . Nothing can have worse effects upon the Clergy than this servitude, for it hinders all good ministers from coming in or staying amongst us . . . it exposes [them] to great poverty and contempt, and makes them base, mean, and mercenary."[6]

Efforts had been made before Spotswood's time to put the Church upon a better footing. Henry Compton, bishop of London from 1676 to 1713, had sponsored the movement, and its incarnation was his representative in Virginia, Commissary James Blair. Governor Francis Nicholson had lent his aid, and despite an untimely quarrel between governor and commissary some progress had been made. William and Mary College had been founded to train young men of the colony for the ministry, though it was a matter of decades before the college was actually supplying Virginia's pulpits. Salaries had been raised a modicum. And while many parishes remained chronically vacant, some advance seems to have

[5] Perry, pp. 324, 325.
[6] Wertenbaker, *op. cit.*, p. 273.

been made toward securing an adequate supply of ministers. But an attempt to render the tenure of the clergy more secure had failed.

In 1711 Spotswood sought to induce the assembly to put the salaries of the clergy upon a better footing. A poll tax of forty pounds of tobacco was to be levied on all tithables,[7] the tobacco sold, each incumbent paid £80, and "the Overplus . . . applyed towards the erecting new Churches where they are wanting, the repairing and adorning the Churches already built, and providing suitable Ornaments." But the burgesses, "a Whimsical Multitude . . . especially where money is required," were not to be drawn into the plan.[8] A few years later, however, the clergy benefited from the tobacco act of 1713 which established a minimum quality for salary tobacco and relieved them of the necessity of traveling the length and breadth of their respective parishes to collect it, since they now received certificates for tobacco deposited at the government warehouse. The convention of the clergy sent a delegation to thank council and burgesses for the passage of this act, and presented an address to the governor in a body.[9] The gain was temporary, and vanished with the repeal of the act in 1717.

Lack of ministers of the establishment gave opportunity to the apostles of dissent. Quakers were numerous in Nansemond, and Spotswood wrote to the bishop of London that one "poor" parish had been for a long time without a minister, which had "given occasion to a Presbyterian preacher to set up a Meeting house, where a great many of the People begin to resort, but more for the sake of hearing Sermons . . . than any inclination to the Doctrine or principles of the Dissenters; it being observable that though in former vacancys of that Parish, several of the Parishioners have gone to the Meeting, Yet whenever they have had the happiness of an

[7] The number of tithables (males and unfree females sixteen years of age or older) was placed at 30,000.

[8] *Letters*, I, 127, 128; *Jour. Burg.*, 1702-1712, p. 303.

[9] *Letters*, II, 49; *Leg. Jour. Coun.*, I, 579; *Jour. Burg.*, 1712-1726, p. 95; *Ex. Jour. Coun.*, III, 388, 389.

Orthodox Ministry they have all returned to the Church."[10] That Spotswood was greatly alarmed by the spread of nonconformity is improbable. Although a good churchman, he was no zealot of the Nicholson type. He indeed called Quakers to account over the matter of oaths, and would have taken strong measures to curb their "Unaccountable Behaviour" during the troubled times of 1711.[11] But these were administrative problems. His disrelish for the spreading of the doctrines of dissent had its rise in large measure from the time-honored belief that "when once Schism has crept into the Church, it will soon create Faction in the Civil Government."[12] His anxiety to appoint George Walker naval officer[13] indicates little hostility to a dissenter *per se*. After all, this was the eighteenth century, and in 1717 the crown disallowed an act of 1663 to prevent the assembling of Quakers without a voice being raised in its favor.[14]

As the king's ordinary, the governor possessed powers of induction and collation which loomed large in his commission. It was to him that ministers were sent by the bishop of London, he in turn recommending them to the vestries, and thus obtaining livings for them. Therefore, when the would-be reformers of the colonial church turned their attention to the insecure tenure of the clergy, the solution of the problem seemed to lie through the governor. So barren was the project in results that it might be dismissed summarily but for the fact that it is tangled inextricably with the struggle occasioned by the divided headship of the church in Virginia. The royal power devolved upon the governor; the commissary represented his bishop. One seems to catch the faint echo of Hildebrand hurling anathema at Henry IV and, be it added, the glimmering reflection of an emporer standing in the snow of Canossa.

[10] *Letters*, I, 26.
[11] *Ex. Jour. Coun.*, IV, 13; *Jour. Burg.*, 1702-1712, p. 303.
[12] *Letters*, I, 38.
[13] *Supra*, p. 65.
[14] *C.O.5/1318*, pp. 235, 305, 306; *B. T. Jour.*, 1715-1718, p. 328.

To follow the induction controversy through all its obscure meanderings would be as tedious as profitless. Yet accurate generalization is difficult. The principal protagonists were not always consistent in their positions, and their attitudes, expressed in terms the definition of which was part of the controversy, cannot be determined with certainty. Reduced to its essentials the matter seems to have been as follows.

Once "inducted" by the governor the tenure of a minister was permanent.[15] Colonial law "requested" the governor to induct a duly qualified minister "into any parish that shall make presentation of him."[16] But the vestries were reluctant to "present" their ministers. Blair therefore urged Nicholson, during his first term, to "induct upon lapse." In other words, if the vestry did not present a new minister for induction within six months after a parish had become vacant, the governor might "collate" a clergyman of his choice, and his collatee would hold the cure for life. Nicholson's term ended before he could do anything, and Andros ignored the question. With Nicholson's return Blair urged the matter once more, backing his position with decisions which he had obtained from the crown lawyers. But at the first move on the part of the governor a furor of protest arose from the vestries, and Nicholson dared not use his power. A few vestries were scared into making presentations, but that was all.[17] When Spotswood arrived in Virginia there were, it seems, but three ministers who had been inducted, all upon the presentation of their vestries.[18]

That Blair was responsible for the removal of both Andros and Nicholson is well known; but the bearing of the question of induction upon his differences with them is less clear. Andros seems to have been indifferent, if not hostile, to this

[15] Though even then it is difficult to see how an unwilling vestry could have been obliged to pay his salary.

[16] Hening, II, 46.

[17] Wertenbaker, *op. cit.*, pp. 269, 272-275.

[18] Perry, p. 315.

as to all other efforts at church reform. Nicholson, on the other hand, appears to have sinned by an over-zealous participation in matters ecclesiastical. He indeed adopted Blair's position on the induction question. But he had "invaded almost all . . . parts of the ecclesiastical Jurisdiction."[19] In the ensuing contest for primacy Blair was victorious. Nicholson like Andros before him being "unmade" by this "surpliced Warwick."[20]

Governor and commissary had failed, and even had they been capable of working harmoniously together they would still have failed, for their reliance was upon law and authority, not upon the affections of the people.[21] Then came Spotswood. It seemed for a while that he had seen the light. "I do not see but that all Ministers of good Life and Conversation are upon as sure a Foot here as if they were inducted," he wrote to Bishop Compton, and later he assured Bishop Robinson that "Your Lo'p's great care in sending hither men of good Character is the surest way of establishing the Clergy upon a sure footing, seeing it makes the Affections of the people concurr with the Rights of the Church."[22] The vision faded. Spotswood was soon flourishing his commission in the face of a hostile province as if it were from parchments that the Church militant derives her strength!

At the very outset of his administration Spotswood was urged by Compton to exercise his power of induction. The governor hesitated. "I hope Yo'r Lord'p will judge it advisable," he wrote, "that by how much this Practice has been neglected by my Predecessors in this Government, with so much the more Caution I am to proceed in the reviving it here, and that as yet it may be too dangerous for me, whilst a stranger, to attempt." "Some Injunction," he thought, "ought rather to be laid on the Pastours not to forsake their Flocks, for it is observable that those Shepherds here oftener

[19] Wertenbaker, *op. cit.*, pp. 272, 273.
[20] *Jour. Burg.*, 1712-1726, p. xlv, *n.*
[21] Wertenbaker, *op. cit.*, pp. 270, 281.
[22] *Letters*, I, 27; II, 158.

leave their Sheep than that the Sheep aim at changing their Shepherd." Only recently the sudden departure of its minister had nearly caused Hungars Parish to lose a fine glebe, bequeathed upon the condition that the parish should never be vacant over six months. It might not be amiss, the governor thought, "to allow a little time to wear off the freshness of this passage." He took up the question of induction in private conversation with burgesses in the fall of 1710, "but I found them so cold on that Subject, and so little disposed to join with me, that I durst not venture to recomend it in a publick manner."[23]

Seven years later Spotswood felt surer of his position. "I am in a particular manner," he wrote to Bishop Robinson, "obliged to thank your Lo'p for [your care in sending over only ministers of capacity,] as it eases me of some trouble w'ch my Predecessors have met with in the settling of the Clergy; but now the People are rather contending who shall have the Gentlemen y'r Lo'p send than disputing my Collating them."[24] It will be noted that the governor speaks of collation, not of induction. The act of assembly upon which the vestries based, in part, their claim of patronage placed no limitation of time upon the exercise of the right of presentation.[25] The royal commission gave to the governor the right of collating to benefices in the colony "as often as any of them shall happen to be void."[26] The intermediary position adopted by Blair, that when the vestry failed to present a candidate within six months of a vacancy the governor should induct upon lapse *jure devoluto*,[27] appears to have been based upon neither colonial law nor royal commission, but upon the

[23] *Letters*, I, 4, 5, 26, 27, 66, 67. Early in his administration Spotswood inducted the Rev. John Skaife into the parish of Stratton Major but this, apparently the sole instance of induction by Spotswood, was done upon presentation of the vestry. Perry, p. 276.

[24] *Letters*, II, 254.

[25] Hening, II, 46.

[26] *Va. Mag. Hist.*, XX, 343. The instructions merely imposed the limitation that the candidate should have his fitness certified by the bishop of London. *Ibid.*, XXI, 349.

[27] Perry, pp. 320, 321.

custom in England. Spotswood seems now to have determined to claim the full powers given him by his commission.

One month before, having permitted himself to become involved in the dispute between Spotswood and Ludwell, Blair had also written to Bishop Robinson. His attempted mediation in this controversy had placed him, he declared, "under the frowns of a great and eminent person in this country" who thought he had been too much Ludwell's friend, "and indeed I do not deny that I thought he had much the better as to the merits of the cause."[28] The two letters seem unconnected. Yet the coincidence in date is striking. Blair, fearing that the exercise of so great a power as that of nominating all ministers in the colony would give the governor an overweening influence in church affairs, may have turned his enemy and fought him on other grounds also. On the other hand, he may have become embroiled with Spotswood in much the same way as did the other councillors, and on this account have opposed him on the matter of collation.

So long as the ministers nominated by the governor were acceptable to their respective vestries, and Spotswood did not attempt to give his nominees permanent tenure, the question of the right of patronage was unlikely to arise. To the vestries the governor's "collations" were simply recommendations, the immemorial method of supplying vacancies. But it was only a matter of time until vestry and governor would each propose a candidate, thus bringing things to an issue. The Rev. John Bagg had come to Virginia in 1709. But a defect in his ordination (he was only in deacon's orders) made him unacceptable to the vestry of St. Anne's, and before Bagg could go to London to be ordained priest the Rev. Giles Rainsford had been chosen instead. Bagg returned with a letter from Bishop Robinson to the governor recommending him for the pulpit in question, whereupon Spotswood collated Bagg, ignoring Rainsford. The latter could hardly

[28] Blair to Bp. of London, May 14, 1717. *Fulham MSS., Virginia,* 1st Box, no. 119.

withstand the governor, and was on the point of giving up his parish when the majority of the vestry came to his rescue and resolved to "present" him to the governor for induction as their minister.[29]

The governor's position was thus squarely challenged. On July 30, 1718, Spotswood laid before the council those parts of his commission and instructions which concerned the filling of ecclesiastical benefices, and stated that it appeared that the king considered all benefices in the colony to be "in his Majestys Gift." "Some Persons," however, had "taken upon them to dispute that right," and a neighboring vestry had placed a minister in their parish upon their own authority without any application to the governor. He asked the council whether he ought to exercise the powers conferred upon him, or whether the vestry was to be allowed "to place or displace Ministers at their Pleasure." The council assumed a "correct" but noncomittal attitude, just as in the later stages of the oyer and terminer dispute. It replied "that the Governor ought to pursue the Powers Granted by his Majesty wch according to the words of the said Commission and Instructions give him authority to supply Vacant benefices."[30] A month later Spotswood laid before the council a paper signed by nine vestrymen presenting Rainsford for induction, asking whether it ought to be received as a legal presentation. That the sympathies of the councillors lay with the vestry seems reasonably certain, but it was little to their interest to give Spotswood another opportunity of denouncing them to the board of trade for failure to uphold the royal prerogative. They therefore avoided the issue by saying that the presentation, "being informal," ought not to be received.[31]

But this was enough for the governor. The next day he sent the recalcitrant vestry copies of the council's decisions,

[29] Perry, pp. 205, 313, 314; *Letters*, II, 253-255.

[30] *Ex. Jour. Coun.*, III, 482.

[31] *Ibid.*, p. 483. Blair later declared that the council admitted the vestry's right of presentation. Perry, pp. 234, 235. The journal is silent on this point.

informing them that the commissary, who it was rumored had urged them to insist on their rights, denied having done so and had "joined" in the proceedings of the council.[32] He presented the case for the crown, backed by commission, instructions, legal decisions, and historical data. "If you are the patrons (as you suppose) you may, as soon as you please, bring a quare impedit, to try your title; and then it will appear, whether the King's clerk or yours has the most rightfull possession of the Church. In the mean time," he continued, "I think it necessary hereby to forewarn you to be cautious how you dispose of the profits of your parish; least you pay it in your own wrong."[33] The vestry did not care to try the issue. It seems to have had no objection to Bagg personally, and he was permitted to retain his parish until his death in 1724.[34] A similar course of opposition to the governor on the part of the vestry of James City had already been abandoned.[35] Thus far the victory was with Spotswood.

The convention held at William and Mary College in April 1719 showed that a majority of the clergy were supporting Spotswood against Blair. Not content with assailing the commissary's position on collation,[36] they questioned the purity of his doctrine, the validity of his ordination, and his zeal in observing the liturgy. They even took the questionable course of supporting the governor in his quarrel with the assembly. The assault was led by Hugh Jones,[37] who had but recently been made professor of mathematics at the college. It is evident that he owed this appointment to the support of the governor, who pushed it through in face of the

[32] Blair, it seems, had denied that he was author and abettor of the contest, but later denied having denied (here was equivocation indeed!) that he had said the vestry had the law and the council on its side. Perry, p. 235.

[33] Perry, pp. 203-208.

[34] *Ibid.*, pp. 313-315; *Letters*, II, 254 *n.* The governor did not induct him, however, and in the year of his death Bagg was recommending that the crown disallow the act of assembly upon which the vestries based their right of patronage.

[35] Perry, p. 205.

[36] While they could hardly do so explicitly, their attitude is clear.

[37] Jones to Bishop Robinson, May 30, 1719. *Fulham MSS.*, 2nd box, no. 233.

opposition of Ludwell and probably of Blair.[38] Jones now went so far as to propose that the governor be desired to suspend the commissary, and the bishop to send another in his place (Jones would have liked to succeed Blair at the head of the Virginia clergy[39]), proposals which the convention rejected "with great indignation."[40] The convention being little more than a deliberative body its actions had slight effect. In an able letter to his bishop Blair admitted and went far to justify his opposition to the governor in the matter of collation. The frivolity of the other charges against him he demonstrated without difficulty.[41]

Blair was not likely to permit Spotswood to rest on the laurels won in his contest with the "twelve bishops of St. Annes." He now transferred the issue to his own parish of Bruton. The cure was an important one. Located at Williamsburg, Bruton Church was becoming something of a colonial Westminster Abbey. When the assembly was in session the bell, salvaged from the wreck of H.M.S. *Garland* in 1711, summoned to church governor, councillors, and burgesses, to say nothing of visitors to the colonial capital. And a governor lay in her churchyard. When therefore the question of rebuilding the church was mooted in 1710, it seemed fitting that the expense should not be borne by the parish alone. Accordingly Spotswood offered to build the governor's pew, and the assembly appropriated £200 to provide accommodation for its members. But the fund was insufficient to carry out the plans which had been prepared and the burgesses declined, two years later, to augment it.

[38] *Letters*, II, 253.

[39] In his *Present State of Virginia* (pp. 98-102), published in 1724, Jones proposes that as an introductory step to a bishopric the office of Dean of Virginia be erected. Having enlarged elsewhere upon the unpopularity of Blair, he says, "This Person [the dean] should be one that is popular, universally acquainted with the People, their Temper and Manners, and one respected and beloved by them." It is difficult to avoid the conclusion that the author is describing himself.

[40] Accounts of the proceedings of the convention are given in Perry, pp. 199-225.

[41] Perry, pp. 226-233.

"I shall Diminish," Spotswood informed them, "the Wings projected for the Public use. . . . Since I perceive you will be Contented with less Room therein."[42]

It was appropriate that the bishop's commissary should be the incumbent of such a parish, and in 1710 Blair accepted the cure upon the invitation of the vestry and with the governor's tacit assent, perhaps with his cordial approval. But in the heat of later controversy Spotswood taxed Blair with having failed to apply to him for collation. Blair apparently suspected that the governor would attempt to supplant him. At all events he accepted the challenge; he induced the vestry to present him to the governor as their minister. In the presentation (Blair saw to it that it was formal) the vestry styled themselves the undoubted patrons of that church. Blair now demanded that the governor induct him.[43] As was to be expected, Spotswood refused.

When in April 1720 a reconciliation took place between governor and council, it was agreed that the vestry bring a *quare impedit* against the governor to settle the right to the advowson. The case was to be tried before the general court, with an appeal to the crown. Since, however, it would be unfair to burden one parish with the cost of prosecuting a case of general concern, the matter was postponed until the next general assembly.[44] Accordingly the assembly appropriated £60, twenty for the trial before the general court and forty for the appeal.[45]

The governor's right of collation was soon being challenged elsewhere. The following year Spotswood informed the bishop of London that a Rev. Mr. Bailey "at first thrust himself into a Parish in this Govt against my will, & even in opposition to one of your Lordship's licensed Missionaries

[42] *Letters*, I, 67; *Cal. Va. State Paps.*, I, 145, 146; *Jour. Burg.*, 1702-1712, pp. 288, 289, 291; 1712-1726, pp. 37-39.

[43] Spotswood to B. T., March 5, 1720. *C.O.5/1318*, p. 735.

[44] *Ex. Jour. Coun.*, III, 524, 525; Perry, p. 315.

[45] *Jour. Burg.*, 1712-1726, p. 301; Perry, p. 315. With Spotswood's removal the suit was dropped, and the money appropriated for its prosecution remained (so said scandal) in the pocket of the commissary. *Ibid.*, pp. 314, 315.

(Mr. Jas. Falconer), who had my collating letter to that Vestry, & as he afterwards got possession of another parish without any letter or act of mine, & has since been treating with a third; I must, how wrong soever I Judge these proceedings to be, remain passive until a weightier judgment than mine decides the controversy or else I shall raise the old combustion in this Govt., & be in danger of Drawing your Lordship's Comry upon my back again."[46]

Knowing the situation as he did, James Blair must have contemplated the outcome of the controversy with some misgivings. The decision of the general court would probably go against the governor, and although the decision was apt to be reversed upon appeal to London, it would prove impracticable for the governor to exercise his vindicated authority once the vestries resolved to resist him. If the vestries gave way, as had that of St. Anne's, Spotswood would hold the clergy of Virginia in the hollow of his hand, a bitter prospect for the commissary. But if the vestries successfully withstood the governor, the clergy would then be once more reduced to the old "servitude" of precarious tenure. For this Blair could have had little relish; he was no more the friend of "congregationalism" than was Spotswood. Would it not be far better if Spotswood were replaced by a governor who would be led by Blair's counsel, and by holding over the vestries the threat of collation upon lapse,[47] would induce them to present their ministers for induction?

That this was Blair's attitude cannot positively be stated. The relative importance of church affairs in the quarrel between Spotswood and Blair is difficult to determine. Certain it is, however, that the commissary now desired a change at the governor's mansion, and that among the differences between these two the contest for the control of the church loomed large.

[46] Perry, p. 249.

[47] The weapon seems innocuous, but it is assumed that Blair was sincere in his repeated advocacy of it.

Chapter X

DEFENSE ON LAND AND SEA

SPOTSWOOD'S administration fell upon troubled times. Up to 1713 Britain was at war with both France and Spain, while a state of war with the latter prevailed in 1719 and 1720. In the intervals of peace the colonies were subject to attacks from pirates by sea and from Indians by land. And there was a constant menace from within, where the rapidly increasing number of Negroes intensified the fear of servile insurrection. One such outbreak had been nipped in the bud shortly before Spotswood's arrival in the colony. The burgesses readily assumed the cost of manumitting the slave who had disclosed the plot, but contended that the charges arising from the arrest, trial, and execution of the conspirators ought to be borne by the counties. The council argued that an insurrection involved the peace of the colony as a whole, and finally secured the insertion of these charges in the book of claims.[1] A bill framed at Spotswood's instance in 1710 to prevent Negroes from holding meetings and possessing weapons was amended to death by the burgesses, while in 1711 a similar measure passed the house, only to be tabled by the council.[2]

At the beginning of Spotswood's administration the militia was regulated by an act of 1705, which made all males of military age subject to militia duty, exception being made of servants and slaves, overseers in charge of four or more slaves, millers, and past and present holders of practically all official positions. The latter, while exempted from musters in order to preserve the dignity of their respective offices, were required to provide themselves with arms and horses,

[1] *Cal. State Paps., Col.*, 1710-1711, p. 177; *Jour. Burg.*, 1702-1712, pp. 270, 288, 294-296; Hening, III, 537, 538; *Letters*, I, 58, 59.

[2] *Ibid.*, p. 42; *Jour. Burg.*, 1702-1712, pp. 250-318, *passim*; *Leg. Jour. Coun.*, I, 521.

and in time of danger were liable for service "in such stations as are suitable for gentlemen." The chief officer of militia in each county had authority to enlist all those subject to militia duty, and to assign them to service in either horse or foot, the basis of selection (each militiaman had to furnish his own outfit) being the ability of the individual to provide himself with a horse and with the more expensive equipment required for the cavalry. General musters were to be held once a year or oftener at the discretion of the chief militia officer in each county, while company musters were to be called at least once every three months by the captains. Militiamen failing to appear at musters fully equipped were to be fined one hundred pounds of tobacco, but not more than five times in any one year! Failure to answer the call in case of alarm was punishable by a fine of £10 or three months' imprisonment.[3] The men of better estate acted as commissioned officers in the militia, hence the military titles to this day associated with the gentry of the South.[4]

In 1710 Spotswood urged upon the assembly the necessity of a more adequate regulation of the militia. But the matter remained locked in committee for two sessions, delay being partly due to the governor's failure to specify the reforms which he desired. Upon being reproved for their inaction, the burgesses returned the rather surprising explanation that in view of the imminence of hostilities[5] they thought it better to await the outbreak of war before making new regulations for the militia. In 1712 a proposition from Princess Anne County "for Establishing the Militia of this Colony on a better foot than it now Stands and for providing the poorer Sort of people with Arms and Ammunition gratis" was rejected.[6]

When, upon the outbreak of the Yamasee War in South

[3] Hening, III, 335-342.

[4] Jones, *Present State of Virginia*, p. 62. These officers were evidently numerous. In 1720 the burgesses rejected the petition of Chichley Corbin Thacker for an allowance for making out eight hundred and fifty commissions for the militia. *Jour. Burg.*, 1712-1726, p. 275.

[5] The Tuscarora War had just broken out in North Carolina.

[6] *Ibid.*, 1702-1712, pp. 240-344, *passim;* 1712-1726, p. 16.

Carolina Spotswood summoned an assembly, he sent the burgesses at their request his recommendations for the reform of the militia law.[7] Affirming the principle that all ought to contribute to the defense of the country in proportion to the estate which they had to defend,[8] the governor pointed out that the law placed the burden of defense upon the poorer class. A poor man might be obliged to leave his farm when his absence meant the loss of the crop upon which his family depended for subsistence, while the well-to-do, practically all of whom held some office or other, were exempt as were also their overseers. The militia officers evidently considered these regulations oppressive, for although half the militiamen of the colony were unarmed few culprits were fined, and still fewer fines were collected. He might have added that although the strength of the militia amounted on paper to some 15,000,[9] he had been unable to secure as many as 200 for active service within the colony against the Tuscarora. The governor proposed that the militia be reduced to 3000 foot and 1500 dragoons, apportioned among the counties in proportion to the number of tithables. Officers and men were to be subject, under penalty, to appear under arms at the call of the governor, but were not to be mustered for more than ten days a year, except by consent of the council in times of emergency. They were to be paid by their respective counties for every day they were called out. Weapons were to be provided at the charge of the estates defended, the firearms to be of uniform bore. An adjutant[10] was to be appointed for each neck, or for every four or five counties, to supervise the training of officers and soldiers and to maintain a uniform system of drill. In time of danger all persons capable of bearing arms were to be liable for military service.[11]

[7] *Letters*, II, 123, 124; *Jour. Burg.*, 1712-1726, p. 128.

[8] This is one of several indications that Spotswood was a good Whig so far as political theory was concerned.

[9] *Letters*, II, 211.

[10] Spotswood intended himself to give these officers adequate military instruction.

[11] *C.O.5/1318*, pp. 201, 202.

A bill was accordingly introduced into the house, but was rejected upon the third reading.[12] In 1720, despite an appeal from the governor and a proposition from New Kent, the problem of providing adequate equipment for the militia was referred to the next session when, the committee on propositions and grievances finding "various difficulties therein," the matter was again deferred.[13] Thus Spotswood's administration passed without a new militia law. Part of the responsibility for this failure must rest with the governor. Had he at the outset submitted his proposals to the burgesses in writing, instead of waiting until the bitter session of 1715, his chances of success would have been much greater. It is evident, however, that the colony as a whole wished no change in the militia law. The opposition of the well-to-do is understandable, for the proposed reforms would have placed the expense upon the county rate-payer. Probably the poorer people preferred the old law which, if more severe in the letter was evaded with comparative ease, to a new measure which the governor evidently intended to enforce. But perhaps the decisive factor was that rich and poor alike shared the belief of Englishmen at home that a strong military force was the right arm of absolutism. What cared Virginia if not one of her militia officers had the benefit of an army training? This was better than having "an Adjutant in every neck to huff and bully ye people" into an instrument by means of which the chief executive might "govern Arbitrarily and by Martial Law."[14]

In 1705 an act for the security and defense of the country in times of danger had passed the general assembly. The governor was authorized to call out the militia in case of invasion or insurrection, and to impress vehicles and vessels for its transportation, together with any other supplies which might

[12] *Jour. Burg.*, 1712-1726, pp. 149-151.

[13] *Ibid.*, pp. 250, 278, 279, 338, 339, 352, 353.

[14] *Letters*, II, 209-212. The deplorable lack of discipline in the militia is clearly indicated in a letter from Robert Carter to the governor, Oct. 12, 1720. *Carter Letter Book.*

be needed. Artisans might be pressed into service. Lookouts were also authorized in Princess Anne, Elizabeth City, and Northampton Counties. The payment for these various services was made a "country charge." The militiamen were to receive pay if they served for more than four days. This act expired June 30, 1708,[15] and therefore no such powers were enjoyed by the executive when Spotswood assumed office, although as he told the burgesses, " 'tis not to be Doubted but That The Reasons on Which They were grounded do Still Subsist." The act of 1705 was therefore revived though only for another two years, and upon its expiration was continued for a similar period. In 1714 a measure to continue it yet another two years passed both houses but the governor, bound by his instructions concerning the reenaction of temporary laws, withheld his consent.[16] No further attempt appears to have been made in Spotswood's day to revive this law. There was thus no provision for the payment of the militia, which doubtless goes to explain Spotswood's anxiety for a new militia law in 1715.

Disappointed by the assembly, Spotswood appealed to the authorities in England for arms and ammunition. In 1702 supplies costing over £3000 had been sent to Virginia, but these had been for the most part distributed for use by the militia among the counties where, since no one was responsible for their care, the weapons became unserviceable and the powder all but useless.[17] Spotswood asked that ships of war touching at Virginia might exchange fresh powder for that in the colony which, he maintained, would be as good as any for signals, salutes, and watch guns, a proposal to which the ordnance board did not take kindly. In the meantime, events in North Carolina were making the need for arms even more pressing, and the governor renewed his requests, adding to

[15] Hening, III, 362-367.

[16] *Ibid.*, III, 296; IV, 30; *Letters*, I, 58; *Jour. Burg.*, 1702-1712, pp. 277; 1712-1726, pp. 103-106, 112; *Ex. Jour. Coun.*, III, 393.

[17] In 1712 the munitions in Virginia belonging to the crown amounted to 1013 muskets, 326 carbines, 296 pair of pistols, 1017 swords, 798 cartridge boxes, 41½ barrels of powder, and 4000 pounds of ball. *C.O.5/1316*, O. 142.

his requisition three hundred tents for the projected expedition against the Tuscarora. Micajah Perry supported his demands. Although the treasury felt that the colonies ought themselves to defray the cost of the munitions which they received, the desired supplies (the ordnance board placed their cost at nearly £2500) were sent.[18] "It was a particular pleasure to me to see so fine a sett of Arms," wrote Spotswood, "for I must confess they are far beyond any usually deliver'd out of the Tower while I serv'd in the Army."[19]

In 1713 Spotswood laid before the council a plan for appointing an armorer to clean and keep in repair the arms at Williamsburg. The armorer was forthwith appointed, at a salary of £12 to be paid out of the two shillings a hogshead, £5 being at the same time deducted from the allowance to the gunner of Jamestown.[20] In 1714 the assembly appropriated for the construction of a brick magazine £200 out of the duty on liquors and slaves, half of which was to be repaid by the Virginia Indian Company. It also voted an annual salary of £20 for a storekeeper, to which the council added the £10 theretofore granted to the gunner at Jamestown.[21] The revenue being greatly in arrears, the governor advanced the money necessary to construct the octagonal building which is to this day one of the historic sights of Williamsburg.[22]

With the outbreak of the Yamasee War, Spotswood re-

[18] *Acts of Privy Coun., Col.*, II, 669; *B. T. Jour.*, 1709-1715, pp. 317-432, *passim; Cal. State Paps., Col.*, 1711-1712, pp, 160-284, *passim; Letters,* I, 95, 106, 133, 166, 167; *Ex. Jour. Coun.*, III, 300; *C.O.5/1316*, O. 105, 123; B. T. to Dartmouth, April 16 and Dec. 6, 1711, *C.O.5/1341; C.O.324/10*, pp. 1, 2.

[19] *Letters*, II, 65, 66. The governor reported in 1716 that there had been sent to Virginia since his arrival 300 firelocks, 300 tents, 154 barrels of powder, 3 ton 7 lb of musket ball, and 2 field pieces with their carriages and furniture, all of which were then in good order. *Ibid.*, p. 140.

[20] *Ex. Jour. Coun.*, III, 339. This left the gunner a salary of £10. *C.O.5/1316*, O. 172; *C.O.5/1317*, pp. 116, 249.

[21] *Ex. Jour. Coun.*, III, 393, 394. The accounts of the revenue of two shillings a hogshead indicate no such transfer during Spotswood's time. The gunner continued to receive his £10 and there is no record of any allowance to the storekeeper. Possibly the two offices were combined, and the salary allowed under the old title.

[22] Hening, IV, 55-57; *Letters*, II, 97.

newed his appeals for arms. He pointed out that Virginia was now equipped to take care of stores of war, and that her central location made her the most convenient place for storing emergency supplies for the other colonies.[23] Early in 1716 the governor wrote that he was moving all the small arms and stores into the new magazine, and in 1718 the arms and stores distributed to the counties in Governor Nott's time were called in and placed in the magazine. But the new regulations were not altogether effective. In 1723 the council decided that if the armorer did not put the arms in better repair his salary should be stopped, and applied for that purpose.[24]

It was not only upon land that Virginia had need to guard against attack. The greater part of her settled area lay within easy access from the sea, and her extensive commerce stood in constant need of naval protection. It was tacitly understood that responsibility for this protection devolved upon the mother country, the colonies contributing indirectly through a trade regulated to favor British interests. Thus the guardships which patrolled their coasts and the men-o'-war which convoyed their trading vessels were furnished not by the provincial governments but by the mother country. The convoy system was resorted to only in time of war, when the tobacco fleet from Virginia and Maryland sailed as a unit. Sailing with the convoy was obligatory, naval officers being under orders not to clear vessels at other times. Exemptions from the crown, commonly known as the queen's letter,[25] were however granted, and sometimes governor and council permitted vessels to be cleared without convoy. These excep-

[23] *C.O.5/1364*, pp. 250, 251; *Letters*, II, 120.

[24] *Ibid.*, p. 140; *Ex. Jour. Coun.*, III, 462; IV, 31, 32. Daniel Jones was armorer in 1714. *C.O.5/1317*, p. 249. Henry Cary may have been the first storekeeper. His resignation is referred to in the council minutes for October 25, 1726.

[25] It will be remembered that it was for changing the date of one of these letters that Gawin Corbin was removed from his post as naval officer for Rappahannock.

tions were usually made in the case of vessels trading with the outports, to whom (since it always proceeded to London) the convoy was of little service in European waters where risk of capture was greatest.[26] Commanders of convoys were not under the direction of the governor, though his power to lodge complaints against them with the authorities in England gave him some semblance of control.[27]

The defense of the long and broken coast line of the tobacco colonies was greatly facilitated by the fact that they faced, not upon the open sea, but upon Chesapeake Bay.[28] They could thus be protected by guardships cruising between the Capes[29] to exclude intruders from the bay. In 1709 H. M. S. *Garland*, a vessel of 40 guns, was sent to Virginia to perform this duty, and another ship was ordered to be bought in New England for the same purpose. The *Enterprize*, also of 40 guns, arrived in Virginia early the following year, but having to go to New York to refit, and then making a trip to the Bahamas, was not ready for duty until August. In the meantime the *Garland* was wrecked upon the treacherous North Carolina coast, and Virginia was for several months without a guardship. Enemy privateers were thus able to prey with impunity, not only upon shipping but upon the more exposed parts of the coast, particularly Princess Anne County. Jennings begged the authorities in England for a fourth rate man-o'-war[30] and a sloop for the defense of Virginia alone, and upon his arrival Spotswood wrote requesting a sloop. This would be invaluable for pursuing privateers into shallow water where larger ships dare not venture, and

[26] *Letters*, I, 2, 3; *Ex. Jour. Coun.*, III, 250, 251, 312, 498, 509-511.

[27] *Letters*, I, 94.

[28] The seaward coast of the eastern peninsula, being without good harbors and scantily populated, stood in need of little protection. *Letters*, II, 107.

[29] That is, Cape Charles and Cape Henry.

[30] A fourth rate was a ship of the line carrying from 50 to 60 guns. Fifth rates carried from 30 to 44, sixth rates from 10 to 30; though vessels carrying less than 20 guns were usually counted as sloops. Clowes, *Royal Navy*, III, 7.

for preventing illegal trade, since it could search all the small ships passing out through the Capes. In the meantime the *Tryton's Prize*, a sixth rate carrying 30 guns, had been sent, and with this Spotswood professed to be satisfied.[31]

One regulation, however, Spotswood sought to have changed. When guardships needed a fresh supply of provisions, or required refitting and careening, they went to New York for that purpose, and Virginia was thus deprived of their protection for considerable periods at a time. Spotswood proposed that an agent victualler be appointed for Virginia, so that the ships might obtain provisions on the spot, and declared that there was a place at Point Comfort which might at small expense be fitted up for careening the largest ships coming to Virginia either as cruisers or convoys.[32] Both suggestions appear to have been adopted. Apparently guardships were deemed of little use in Virginia during the winter months, and it was feared that they might be damaged by ice while lying in the open roadstead. Accordingly in November 1710 the *Enterprize* was sent at the request of some Virginia merchants to convoy a number of small vessels to Barbadoes, and did not return before March. The following winter both guardships were sent, and while in the West Indies, in company with some of the naval ships there, attacked a French fleet of seventeen sail bound for Martinique. Twelve were captured, the *Enterprize* taking the man-o'-war which convoyed them. In the summer of 1711 the *Enterprize* also captured at the Capes a French privateer carrying eighty-eight men. These prisoners were kept in Virginia for seven weeks before they could be sent to England. The governor was unwilling, he said, to send them by flag of truce to the French West Indies, for he wished to be above all suspicion of illegal trade with the enemy, and hoped (he himself had seen the inside of a French prison) that by sending them to England they might be exchanged for an equal number of

[31] *C.O.5/1363*, pp. 182, 184-187, 192-203; *B. T. Jour.*, 1709-1715, pp. 49, 144; *Cal. State Paps., Col.*, 1710-1711, pp. 104, 177; *Letters*, I, 3, 11, 15, 16, 33.

[32] *Ibid.*, p. 34; *Cal. State Paps., Col.*, 1710-1711, p. 243.

British prisoners held by the French.[33] Apparently in 1713 the *Enterprize* went to England and was replaced by the *Success*. In 1715 the *Success* also went to England. In 1716 the *Shoreham* was on duty in Virginia waters.[34]

The guardships would doubtless have rendered more effective service had there been closer cooperation between their commanders and the provincial government. The governor, though titular admiral of Virginia, had only a tenuous authority over these officers. The guardships were said to neglect the defense of the coast in order to engage in trade and carry freight. They usually obeyed the orders of governor and council, but where they declined so to do the governor's only recourse was to complain to the admiralty. In 1715 the board of trade suggested that to promote a good understanding between them, the commanders of the attending ships be made subject to the governors of the plantations "as formerly" while on duty in the colonies. This the admiralty was unwilling to concede. The commanders of vessels in colonial waters were receiving instructions "to employ the said ships in such manner as may be most for the service of the Islands, or Government, and therein to advise with the Governours, and follow their directions." This, it contended, was better than making them subject to the caprice of the governor, who might divert them from their regular line of duty. In 1720 the house of burgesses proposed, in an address to the crown, that the guardships be placed under the immediate direction of the governor. No such change, however, appears to have been made.[35]

When many of the inhabitants of Europe were willing to work out their passage to America by as much as seven years'

[33] *Lettters*, I, 68, 91, 104, 162, 163. Spotswood evidently expected that the expense of keeping these prisoners while in Virginia would be borne by the commissioners for sick and wounded in England, but was informed that the dominions were expected to defray the expense of maintaining their own prisoners. The claim of Susanna Allen, who had supplied the prisoners, amounting to £100.14.8, was thereupon presented to the assembly, but the house voted that, although a just claim, it was not a "country charge." *Jour. Burg.*, 1712-1726, p. 14.

[34] *Letters*, II, 22, 45, 107, 168.

[35] *B. T. Jour.*, 1715-1718, p. 3; 1718-1722, p. 238; *Jour. Burg.*, 1712-

labor, it is not surprising that seamen deserted their ships in American waters, thus to obtain their passage at no greater price than the forfeiture of pay for the outward voyage. Both merchantmen and men-o'-war were handicapped by such desertions. In 1710 Spotswood issued a proclamation forbidding the harboring of seamen who could not give a good account of themselves, and requiring shipmasters and all officers of the government to arrest all straggling seamen, and have them put on board the warships. Upon the conviction of anyone for harboring runaway seamen, the informer was to receive £5.[36] In the fall of the same year a bill was passed establishing rewards of from fifteen to thirty shillings for the recapture of runaway seamen, to be paid by their respective ships.[37] Constables who permitted seamen to escape were to be fined five hundred pounds of tobacco, while those concealing runaways were to forfeit the same amount to the informer, and pay costs. If unable to pay, they were to receive twenty lashes. This act ran for only two years, but was revived and made perpetual in 1713.[38] In 1717 complaint of the desertion of seamen from the captains of the guardships provoked another proclamation ordering officers to enforce the laws.[39] The latter, it would seem, were none too effective.

Although guardships were the best protection against attack by sea, prudence demanded that they be supplemented by some sort of coast defense. They were at times absent from the colony, and while the fourth and sixth rates which patrolled the Chesapeake outclassed the small pirates and privateers infesting Virginia's coasts, they would have been swept away like straw if an enemy attacked in force. In 1710 Spots-

---

1726, pp. 261, 310, 311; Jones, *Present State of Virginia*, p. 78; *Cal. State Paps., Col.*, 1714-1715, pp. 121, 138, 139.

[36] *Letters*, I, 3, 56; *C.O.5/1316*, O. 64.

[37] *Jour. Burg.*, 1702-1712, p. 287 ff. Since an act of assembly could not bind the officers of the navy, Spotswood asked the admiralty to instruct the captains of the naval ships coming to Virginia to pay the rewards according to law. *Letters*, I, 68.

[38] Hening, III, 486-489; IV, 46; *Jour. Burg.*, p. 51 ff.

[39] *Ex. Jour. Coun.*, III, 458; *C.O.5/1318*, pp. 459, 460.

wood proposed to the board of trade the erection of a small fort at Point Comfort, and Elizabeth City County petitioned the assembly to the same end. The petition was rejected, for although the cost of erecting such a fort was not great the assembly would do nothing without the assurance that it would not have to maintain the garrison. Spotswood therefore proposed that a company of invalids be sent over to do garrison duty. They would cost the government no more than at Greenwich Hospital, and had this advantage over other soldiers that their physical handicaps would prevent them from deserting to the merchant marine or turning planters! When attack threatened the garrison could be reenforced by the militia "who would make a better figure in the Company of experienced Soldiers, and having Walls to befriend them, than I'm afraid they will do by themselves without those advantages." The board of trade reserved judgment.[40]

The situation was thus not auspicious for the erection of coast fortifications, but an emergency gave the governor the authority to accomplish this work. In the summer of 1711 an elaborate attack was launched against Canada both by sea and land, and it was feared that while the colonies were thus stripped of their military strength a counter-attack would be made by the French fleet to force the withdrawal of the expedition. Virginia's contribution to this campaign was indeed slight, consisting of some 700 barrels of pork, purchased in Virginia and North Carolina, and paid for partly out of the quit rents, and partly by the governor and other prominent men, who were eventually repaid by the treasury in England. No funds or supplies were voted by the assembly, and no troops were sent. But the guardships went to join the fleet, and Virginia shared the general fear of an attack. The militia was mustered and drilled, an armed sloop was sent to cruise at the Capes, and signals were provided that the whole colony might promptly be warned of the approach of the

[40] *Letters*, I, 11, 12, 88; *Cal. State Paps., Col.*, 1710-1711, p. 243; *Jour. Burg.*, 1702-1712, p. 249.

enemy. Batteries were erected at Point Comfort, Tindal's Point, Yorktown, and Jamestown, mounting in all seventy guns, while a line of secondary defenses was marked out to protect Williamsburg, to be constructed only if the enemy succeeded in penetrating beyond Point Comfort. Ten small pieces of ordnance were ordered mounted on carriages. Pursuant to the act for defense of the country in time of danger, the necessary artisans and laborers were impressed, and lookouts were appointed in the counties of Elizabeth City, Princess Anne, Northampton, and Accomac. Spotswood complained that he was handicapped by the opposition of the Quakers who refused either to work themselves or to permit their servants to be employed upon the fortifications, declaring that their consciences would not permit them to contribute to the defense of Virginia in any way, while if the French were to come there they would be obliged, in conscience, to feed their enemies. The governor put the laws of the colony into execution against them, and anticipated that both they and their brethren in England would raise a cry against him.[41]

When the assembly met in the fall of 1711 Spotswood broached the question of defense. "I cannot but wonder," he declared, "at the Supine notions of many people here who argue that either their poverty will discourage or their wilderness[s] frustrate any Invasion—Surely they do not consider, that a fleet which happens to want Sustenance and Refreshment will long more for the Stocks and Plantations of *Virg*[a] than for the Mines of *Peru*.[42] To the profuse thanks of the house for the measures he had taken he tersely replied, "I shall be glad of y[e] Occasion to return y[e] like thanks to you Gentlemen of the House of Burgess[s] for your Labouring as cheerfully as Sincerely and as free from all Self Interest as I have done for y[e] Gen[ll] good of this Colony."[43] The burgesses, indeed, were in a quandary. They recognized the value of the precautionary measures which the governor had taken, and

[41] *Ex. Jour. Coun.*, III, 282, 283; *C.O.5/1316*, O. 104.
[42] *Jour. Burg.*, 1702-1712, p. 302.
[43] *Ibid.*, pp. 314, 315.

realized, too, that since they were done in the face of danger of actual attack the assembly was committed, by the act for security and defense, to meet the expenses incurred.[44] Yet, with the true Englishman's wariness of precedent, they were anxious to avoid any committal to the permanent maintenance of the fortifications. They resolved, however, "That the Charge of ye present Batterys is a Country Charge by the Law—" and that it be paid in tobacco, levied by the poll.[45] Thereafter little attention was paid to the fortifications until the pirate scare of 1721.

In 1713 Spotswood scouted the idea that Virginia needed additional protection against pirates.[46] Three years later he was requesting the admiralty to reenforce the guardship by another of equal or greater strength. For the menace of buccaneers had assumed alarming proportions, and was to hang like a black cloud over the commerce of the plantations for the remainder of his administration. Survivors from wrecks[47] and other desperate characters, under the leadership of a former mate, Thomas Barrow by name, had established a reign of terror upon New Providence Island in the Bahamas.[48] Having seized in March 1716 a French ship of thirty-two guns, they began to commit depredations upon French and Spanish shipping. Nor was much faith to be put in their declaration that they would spare the English for, Spotswood declared, they had already taken and plundered vessels belonging to New England and Bermuda. From Providence Island the pirates could dominate Florida Strait, and thus

[44] The spy sloop furnished an exception. The governor was indeed empowered to employ shipping, but only for the transportation of troops. While the house considered the claim of Nicholas Curle, who had furnished the sloop *Fanny and Mary*, a just claim, it held that it should be paid out of the two shillings a hogshead. *Jour. Burg.*, 1712-1726, p. 14.

[45] *Jour. Burg.*, 1702-1712, pp. 307,317.

[46] *Letters*, II, 45.

[47] According to another account, the crews of several vessels, fitted out in Jamaica "for fishing on ye Wrecks" had committed piratical attacks upon the French and Spanish, and established themselves on Providence Island because they were afraid to go home. *Letters*, II, 168.

[48] Deposition of John Vickers, a resident of Providence, and Alex. Stockdale, a merchant of Barbadoes. *C.O.5/1317*, pp. 495-497.

the trade of Jamaica and the South Sea Company would fall into their hands. Indeed, the trade of the entire continent might be jeopardized if measures were not speedily taken to check this growing evil. The pirates expected reenforcements "of loose disorderly people from the Bay of Campeache, Jamaica and other parts," and could easily supply themselves with suitable ships from passing merchantmen. As Spotswood was the nearest royal governor to the Bahamas[49] and held a commission to appoint officers of the admiralty for those islands, he felt obliged to investigate. He therefore encouraged Harry Beverley, master of the sloop *Virgin* bound for the Bahamas on a trading voyage, to carry an extra strong crew, and instructed him to ascertain the number, strength, and designs of the pirates at Providence. In the meantime the governor suggested that if another guardship were sent to Virginia to cooperate with the *Shoreham* the pirates might be attacked in their stronghold before they grew too formidable.[50] When these tidings reached the admiralty, that body shifted to the board of trade the responsibility of proposing a remedy.[51]

The following year pirates began activities in Virginia waters. In April a ship of twenty-eight guns and two hundred men and a sloop of ten guns were reported cruising about the Capes, and a number of vessels were captured. The *Shoreham* being absent in South Carolina, the colony was helpless to defend its shipping.[52] In May Spotswood repeated to Secretary Methuen his request for another guardship. "Experience has shew'd how just my fears were," he wrote, "Our Capes have been for these six Weeks pass'd in a manner blocked by those Pyrates, and diverse Ships, inward bound, taken and plundered by them." They had one large ship and a number of sloops, and were constantly increasing

[49] In 1717 the board of trade urged that the crown resume the government of the Bahamas. The following year the proprietors surrendered their rights, and royal government was established. *Cal. State Paps., Col., passim.*

[50] *Letters*, II, 168-171; *B. T. Jour.*, 1715-1718, pp. 182, 183; *Ex. Jour. Coun.*, III, 428.

[51] *B. T. Jour.*, 1715-1718, p. 196.

[52] *Ex. Jour. Coun.*, III, 443, 444.

in strength. The *Shoreham* had returned, but since she carried only thirty-two guns it seemed hazardous to attack so formidable a foe, and she was kept acting on the defensive. It was arranged, however, that while the danger lasted she should convoy the shipping of Virginia and Maryland out to sea. By August the desired ship had been sent, and Spotswood reported "a Respite from the Insults of the Pyrates."[53]

So helpless did the authorities appear before the pirate menace, that the government in England found it necessary upon two occasions to grant a general amnesty to pirates surrendering before a specified date.[54] But such methods were uncertain. Pirates might indeed reform for a time in order to escape punishment, but were all too apt to resume their former practices when opportunity presented itself. In May 1718 certain pardoned pirates were ordered arrested in Virginia, while in July the suspicious conduct of others who had been pardoned in North Carolina called forth a proclamation to prevent the illegal concourse of such persons. One of these pirates, William Howard, quartermaster of Edward Thatch, was arrested for attempting to form a company of sailors to engage in another piratical enterprise. It was then discovered that he had forfeited the royal pardon by committing piracy after the expiration of the time limit. He was brought to trial,[55] convicted, and executed.[56]

At the trial of Howard it came out that although Thatch and his crew had surrendered to the governor of North Carolina and obtained pardon, they had since January 5, 1718[57] plundered nearly twenty vessels. It was thus evident that

[53] *Letters*, II, 249, 250, 256; *C.O.5/1318*, pp. 125-130.

[54] *C.O.323/7*, K. 127; *B. T. Jour.*, 1715-1718, p. 429; *Letters*, II, 317, 353.

[55] Howard was tried without a jury, under the act of 11 and 12 William III, c. 7. The council was willing that pirates should be tried by jury in accordance with 28 Henry VIII, c. 15, but a commission for that purpose was lacking. *Ex. Jour. Coun.*, III, 484.

[56] Circumstances connected with the trial of Howard and others suspected of piracy led to an estrangement between the governor and John Holloway, judge of the court of vice-admiralty. Spotswood accused Holloway of collusion with the pirates, and as a result of the dispute appointed John Clayton, the attorney-general, in his place. *Letters*, II, 352-354.

[57] The time limit allowed by the pardon.

they intended to continue their desperate trade, and rumor had it that they were determined to make reprisals upon the shipping of Virginia for the arrest of Howard. The guardships could not venture into the shallows along the Carolina coast. Governor and council therefore proposed that rewards be offered for the capture and conviction of the gang, ranging from £100 for Thatch to £10 for each common hand of his crew. To this the burgesses assented,[58] but insisted that the expense of trying and executing pirates be paid out of the two shillings a hogshead.[59]

Without waiting for the conclusion of the action of the assembly, without even consulting the council, the governor fitted out two sloops at his own expense, and manning them with two officers and fifty-five men from the guardships, sent them to seek Thatch in his place of refuge in North Carolina. So swift and secret was this expedition that, despite the numerous well-wishers which they appear to have had in Virginia, the pirates were taken completely by surprise. "They came up with Tach at Ouacock Inlett on the 22nd of last month, he was on board a sloop wch. carryed 8 guns and very well fitted for fight. As soon as he perceived the King's men intended to board him, he took up a bowl of liquor and calling out to the Officers of the other sloops, drank Damnation to anyone that should give or ask quarter, and then discharged his great guns loaded with partridge shott, wch. killed and wounded twenty of the King's men who lay exposed to his fire without any barricade or other shelter; he resolutely entered the first sloop which boarded him, nor did any one of his men yield while they were in a condition to fight. His orders were to blow up his own vessell if he should happen to be overcome, and a negro was ready to set fire to the powder, had he not been luckily prevented by a planter forced on board the night before and who lay in the hold of

[58] *Jour. Burg.*, 1712-1726, pp. 223-233. That in this time of strained relations between assembly and governor this entire matter should have been transacted in eleven days indicates the alarm with which pirates were regarded.

[59] *Ex. Jour. Coun.*, III, 489, 490.

the sloop during the action of the pyrats. Tach with nine of his crew were killed, and three white men and six negros were taken alive but all much wounded. The loss of the King's men is very considerable for the number, there being ten killed in the action, and four and twenty wounded of whom one is since dead of his wounds."[60]

At the request of his council, Governor Hart of Maryland wrote Spotswood a letter of thanks, but in North Carolina considerable umbrage was taken at his action. He had neglected to consult the governor of that province. The piratically taken goods seized by the expedition should have been condemned in North Carolina, not in Virginia. It was even declared that Thatch and his crew had not been guilty of any piracies since they first surrendered, and were therefore within the benefits of the royal pardon. Spotswood wrote to Lord Cartwright, one of the proprietors, that (so necessary was secrecy) he had not even consulted his council, while the governor of North Carolina, lacking an armed force, would have been unable to offer assistance, and in case of failure would have been exposed to the resentment of the pirates. To the second complaint Spotswood replied that if the proprietors had a right to the goods seized they would profit by their sale in Virginia, where prices were better and payment more prompt. The third he doubtless regarded as proof of his contention that an influential faction in North Carolina was in league with the pirates.[61]

The hope that the overthrow of Thatch would end the activities of buccaneers was doomed to disappointment. In 1720 the council and burgesses presented to the governor an address enlarging upon the frequent depredations of pirates and privateers[62] off the coast of the colony. They begged him to represent to the admiralty the danger to which the com-

[60] *Cal. State Paps., Col.*, 1717-1718, p. 431.

[61] *Letters*, II, 272-275, 305, 306; *Ex. Jour. Coun.*, III, 495, 496; *C.O.5/1318*, pp. 812, 813. Spotswood intimated to the board of trade that he expected criticism. The board endorsed his conduct, saying that no complaints upon that score had been received. *C.O.5/1365*, pp. 217, 218.

[62] It will be remembered that at this time Britain was at war with Spain.

merce of Virginia and Maryland was exposed, and to request that in place of a sixth rate a ship of forty guns be sent to Virginia, together with a man-o'-war sloop to pursue small craft into shoal water. They further proposed that the guardships be prevented from going to New York, Barbados, and elsewhere upon various pretexts, and that they be placed, while attending Virginia, under the comand of the governor. Spotswood replied that he agreed in great measure with their views, and promised in so far as he did so to urge favorable action in England.[63]

In May 1721 Captain Turner of the ship *Jeremiah* arrived in Virginia with the news that he had been captured by two pirates, one a ship of fifty guns and two hundred and forty men, the other a brig of eighteen guns. They expected shortly to be joined by another vessel of forty-six guns, and then intended to sail to Virginia, their leader, Roberts by name, swearing that he would avenge the hanging of certain pirates there.[64] Captain Whorwood of the guardship *Rye* declared that it was impossible for him to resist so great a force with the ship under his command. Governor and council hastily conferred, and measures were adopted similar to those taken to withstand the French fleet ten years before. Lookouts were appointed, beacons prepared to spread the alarm, and batteries erected.[65] The governors of New York, New England, and South Carolina were asked to send their men-o'-war to join the *Rye* in an effort to intercept and destroy the pirates.[66] The policy of constructing defenses was continued even after this immediate scare had passed, and in

[63] *Jour. Burg.*, 1712-1726, pp. 310, 311, 313. The following summer the *Enterprize* arrived in Virginia. Captain Yeo, her commander, was instructed by the admiralty that pirates running into shoal water where he could not follow were to be pursued by a lieutenant with a sufficient number of men in a sloop to be furnished by the government of Virginia. *Ex. Jour. Coun.*, III, 550.

[64] An account of the capture, trial, and execution of these pirates is to be found in *Letters*, II, 337, 338. The council journals of this period contain numerous references to the trial and execution of pirates. Some were pardoned and sent to serve on the men-o'-war.

[65] The act for security and defense having long since expired, the expense had to be defrayed out of the two shillings a hogshead.

[66] *Ex. Jour. Coun.*, III, 542, 543.

June 1722, when preparing for his trip to Albany, Spotswood wrote to the board of trade that the coast was protected against pirates by a number of substantial batteries, upon which sixty pieces of cannon were already mounted. Such precautions were not misplaced, for the depredations of buccaneers continued in Drysdale's time.[67]

It is hardly to be wondered at if the activities of the pirates, who appear for the most part to have been British subjects, led to friction with the Spanish authorities. As we have seen, it was the declared intention of the pirates to prey not upon British, but upon French and Spanish shipping. The former part of this resolution they broke, but their adhesion to the latter cannot be doubted. In 1716 one Captain Josiah Forbes was in custody in Virginia for firing on the forts which the Spanish had erected upon the Florida coast to protect wrecks.[68] British interlopers were active in the forbidden trade with Spanish America. The Spanish authorities were thus prone to regard all British ships with suspicion, and their irritation led them at times to mete out hard usage to vessels on legitimate business.

In June 1716 Captain Harry Beverley of the sloop *Virgin* left Virginia for the Bahamas. To judge from the instructions given him by Spotswood, the expedition had several diverse purposes. Besides trading, he was to investigate the number and nationality of the inhabitants, and the fortifications in those islands, paying particular attention to the situation at Providence Island. He was also to locate certain wrecked Spanish galleons. If he found them within or near British possessions he was to recover what he could, asserting the claim of the king according to the law of nations. While Beverley was ordered not to commit any act of hostility against subjects of friendly nations, Spotswood must have realized the danger of disputing with the Spanish the right to salvage sunken galleons.[69]

The day after the *Virgin* sailed she was struck by a violent

[67] *C.O.5/1319*, pp. 132, 415-422.
[68] *Ex. Jour. Coun.*, III, 427, 428.
[69] *C.O.5/1317*, pp. 499-501.

storm and driven as far east as Bermuda. Five days out, she was captured by a Spanish man-o'-war, and taken to San Domingo. Here Beverley's petition for a trial was refused. In a letter to Virginia he complained of the injustice of the seizure and of the ill treatment which his crew had received, expressing fear that he and his men would be sent to the mines. At the instance of Peter Beverley, brother of Harry, the case was represented by governor and council to the authorities in England.[70] The board of trade communicated the matter to Secretary Addison, expressing grave concern over the situation created by the pirates in the Bahamas. The case of the *Virgin* was finally ordered transmitted to the envoy extraordinary at the court of Spain, that he might endeavor to secure redress.[71] In the meantime Beverley and his men were taken to Vera Cruz, where he was detained seven months without trial. No rations were issued them, except what the assiento factory gave them out of charity. Several died, others lived by begging "till they could find opportunitys of getting off." The ship and cargo were confiscated. Beverley finally managed to escape, and was back in Virginia in August 1717. The treatment accorded to Beverley, Spotswood declared, was shared by the English at Campeche and others whose misfortune it was to fall into the hands of the Spanish.[72]

Any attempts made at the Spanish court to secure redress for Beverley and his crew were doubtless cut short by the breaking out of war with Spain. As a result, commerce was menaced by Spanish privateers as well as by pirates. Nor did the return of peace put a prompt stop to these depredations. After he had been notified of the cessation of arms by the governor of South Carolina, though before he had received noti-

[70] *Ex. Jour. Coun.*, III, 441; *Letters*, II, 245, 250; *C.O.5/1318*, pp. 117-121.

[71] *B. T. Jour.*, 1715-1718, p. 254; B. T. to Addison, Aug. 6, 1717, *C.O.5/1342*; *C.O.5/1365*, p. 40.

[72] *B. T. Jour.*, 1715-1718, pp. 294, 295; *Letters*, II, 259. The account of this incident is gleaned exclusively from English sources. The Spanish may have had another tale to tell. Spotswood's instructions concerning the wrecks give grounds for suspicion. It seems to have been generally agreed that these wrecks were upon the Florida coast.

fication from Spain, the governor of St. Augustine appears to have commissioned privateers to prey upon British commerce. One of these, a brigantine, arrived off the Capes of Virginia while the *Rye* was being cleaned in Elizabeth River. Some of her crew manned two sloops and retook one of the prizes, thereby discovering whence the privateer had received her commission. It being impossible to get the *Rye* ready for sea in time to intercept the privateer, Captain John Martin, who had had a sloop captured, was commissioned to proceed to St. Augustine under flag of truce in the *Ranger*, another sloop of his own, to secure if possible the restoration of the prizes.[73] His crew of fifty men was supplied by the *Rye*, and he was equipped by the government with eight guns.

Upon reaching St. Augustine, Martin found the privateer and three brigs which she had captured. Of her other prizes some had been sent to Havana, while others had been wrecked upon the bar of St. Augustine. The Spanish governor denied commissioning the privateers to cruise on the Virginia coast. He directed the release of a London ship taken in ballast, and a Philadelphia sloop laden with bread and flour, but requisitioned the cargo of the latter for his garrison, giving for it a note for 2098 pieces of eight, "w'ch is of no value to the Owners, seeing they dare not send to demand it at any place where their Vessels are lyable to be Seized upon the most trifling pretences." The third and most valuable prize, a London sloop with a cargo of Negroes, was claimed as a lawful prize because it had redwood on board, "w'ch he said was the Growth of the Spanish Plantations, tho' it was evident the same was brought from the Coast of Africa." No reparation could be obtained for the prizes which had been wrecked or sent to other Spanish ports. The *Ranger* was itself wrecked upon the bar of St. Augustine and proved a complete loss, a number of her crew losing their lives in the disaster.[74]

[73] *Ex. Jour. Coun.*, III, 529-531.

[74] *Letters*, II, 346-348. Governor and council proposed that Martin be compensated for the sloop and the expense of fitting her out, and that suitable rewards be granted both to him and to others suffering because of the ex-

The expedition to St. Augustine at least had the good effect of stopping, for the time being, the further molestation of Virginia's trade by Spanish privateers. "But," wrote Spotswood to the board of trade, "notwithstanding the Trade of this Colony remains for the present undisturb'd, I cannot forbear representing to Yo'r Lord'ps how necessary it is that some more Effectual care be taken to preserve the freedom of Navigation to and from the West Indies, and especially from the Insults of those of St. Augustine, w'ch seems rather to be the resort of Banditto than deserving the name of a Government." Proceeding to give the board some recent instances of Spanish injustice, the governor voiced a complaint, widespread among the British traders, against the Spanish custom of considering the presence of "any Commoditys of the like species w'th those w'ch are produced in the Spanish Plantations, nay even a pistole or p's of 8/8 w'ch is the common currency of these Colonys," sufficient evidence of illegal trading and therefore "a sufficient Ground for making Prize of the Vessel in w'ch the same are found." Such was the expense and difficulty met by private persons seeking redress at the court of Madrid that "the remedy seems as intollerable as the Disease; And I hope while a new Treaty is on foot with that Crown Yo'r Lo'ps, w'll be please to represent this growing Evil so powerfully as that it may be restrained for the future." He declared that besides the losses to private persons the depredations of the Spanish had cost the government of Virginia nearly £1000.[75]

---

pedition. The burgesses voted £200 for Martin and a like sum for the other victims, but refused to make good the loss of the *Ranger* or to defray the cost of fitting her out "since this Expedition was projected and carryed on . . . with a View to the General Benefit and advantage of all his Majesties Subjects trading to these parts." The council therefore ordered that £200 be paid Martin out of the two shillings a hogshead and that the rest of his expenses be met out of the same fund. As late as 1723 he was ordered paid £30 as wages on his trip to Florida. *Jour. Burg.*, 1712-1726, pp. 304-309; *Ex. Jour. Coun.*, III, 536, 538, 540; IV, 43.

[75] *Letters*, II, 348, 349.

Chapter XI

THE WEST

VIRGINIA, a young community in which land was plentiful, was growing rapidly during the early eighteenth century. In 1702 the number of tithables[1] was 25,099; by 1724 it had grown to 43,877,[2] an increase of 75 per cent in twenty-two years. The total population had doubtless increased somewhat less rapidly, for the ratio of blacks to whites was constantly becoming greater, and a larger proportion of the former were subject to the poll tax. More significant than the growth in the total number of inhabitants is the removal westward of the center of population. In each of the "necks" of Virginia the tithables had increased far more rapidly in the western counties in contact with the open frontier than in the eastern divisions now entirely surrounded by settlement. In the Northern Neck the increase was 92 per cent for the western counties, 39 for the eastern; between Rappahannock and York the count was 193 to 35; between York and James, 150 to 34;[3] while south of the James the western counties showed an increase of 115 per cent against 49 for the eastern. The Eastern Shore showed the slowest advance of all, 32 per cent.[4]

The quit rent accounts tell a similar story. In the eastern counties most of the desirable land had by the turn of the

[1] That is, those subject to the poll tax, all males and unfree females sixteen years of age and above.

[2] Two years later it was 45,857. *C.O.5/1320*, p. 111.

[3] The figures for Charles City in 1702 include Prince George, which began its separate existence that year. The proportion in the two counties has therefore been calculated upon the basis of that of 1714 with the result that the figure for the eastern counties between York and James is probably a trifle high, and that for the western counties south of the James a trifle low. Other changes in county lines do not complicate the problem.

[4] *Va. Mag. Hist.*, I, 364-373; *C.O.5/1319*, p. 439. The figures for 1714 and 1722 are also suggestive. See *Va. Mag. Hist.*, II, 3-14; U. 65. Va. Hist. Soc.

century already been patented. Indeed in 1713 Elizabeth City paid quit rents on nearly 98 per cent of the total area of the county,[5] and although more land lay unpatented in the other eastern counties, little was taken up. Swamp and waste land was of little use except for pasturing cattle and furnishing fire-wood, and since one might employ it surreptitiously for these purposes, there was little incentive to incur the trouble and expense of securing a patent and paying quit rents.

In the frontier counties, on the other hand, the rent roll grew rapidly during Spotswood's administration. South of the James, in Isle of Wight, Surry, and Prince George, it increased 148,000 acres; between York and James, in Henrico, New Kent, and Hanover,[6] 145,000; north of York River in King William, King and Queen, and Essex, 197,000.[7] While data are lacking for the Northern Neck, there was presumably a comparable increase in the quit rents of Lord Fairfax. Proportionately, however, the increase in patented land was not so great as that in population. The settled area of Virginia was expanding; it was also becoming more densely inhabited.

As the colony expanded, county and parish boundaries frequently needed readjustment. Settlement had followed the rivers, and transportation in the early days being mostly by water, a county was apt to lie on both banks of a stream. Later when roads came into use this became a serious inconvenience.[8] The lower counties, the first to be settled, were small, while those further up the river were frequently of great length. The same was true of the parishes. The divisions with the least population were naturally subject to the heaviest rates

[5] *C.O.5/1316*, O. 170.

[6] Hanover was formed from the western part of New Kent in 1720.

[7] *Ibid.*, O. 100, 131, 170; *C.O.5/1319*, pp. 113, 143, 243. Since the quit rent accounts were frequently in arrears, the figures given are an only approximate indication of the increase in patented land. For the region between Rappahannock and York the figures for 1720 are used, since the peculiar situation created by the erection of Spotsylvania County make those for 1722 misleading.

[8] Charles City before the formation of Prince George in 1702 is a case in point. "For many years, rather than submit to a division, the legislature established two courts, the one on the north, the other on the south side of James river." Hening, III, 223.

per capita. Boundaries were apt to be arbitrary. Inhabitants were frequently much closer to the courthouse of a neighboring county than to their own. In the frontier counties it was frequently difficult to induce justices to serve, so long was the monthly journey to the county courts. Yet the influence of burgesses who did not wish a change in their constituencies, that of parishioners who were unwilling to submit to an increase in the rates, and the fondness of the colonists for their "old Customs and Constitutions," made reform by legislative action exceedingly difficult.[9]

When the legislature refused in 1710 to add to Charles City County the part of James City on the right bank of the Chickahominy,[10] Spotswood reported the situation to the board of trade. His instructions still authorized the governor to bound parishes, though the power had not been exercised in years, and in Lord Howard's day he had enjoyed the right of bounding counties as well. Spotswood proposed that these functions of the prerogative be revived. It was only the desire "to do equal justice to all my fellow subjects," he declared, which made him "ambitious of a power in the execution of which I must expect to disoblige several men of Consid'ble figure in the Government."[11] To this proposal he received no reply. In 1713, at the earnest instance of the parishioners, Spotswood assented to an act for dividing St. Mary's parish, though he evidently retained his conviction that it would be better to determine the boundaries of parishes and counties by executive action.[12] All things considered, it was perhaps well for the tranquillity of his administration that no such power was granted him.[13]

Unquestionably the greatest attraction of the west lay in its unexploited land suitable for the growing of tobacco. The

[9] *Letters*, I, 36-39.

[10] *Jour. Burg.*, 1702-1712, p. 273. The change was finally made in 1720. Hening, IV, 94.

[11] *Letters*, I, 20, 36-39.

[12] *Ibid.*, II, 56.

[13] A comprehensive reorganization of both parish and county lines was enacted by the legislature in 1720. *C.O.5/1319*, pp. 89, 90.

era of large-scale production ushered in by the coming of the Negro involved not only larger plantations than most men were able to acquire in the more settled regions but unexhausted soil; for the methods by which the thrifty yeoman could coax year after year a crop from his holding could not well be employed in cultivation by the slave gang. The proportion of tithables employed in tobacco culture in 1724, ninety-one per cent for the colony as a whole, was as high in the frontier counties as elsewhere.[14] But it was not to the tobacco planter alone that the west appealed. The activities of the fur trader, reaching far ahead of the more prosaic process of permanent settlement, have already been considered.[15] For the miner also the west had a magnetic appeal.

In 1709 Baron Christoph de Graffenried and other promoters proposed to establish a colony of Swiss upon the southwest branch of the Potomac. The merchants Perry and Hyde assured the board of trade that this would both strengthen Virginia's frontiers and increase her trade, and the board recommended the order in council which authorized the settlement.[16] This project was not carried out, de Graffenried's interest being transferred to the Neuse River in North Carolina. After his terrible experience with the Tuscarora, however, de Graffenried once more turned his attention to Virginia,[17] but encountered difficulties in the claims of the proprietors of the Northern Neck and of Maryland to the lands which he hoped to obtain there by royal grant.[18] Since he expected to engage in silver mining, he was also discouraged by the fact that the royal share of precious metals found in Virginia had never been determined. Seconded by Orkney, Spotswood proposed that the crown receive one-fifth of the gold and one-tenth of the silver, as in the Northern Neck.[19] The

[14] *C.O.5/1319*, p. 439.

[15] *Supra*, p. 80 ff.

[16] *B. T. Jour.*, 1709-1715, pp. 53, 55; *Acts of Privy Coun., Col.*, II, 608, 609; *C.O.5/1316*, O. 43 and elsewhere.

[17] *Letters*, I, 143; *B. T. Jour.*, 1709-1715, pp. 397, 398.

[18] *Letters*, I, 152, 153; *B. T. Jour.*, 1709-1715, pp. 405, 406.

[19] *Ex. Jour. Coun.*, III, 266, 267; *Letters*, II, 161, 162, 168; *C.O.5/1316*, O. 157.

board of trade considered the matter at length,[20] but whether final action was taken by the crown is not known and indeed matters little, for it was not in the precious metals that the mineral wealth of Virginia consisted.

With Spotswood's approval, and perhaps upon his initiative,[21] propositions were introduced into the assembly of 1710 for raising money to exploit certain iron deposits at the falls of the James. The burgesses resolved that the work was worthy of encouragement, and referred the matter to the next session, proposing that the persons subscribing these propositions submit an estimate of the expense.[22] Construing this action to mean that the assembly intended to do nothing, Spotswood proposed to the board of trade that the crown take over these mines, using the quit rent revenue to develop them. The ore was very rich, he declared. The iron could be sent home as ballast, and the cost of transportation would therefore be so slight that it would not pay to manufacture iron in Virginia, the only ill consequence to the trade of Great Britain which Spotswood could foresee if the project were undertaken.[23] Thus Spotswood first attempted to promote iron mining in Virginia as a public enterprise.

But the time was not propitious for getting the British government to encourage the iron industry in America. A duty of 54*s*. a ton had in 1689 been imposed upon foreign unwrought iron,[24] but in 1703 a drawback of 50*s*. 6*d*. was allowed upon reexportation.[25] This enabled the colonies to import unwrought iron at a comparatively low figure, lower probably, than it could be obtained in England. The colonists, notably the New Englanders, were thus encouraged to manufacture for themselves, with the result that the decade before 1710 showed a marked increase in the exportation of unwrought iron to the colonies, while that of steel remained

[20] *Acts of Privy Coun., Col.*, II, 676; *B. T. Jour.*, 1709-1715, pp. 518, 519, 533; *C.O.5/1316*, O. 157, 158; *C.O.5/1364*, pp. 31-33.

[21] *Letters*, I, 21.

[22] *Jour. Burg.*, 1702-1712, p. 279.

[23] *Letters*, I, 41.

[24] 1 & 2 Wm. & My., c. 4.

[25] 2 & 3 Anne, c. 9.

practically at a standstill.[26] English iron manufacturers believed that were the drawback[27] discontinued, they could sell their ironware in the colonies at a price sufficiently low to swamp the infant industry of New England.[28] The board of trade was debating this problem when it received Spotswood's proposal for mining iron in Virginia, and finally recommended that the drawback be discontinued.[29] This move being designed to discourage iron manufacture in the plantations by cutting off their supply of cheap unwrought iron, it was not to be expected that a project to stimulate iron mining would be greatly countenanced. The governor was therefore told not to assent to any act for encouraging iron mines without a suspending clause, and the board of trade appeared well satisfied when the assembly failed to act.[30]

A number of letters written by Spotswood to Blakiston indicate that his interest in mining was by no means exclusively of a public nature. The extracts from this correspondence found in the governor's letter book are suggestive rather than explicit, but they indicate that he and others, de Graffenried and probably Orkney among the number, were concerned in mining enterprises. To make their position secure, they wished to obtain a grant from the crown. Presumably it was silver mining in which they wished to engage, and the grant was to determine the royal share of the product. It was hoped to obtain a private grant, but this was a delicate matter, and Spotswood thought it likely that it could be handled only by representing the grant as a public benefit to the colony. Were it passed in this form, Blakiston was to be reimbursed out of

[26] *C.O.323/7*, Bund. K. 7.

[27] The total or partial repayment of import duties, upon the reexportation of the goods.

[28] *B. T. Jour.*, 1709-1715, p. 222.

[29] *C.O.323/7*, Bund. K. 8; *B. T. Jour.*, 1709-1715, pp. 229, 232, 233, 236.

[30] *Cal. State Paps., Col.*, 1710-1711, pp. 347, 570. No notice seems to have been taken of the proposal that the crown take over the mines, although Spotswood again called the board's attention to the matter. *Letters*, I, 88. Nor does the assembly appear to have been concerned by the scarcity of iron in Virginia. On two occasions it rejected proposals from Northampton that the exportation of old iron be prohibited. *Jour. Burg.*, 1712-1726, pp. 14, 192.

the public revenue for the incidental expenses. If, however, a private grant were secured, those engaged in the project would repay him.[31] Nothing, the governor declared, could be undertaken until the grant were obtained, "without the hazard of raising so great a Clamour, especially when Mr. Nicholson arrives."[32] The desired grant was not obtained before the queen's death,[33] and Blakiston was instructed to renew his applications to her successor.[34] In the meantime Blakiston sent over a number of de Graffenried's miners, partly at Spotswood's expense. The governor was somewhat apprehensive of the outcome of the venture "when, besides, it seems, I run the risque of the same Censure, as you say others have undergone, for transporting Forreigners into these parts," but added philosophically, "however, 'tis in vain to look on the worst side of a business wherein one is so far engaged, and must go through."[35]

When the Germans arrived in the spring of 1714 Spotswood, concealing from the council his part in bringing them over, proposed that they be settled at the falls of the Rappahannock as a barrier against the Indians. The council approved the governor's proposal to build a fort and clear a road for them, and to carry two cannon and ammunition thither at the public expense, since the settlement was held to be for the benefit of the colony at large. Since the Germans had arrived too late in the year to cultivate any land for their own subsistence, they would of course be unable to pay any public levies. They were technically counted as rangers, to exempt them from this obligation. That they might better maintain themselves by hunting, all others were forbidden to hunt on unpatented land near their settlement.[36] The following fall, at Spotswood's suggestion, the Germans were exempted by

[31] *Letters*, II, 28, 33.

[32] *Ibid.*, p. 66. Former Governor Francis Nicholson was about to proceed to America to conduct a comprehensive investigation of conditions in the various colonies.

[33] This event terminated Nicholson's commission, thereby removing whatever cause for alarm Spotswood had from that quarter.

[34] *Letters*, II, 78.

[35] *Ibid.*, p. 66.

[36] *Ex. Jour. Coun.*, III, 371, 372.

the assembly from the payment of public, county, and parish levies. At the same time the parish of St. George was created, it being understood that the Germans would support a minister of their own choice.[37]

The fortified settlement which Spotswood constructed was surrounded by a stockade in the form of a regular pentagon, "with stakes stuck in the ground, and laid close the one to the other and of substance to bear out a musket-shot." In the very center was a blockhouse, also of five sides, the loopholes of which commanded the entire enclosure. The following summer there were nine families there, "and they have nine houses, built all in a line; and before every house, about twenty feet distant from it, they have small sheds built for their hogs and hens, so that the hog-sties and houses make a street." The existence eked out by the minister and his flock was miserable enough.[38] How long the Germans continued in the search for silver, if indeed silver was the object of their search, it would be hard to say. The suspicion will not down that the agitation concerning silver was designed to throw dust in the eyes of the British authorities, the real object being the mining of iron.[39]

Contributing to the importance of the west was the opportunity which its forests afforded for the production of naval stores. The early proponents of colonization in North America urged that this would relieve the mother country of her dependence upon the Baltic. Time passed, however, with this hope still unrealized, and a century after the founding of Virginia Britain was still importing the greater part of her naval stores through the Sound. The supply of commodities vital to the safety and prosperity of the country was thus contingent

[37] *Jour. Burg.*, 1712-1726, pp. 79-116, *passim.*

[38] Maury, *Huguenot Family*, pp. 268, 269.

[39] Fontaine's diary for August 25, 1716, contains the following entry: "After dinner we went to see the mines, but I could not observe that there was any good mine. The Germans pretend that it is a silver mine; we took some of the ore and endeavored to run it, but could get nothing out of it, and I am of opinion it will not come to anything, no not as much as lead. Many of the gentlemen of the country are concerned in this work." *Ibid.*, p. 282.

upon the caprice of foreign princes. The forests of the New World offered unlimited resources for the making of pitch and tar but, due possibly to lack of skill, the colonial products were usually found to be inferior.[40] The greater cost of transportation from the colonies was also a serious factor.[41]

The low price of tobacco in the early years of Spotswood's administration led Virginians to turn to other occupations which, it was feared, might in time compete with the industries of Great Britain. It would be well, Spotswood thought, to encourage them to produce naval stores. The land which would grow the poorer grades of tobacco was suitable for pitch, tar, and hemp. Pitch and tar were already exported to the West Indies and even to Great Britain, while hemp was raised for local consumption. A recent act of parliament had failed to encourage this industry, due to the lack of skilled workers, the uncertainty of obtaining bounties, and the inertia which led people to continue to plant tobacco. The production of naval stores in Virginia would be greatly stimulated if they were accepted at market value in payment of the British import duties on tobacco. The Virginia trade always had sufficient convoy, and naval stores might thus safely be shipped in time of war.[42]

With the return of peace, the revival of the tobacco trade precluded the development of manufactures in Virginia, but the British government retained its interest in the production of naval stores.[43] In 1717 William Byrd told the board of

[40] *B. T. Jour.*, 1715-1718, pp. 105, 106. There were those who asserted, however, that the plantation naval stores were of excellent quality. *Ibid.*, pp. 215, 218.

[41] In 1710 the board of trade was informed that in war time freight from Carolina was £10 a tun, from New England, £8, and from New York, £7.10. While in time of peace it would probably be only £5 from the northern colonies, freight from Sweden was but £3 a last (two tuns). *B. T. Jour.*, 1709-1715, p. 123.

[42] *Letters*, I, 72-74.

[43] The rapid increase in the production of naval stores in America is shown by the premiums paid upon those imported thence into England. For the first five years of peace the figures are as follows: 1713, £5,783.19.10; 1714, £6,860.8.10; 1715, £10,135.10.9; 1716, £27,410.7.9; 1717, £40,354.0.3. Other premiums were pending. *C.O.323/7*, K. 121.

trade that without doubt America could supply naval stores of as good quality as those produced in the Baltic, but encouragement would be necessary. He proposed that the bounties offered by act of parliament be continued for twenty years, and that they be paid promptly, with interest from the time of importation, that all naval stores from the plantations be admitted duty free, and that the fees of custom-house officials for examining the stores and issuing certificates of importation be moderated.[44] Both premiums and the price of the naval stores imported from the plantations, Byrd declared, would be paid not in specie but in British goods, and the trade would thus be of double benefit to Great Britain. He had raised hemp in Virginia for his own use for the past six or seven years, and "the rope-makers declare they never saw better from the east country, it having a fine grain and taking tar as well as any." The lands in Virginia suited to raising hemp were not fit for tobacco.[45] The tar formerly made in the plantations burned the cordage. This was due, Byrd said, neither to trees nor to climate, but to the use of knots without trunks. When made by the methods employed in Norway and Sweden, it would prove as good as theirs. Byrd also proposed a premium of £3 a ton and exemption from duties to encourage the importation of bar iron from the plantations. At that time, he said, most of Britain's iron was imported from Sweden.[46] A representation upon the encouragement of the production of

[44] The officials had been guilty of great extortion, Byrd declared.

[45] Both Byrd and Spotswood sought to allay the fear that the production of naval stores would reduce that of tobacco, and thus diminish the British customs duties. See *Letters*, I, 74. The pine lands of Virginia, which of course were those used for making pitch and tar, were generally regarded as unsuitable for tobacco. Hening, IV, 96; Jones, *Present State of Virginia*, p. 57.

[46] *B. T. Jour.*, 1715-1718, p. 218; *C.O.323/7*, K. 79. Byrd was not alone in advocating the encouragement of the importation of iron from the plantations. Sir Thomas Johnson, member of parliament from Liverpool, Joshua Gee, Micajah Perry, Captain Hyde, and Mr. Bradley all aired similar views before the board. *B. T. Jour.*, 1715-1718, pp. 215-217. A Thomas Coram proposed that the bounties upon naval stores and iron be paid, not by the British government to the importer, but by the provincial governments to the producer. *C.O.323/7*, K. 83. Whether the board had by this time abandoned its previous attitude of hostility to the production of iron in the plantations is not known.

naval stores in America was agreed to by the board on March 28, 1717.[47] The spring of 1719 saw further discussion of the matter.[48]

In August 1717 the Virginia council attempted to stop the practice of holding land for years upon a bare entry or survey and using it for making pitch and tar without patent, and therefore without obligation to pay quit rents. It was ordered that where application was not made for a patent by the last day of the general court following the completion of the survey the entry was to be void, and others might take up the land. Those gathering lightwood or making other use of lands before taking out a patent were to be prosecuted for trespass, even though they had made entry or survey.[49]

The following year Spotswood received from the board of trade a letter complaining of the badness and fraudulent packing of naval stores shipped from Virginia, and proposing that the assembly remedy this abuse. Spotswood replied that it would be difficult to secure the passage of laws to regulate this or any other branch of the trade of Virginia. Those engaged in the making of pitch and tar were "of the meanest of the people," who while caring nothing for the reputation of their products in England had great influence in the election of burgesses. Such a law, even if passed, might be nullified by colonial opposition. "Besides," added Spotswood significantly, "it is evident that the Virginia Merch'ts, tho' they are apt at empty Clamour against frauds in this Country's Manufactures, are the most difficult to be pleased in any regulations that are made therein here." Had they not secured the disallowance of the laws regulating the tobacco and fur trades, despite their beneficial effect upon the commerce of Virginia?[50] He there-

[47] *B. T. Jour.*, 1715-1718, p. 221.

[48] See *C.O.323/7*, K. 134, 136, 139, 150, 153; *B. T. Jour.*, 1718-1722, pp. 16-23, 27, 28, 45, 46.

[49] *Ex. Jour. Coun.*, III, 454, 455.

[50] The solicitor-general, Spotswood pointed out, had declared that the fee paid to the tobacco agents under the act of 1713 was a tax upon trade, and that the governor's assent to that act was therefore a breach of his instructions. An act regulating the production of naval stores would have to provide fees for inspectors, and a still more stringent instruction against acts affecting

fore proposed that the merchants prepare "a Scheme of such Regulations as they w'll be content to submitt to," which he would then do his utmost to have enacted into law.[51] Meanwhile a proclamation was issued to enforce the laws against those fraudulently packing pitch and tar for sale.[52] Shortly after, parliament passed a law regulating this matter[53] and the governors of the plantations were sent directions for making pitch and tar, which had in future to be followed in order to secure bounties.[54]

In the winter of 1721-1722, in view of the shortage of lumber in Great Britain, the board of trade pondered the advisability of placing that commodity upon the enumerated list. Questioned upon this score, William Byrd said that this would not affect Virginia, which so far as he knew sent no lumber to Portugal and the Mediterranean, as the northern colonies were said to do.[55]

In 1722 an act was passed by parliament to encourage the production of naval stores in the plantations and their exportation thence to Britain. Upon Spotswood's proposal, the Virginia assembly furthered this policy by appropriating £1200 current money for bounties upon tar and £4000 for bounties upon hemp. Two shillings was to be paid for every barrel of tar, and four shillings for every gross hundredweight of hemp, produced in accordance with the regulations laid down by parliament. No mention was made of pitch, and the burgesses resolved to give no bounty upon "Iron Cast in this Colony."[56]

The west beckoned. Its resources of peltry, of mineral wealth, and of forests invited exploitation. Its virgin soil furnished an opportunity for the planter whose lands were ex-

---

trade having been issued in the meantime, should the governor assent to such a measure, it "would surely be charged upon me."

[51] *Letters*, II, 300-302.

[52] *Ex. Jour. Coun.*, III, 484, 485.

[53] B. T. to Spotswood, June 29, 1719, *C.O.5/1365*, p. 202.

[54] *B. T. Jour.*, 1718-1722, pp. 96, 102.

[55] *Ibid.*, p. 328.

[56] *Jour. Burg.*, 1712-1726, pp. 330-353, *passim;* Hening, IV, 96-99. Apparently the tar had to be exported in order to obtain the bounty, while the hemp did not.

hausted, for sons left without a patrimony, and for new arrivals from Europe. For the time being, the English needed only to move west and take possession. There was reason to believe, however, that such might not always prove the case. The interests of a great rival were also involved, and if Britain delayed occupation, her heritage might pass forever.

In Virginia's relatively sheltered position[57] there was both gain and loss. With the farmer's frontier she was in direct contact, but from that of the fur trader she was now separated by mountains or by boundaries of other provinces. She thus had easy access to all the land which she would need for several years in a region where Indian attacks might perchance harass her settlements, but could scarcely imperil their existence so long as her sister colonies remained intact. On the other hand, the very barriers which shielded her from hostile Indians made difficult her trade with those who were friendly. And a governor who sought to play a stellar rôle in the conquest of a continent might find his sphere of activity somewhat confining. The territory east of the Blue Ridge and the valley beyond would have to be settled before Virginia grappled at close quarters with the *coureurs de bois* and their savage allies.

A former officer of Marlborough's was apt to be susceptible to Francophobia, and South Carolina's blockade of Virginia's Indian trade made desirable a more direct route to the western tribes. Spotswood therefore welcomed an application which he received shortly after his arrival in the colony for permission to go exploring over the western mountains. The council authorized the governor to commission a fit person to command the party. He was not to make war on any persons whatsoever, and was to submit to the governor upon his return an exact journal of his proceedings and observations.[58] This expedition, in the late fall of 1710, found the mountains to be within a hundred miles of the outlying settlements, and ascended on horseback to the crest of the ridge. The year being well advanced, the explorers did not descend into the valley

[57] *Supra*, p. 70.
[58] *Ex. Jour. Coun.*, III, 253, 254.

beyond but this, they informed the governor, appeared no more difficult than the ascent. In reporting this expedition to the board of trade Spotswood made his first proposal for the encouragement of westward migration, namely the granting of land upon one bank of the James upon more favorable terms than elsewhere in the colony. This, he held, would thrust a spur of settlement to the very source of the James, thus facilitating trade with the western Indians, and severing the communication which the French had established between the Great Lakes and their settlements on the Mississippi.[59]

The years which followed brought to Spotswood a more intimate knowledge of frontier conditions. Protection of the outlying settlements from Indian attack; reorganization of Virginia's Indian relations; promotion of the fur trade and of mining; these and other problems engaged his attention. One episode in particular has captivated the imagination of posterity. In June 1716 Spotswood informed the council that the rangers having recently discovered a passage over the mountains to the westward of the colony, he intended the following August to send a greater body on further discoveries. The council approved the project.[60]

Better than his word, the governor led the expedition in person. Accompanied by Lieutenant John Fontaine, a Huguenot who had served in the British army, he left Williamsburg for Germanna. There the party assembled and the horses were shod, for the excursion over the mountains would be rougher going than travel in the tidewater region. On August 29 they set out. No great privations awaited the dozen gentlemen who, accompanied by their servants, guided by four Meherrin Indians, and reenforced by two troops of rangers of an officer and six men each, proceeded westward in eight daily stages

[59] *Letters,* I, 40, 41. It must be remembered that Spotswood was handicapped by a total lack of exact knowledge of western geography. His opinion of the advantage of his project is therefore more pardonable than his naïve supposition that the slight concession proposed would have produced such a result.

[60] *Ex. Jour. Coun.*, III, 428.

averaging some nine miles a day. Hornets pestered both horses and riders, rattlesnakes enlivened things, and one of the party had rather a close call with a bear. But sickness was probably a more serious drawback than the native fauna, the principle function of which was to provide very good hunting. On the eighth day they ascended the Blue Ridge. In places axmen had to clear the way, and the incline sometimes obliged the horsemen to dismount. By one o'clock the summit was reached, "and we came to the very head spring of the James River, where it runs no bigger than a man's arm, from under a large stone. We drank King George's health, and all the Royal Family's, at the very top of the Appalachian mountains." Several of the company were now for turning back, but the governor persuaded them to continue. Following an Indian trail they descended into the Shenandoah Valley and encamped that night upon the bank of the river, which they dubbed the "Euphrates." The following day, September 6, they found a ford and crossed to the other side. Liberal potations were drunk to the healths of royalty and governor, and in one of the numerous bottles emptied the governor buried a paper "on which he writ that he took possession of this place in the name and for King George the First of England." The rangers were sent on to explore farther. The rest of the party turned homeward on September 7, and three days later were back at Germanna.[61]

It cannot be doubted that one object of the expedition was to discover a direct route to the Cherokee country. And interest was displayed in the mineral wealth of the country traversed. But the halo of romance which surrounds the "transmontane order" is by no means to be dissipated by the imputation of economic motives. Of the gentlemen adventurers who accompanied Spotswood only one, William Robertson, is known to have been a member of the Virginia Indian Company. The appeal of a continent had seized the gover-

[61] Maury, *Huguenot Family*, pp. 281-292.

nor's imagination, and it was to kindle the imagination of others that he restricted the right to wear the golden horseshoe to those who had drunk the royal health on Mount George.[62]

In December 1717 the board of trade received from Richard Beresford, agent for Carolina, a memorial voicing colonial apprehension at the activities of the French on the Mississippi. It was feared that the recently chartered "Western Company of France" was about to embark upon an active policy of colonization, which by hemming in the English colonies and winning the Indians away from their interest would be the first step in a movement to drive the British out of America.[63] This memorial the board sent to Spotswood, desiring him to verify its assertions and state what measures he considered necessary to protect the British from the encircling settlements of the French.[64] Having, so he wrote to the board, "of a long time endeavour'd to inform myself of ye sictuation of the French to the Westward of Us," Spotswood was not reluctant to air his views. Although the English colonies had been established so many years, no attempt had been made to discover the sources of their rivers or to establish relations with the Indians to the westward, despite the knowledge that the French were surrounding them with settlements. The chief object of his expedition two years previously was to determine the practicability of reaching the Great Lakes by crossing the mountains, and he was convinced that, once a road was cleared,

[62] Jones, *Present State of Virginia*, p. 14; *Letters*, II, 295.

[63] *C.O.323/7*, K. 116. This memorial was part of a vigorous campaign which the Carolinians were waging to convince the crown that the French constituted so grave a menace as to necessitate the substitution of royal for proprietary government. Verner W. Crane, *The Southern Frontier, 1670-1732* (Durham, 1928), pp. 208, 209. The lax frontier policy of the proprietors was a fundamental cause of the revolution of 1719. "I can't think Subjects are to be indulged in the practice of throwing off a Lawfull Authority and setting up a new frame of Government for themselves," wrote Spotswood to the board of trade upon that occasion, "and for that Reason have declined answering the Letter Colo James Moor sent me notifying me of the People's Election of him for their Governor. Yet if, (as they alledge,) their Proprietors are unable or unwilling to protect them, it w'll deserve the attention of his Maj'ty's Ministers to preserve so considerable a Province from falling into the hands of a fforeign Power." *Letters*, II, 336, 337.

[64] B. T. to Spotswood, Jan. 29, 1718, *C.O.5/1365*, pp. 42, 43.

Lake Erie would be only five days' march from the pass which he had discovered, the mountains to the west of the "Great Ridge" being smaller than those on the east.[65] Spotswood then proceeded to give a generally accurate account of the route of "that extensive Communication w'ch the French maintain by means of their water Carriage from the River St. Lawrence to the Mouth of the Mississippi" by way of the Great Lakes, the Maumee, and the Wabash, which he had obtained from three Frenchmen who were familiar with the route.[66] This line of communication, along which the French had already built several forts, put them in a position to win over the Indians, thus to monopolize the fur trade and harass at will the English settlements. The protecting mountain wall would be changed to a menace if the English neglected to secure the passes before the French did so. Spotswood therefore urged that during the interval of peace, and while the French were still unprepared to occupy the vast tract lying west of the English plantations, the mountain passes be secured and settlements be made on the lakes. He thought Lake Erie, located in the center of the French line of communication, the most proper place for a settlement, and the recently discovered pass the logical base of operations, "and as I flatter my Self I have attained a more exact knowledge than any other Englishman Yet has of the Situation of the Lakes, and the way through w'ch they are most accessible over Land, I shall be ready to Undertake the Executing this project if his Majestie thinks fitt to approve of it."[67] He thought that there was a sufficient

[65] *Letters*, II, 295, 296, 304. Besides underestimating the extent of the Appalachians, Spotswood seems to have misconceived the location of Lake Erie. A subsequent letter shows that he thought Lake Ontario to be in the latitude of Pennsylvania (*ibid.*, p. 336) and he doubtless also placed Lake Erie a considerable distance further south than its actual location, and thus closer to the Virginia frontier.

[66] *Ibid.*, p. 296.

[67] *Ibid.*, pp. 296, 297. Spotswood, whose estimate of his own knowledge may well be questioned, proceeded to inform the board that there was no great pleasure in an expedition of that nature, "Yet having been from my Infancy employed in the Service of my Country, I shall not grudge any fatigue w'ch may contribute to its benefits." Had the proposed settlement of the Lake Erie region with Virginia as a base proved feasible and become a reality, the major portion of New

balance of the quit rent revenue on hand to pay for a reconnoitering expedition preliminary to actual settlement. The settlement once made, the French would have no ground upon which to dispute the right of the British to possession, "the Law of Nations giving a Title to the first Occupant,"[68] and should the French try to oust them by force, "We are nearer to Support than they to attack."[69] These views of Spotswood, together with a letter from Governor Hunter of New York upon the same subject were communicated to Secretary James Craggs,[70] and the board of trade wrote to Spotswood that it would be glad to hear from him further upon the matter.[71]

In December 1719 Spotswood laid before the council queries from the board of trade regarding the boundaries of Virginia, particularly where contiguous to settlements of the French or other foreign nations, and the condition of the French and Spanish holdings of the southwest. The councillors could only propose a reward for information as to the western boundaries of Virginia, upon the basis of which a general map of the colony could be made, declaring that they had no knowledge of the Spanish settlements at St. Augustine and the French colonly on the Mississippi, but that if anything material came to their notice they would communicate it to the governor.[72] It is suggestive of Virginia's relatively sheltered position that the political controversy seems to have loomed larger in the vision of the council than the wider problems of empire.

The following February Spotswood wrote to the board regarding Louisiana and Florida. Reiterating his former warning of the encircling French settlements, he was more explicit as to their probable effect upon British trade. Tobacco, rice,

---

York's Indian trade would have been diverted to the southern province. Spotswood may well have been aware of this.

[68] Spotswood did not, however, apply this maxim to the French settlements in Louisiana, maintaining that British charters, which antedated the French settlements, gave the English the right to that region. *Letters*, II, 336, 337.

[69] *Ibid.*, pp. 297, 298.

[70] *B. T. Jour.*, 1715-1718, pp. 434, 437, 438; 1718-1722, p. 40.

[71] *C.O.5/1365*, p. 202.

[72] *Ex. Jour. Coun.*, III, 518.

and other commodities now supplied to Europe by the British plantations would doubtless be cultivated in Louisiana, "and they w'll become our Rivals in that Trade in all fforeign Mark'ts."[73] By a map which Spotswood enclosed[74] he endeavored to demonstrate that most of the Indian settlements were closer to the French than to the English. They had hitherto been kept in the British interest only by trade. But the French were now opening trade with them at the very time that the English were discouraged by the low prices and high duties to which skins and furs were subject in England. South Carolina had already abandoned trade with the Cherokee, and Virginia was on the point of giving it up. The prospect of this nation being won over by the French was particularly alarming, for "as these are the nearest and most considerable Body of Indians on our Southern ffrontiers, and consist of upwards of four thousand fighting Men, so they have generally been very friendly and Affectionate to the English, and are the only Indians we ought to depend on to balla. the North'n Nations if they should attempt to be troublesome to these Plantacons."[75]

The advance of the French, Spotswood thought, could best be checked by the establishment of British settlements in Florida "as near as can be to cramp their's." His opinion as to the advisability of taking St. Augustine, requested by the board, was therefore a hearty affirmative, and he proposed that St. Marks also be seized. Holding St. Augustine on one side of Florida Strait and the Bahamas on the other, Britain would in time of war have all the commerce of France and Spain from Central America and the West Indies at her mercy. St. Marks would serve as a base for British settlements in the Gulf region, while it seemed likely that a port could be established among the islands at Florida Cape, both as a haven for British commerce and a base for British privateers. The

[73] *Letters*, II, 329.

[74] Copied from the original draft of the Carolina planter and explorer, Price Hughes. Indeed, much of Spotswood's knowledge of the west seems to have been derived second-hand from Charleston. Crane, p. 223.

[75] *Letters*, II, 331.

recent seizure of Pensacola by the French indicated, Spotswood thought, their intention to acquire all Florida. The English must forestall them.[76] The expedition against Florida and the securing of the lakes to the westward of Virginia were matters a full discussion of which he was unwilling to trust to the uncertainty of the mails. Spotswood therefore proposed that he be given a year's leave of absence in order that he might return to England to take up these projects with the authorities there.[77] The conclusion of peace with Spain prevented the expedition against Florida, but the board of trade proposed to Spotswood that the large balance on hand of the duty on liquors and slaves be applied towards extending the frontier settlements of Virginia and building forts at the sources of the rivers. It held, with much truth, that governor, council, and assembly being closer in touch with the situation were better qualified to undertake such measures than the authorities in England.[78]

After his unpleasant experience in 1718, Spotswood may well have doubted the willingness of the assembly to reduce its cherished surplus to forward his schemes for the development of the west. He nevertheless broached the matter to the representative body in 1720.[79] The result was gratifying. In a series of conferences the two houses decided upon several important forward steps. The region west of the settled part of Virginia, bounded roughly by the Roanoke, the Rappahannock, and the Shenandoah,[80] was divided into two counties, Spotsylvania to the north, and Brunswick to the south.[81] The

[76] *Letters*, II, 330, 331.

[77] *Ibid.*, pp. 331-333. Spotswood asked that in this event he continue to receive his half of the governor's salary, and be provided with a warship to conduct him safely through the pirates, whose hatred he had incurred by his vigorous measures against them.

[78] *C.O.5/1365*, pp. 218, 219. In its report on the state of the plantations made to the crown in 1721, the board of trade stressed the necessity of fortifying the mountain passes, and of going beyond them to form settlements on the Great Lakes, this being part of a general program of border defense. *N. Y. Col. Docs.*, V, 623-625.

[79] *Jour. Burg.*, 1712-1726, p. 250.

[80] It was not yet called by this name.

[81] The boundary of Spotsylvania was Snow Creek up to the mill, thence

settlers in these two counties were exempted for the ten years following May 1, 1721, from all public dues, and £2000 was appropriated, half to be used for arming the settlers and half for the erection of a church, court house, prison, pillory, and stocks in each of the counties.[82] Fifteen hundred pounds was entrusted to Spotswood, the five hundred for the erection of the public buildings in Brunswick being turned over to three other gentlemen. The whole county of Brunswick was made the parish of St. Andrew, while Spotsylvania was erected into that of St. George.[83] At the same time both houses joined in an address to the king, setting forth the strategic importance

---

southwest to the Northanna, up that river "as far as convenient," thence over the mountains to the Shendandoah, so as to include the "northern passage" which modern authorities have identified with Swift Run Gap, down the Shendandoah to a point opposite the source of the Rappahannock, and down Rappahannock to the mouth of Snow Creek. The boundaries of Brunswick were even more indefinite, but were to include the "southern pass." Hening, IV, 77. This southern pass was known of only upon the evidence of Indians and traders. It was described by Spotswood as being at the head of Roanoke. This, however, does not place it with any accuracy. Spotswood stated also that the northern pass was at the head of Rappahannock, while the act for the erection of Spotsylvania implies that the head of Rappahannock was some distance northeast of the pass. The truth of the matter is that the Virginia rivers had so many tributaries that it was difficult to say which was the head. It is nevertheless somewhat strange that Spotswood, who with a view to making the Northern Neck as small as possible had called the southern branch of the Rappahannock the Rapidan, should refer to the northern pass, which was still further south, as being at the head of Rappahannock. Spotswood declared that he was told by Indians and traders that there were no other passes between these two (Spotswood to B. T. Jan. 16, 1721, *C.O.5/1319*, pp. 11, 12). If, however, as seems most plausible, the southern pass was that of the Staunton River, he was misinformed, for between this and Swift Run Gap lies the greatest pass of all, that made by the James. In view of his earlier plans to win the interior by promoting settlement along the course of the James (*supra*, p. 238), it is difficult to understand how Spotswood could have failed to realize this.

[82] At the same time King George County was formed by the division of Richmond, while Hanover was erected out of New Kent. The privileges conferred on Spotsylvania and Brunswick were not extended to these new counties, which were already fairly well settled, and did not extend so far west. Hening, IV, 95; *Jour. Burg.*, 1712-1726, pp. 265-315, *passim.*

[83] Hening, IV, 77-79; *Jour. Burg.*, 1712-1726, pp. 263-315, *passim.* This involved the repeal of the act of 1714, which had erected the parish of St. George for the benefit of the Germanna Palatines. Provision was made, however, to exempt the Germans from the payment of parish levies provided they maintained a minister of their own. This exemption was renewed by order in council in 1735. *C.O.5/1323*, p. 239.

of encouraging settlement in the west, and requesting that the inhabitants of Spotsylvania and Brunswick be exempted from the payment of both treasury rights and quit rents for ten years. "And this Bounty We are the more Encouraged to Beg because we are fully perswaded that in a few yeares it will prove a considerable Augmentation of your Majesties Revenue here." They also asked that the crown employ the quit rents to erect a fort at each of the passes over the mountains, each to be garrisoned by fifty soldiers, exclusive of officers, in the royal pay. Spotswood promised to second the address with "the most powerful Intercession that I can make,"[84] and while doubtless realizing the difficulty of persuading the crown to assume the burden of garrisoning the Virginia frontier, he made out as strong a case as he could for the erection of the forts. The expense of erecting them would not be large, there being plenty of stone upon the spot. Were he on the French side he could with one company of men construct a fortification in the pass which he had seen,[85] so strong that all the military strength of Virginia could not dislodge him. The French whose settlements were farther away, would find it even more difficult to capture the pass, and the militia would be near to support the regular garrison. Only a thorough conviction of the necessity of such protection, the governor asserted, could have induced a people so averse to a military power as were the Virginians to make such a request.[86]

The act erecting the two new counties and the address of the Virginia assembly were referred by Lord Carteret to the board of trade. Both Orkney and Blakiston urged expedition and the matter was considered at several sessions. The new proposals did not fail to arouse opposition. Horace Walpole expressed the opinion that the exemption from quit rents

[84] *Jour. Burg.*, 1712-1726, pp. 298, 299, 316.

[85] Spotswood declared that it would be necessary for him also to make an expedition to the southern pass before plans for fortifying it could be perfected. *C.O.5/1319*, p. 12.

[86] Spotswood to B. T., Jan. 16, 1721. *Ibid.*, pp. 10-18. In this connection it might be noted that the assembly had requested the crown that the proposed garrison be placed under the command of governor and council. *Jour. Burg.*, 1712-1726, pp. 271, 299.

would reduce the revenue of the crown without benefiting the colony. There was reason to suspect that private persons were endeavoring to secure large tracts in these new counties for the sake of securing exemption. The quit rents of Virginia "are now in an extraordinary good method," and people, he thought, would take up lands in the new settlements upon the former conditions. John Hart and Nathaniel Blakiston, both former governors of Maryland, took a more favorable attitude. They asserted the necessity of securing the mountain passes, but pointed out the obstruction to settlement occasioned by large tracts of land secured for speculative purposes, and upon which no improvements were made. They therefore thought the size of grants should be limited. Blakiston favored the remission of the quit rents, declaring that this would not amount to much during the first ten years, but would greatly encourage settlement. Hart, however, thought that the quit rents should be collected and applied to encourage the new settlements.[87]

The report which the board of trade made to Lord Carteret in June 1721 was entirely in sympathy with the proposals from Virginia. Urging the necessity of seizing the passes before the French reached them, it recommended that the crown consider the expediency of erecting forts at the expense of the quit rents. Before this was done, however, an estimate of the cost would have to be furnished by the governor, and in the meantime stockades might be built by Virginia at the passes at small expense.[88] As to the two companies, the board declared it had long held that it was impossible to maintain, let alone to extend, the empire in America without sending a military force thither. It believed that the two companies could not be employed upon a more important service. It thought that both treasury rights and quit rents should be remitted in the new counties for the desired ten years, but that persons having land in other parts of Virginia should give security for the

[87] *B. T. Jour.*, 1719-1722, pp. 273-299, *passim.*

[88] Blakiston had already promised the board that he would propose such measures to the gentlemen of Virginia. *Ibid.*, p. 299.

continued payment of quit rents thereon before being allowed to take up land on the new terms. Not more than 1000 acres should be alloted to any one person. These and other appropriate regulations might be made by instructions to the governor.[89] This, however, proved to be one of the few occasions upon which the privy council failed to adopt the board's recommendation. The report was referred to the committee of the council,[90] and action was delayed for twenty months.

In December 1722 governor and council urged expedition. The prospect of the desired concessions had greatly stimulated the taking up of land in the two frontier counties, but as the crown delayed action men were becoming discouraged. Much good land closer to water carriage lay unpatented in other counties which, other things being equal, would be taken up before that in Spotsylvania and Brunswick. The easier terms offered in the neighboring proprietary provinces were attracting settlers from Virginia. About one-tenth of the frontier counties consisted of fertile valleys, fit for the production of tobacco and hemp, "which are the two Manufactures that Virginia seems now most bent upon." Under ordinary circumstances, only these would be taken up, the intervening barren land being merely used as pasture, "nor that neither in a longer time than ten Years." But if quit rents and rights were remitted, all land, regardless of fertility, would probably be taken up! The revenue lost to the crown during the first ten years would thus speedily be regained. As to treasury rights, most of the land would doubtless be taken up on the basis of head rights, which could be obtained at little expense, though at considerable trouble, in Virginia, and the crown would thus gain little by insisting upon them. Treasury rights in the new counties would probably amount to not more than £50.[91] The removal of the fear of Indian incursions, which had always

[89] B. T. to Carteret, July 17, 1721, *C.O.5/1365*, pp. 229-236.

[90] *C.O.5/1319*, p. 77; *B. T. Jour.*, 1719-1722, p. 310; *Acts of Privy Coun., Col.*, III, 22.

[91] Twenty times that sum would doubtless have been a low estimate.

come through the mountain passes, would encourage the inhabitants to make greater improvements upon their lands.[92]

In March 1723 the committee of the council referred the matter to the treasury[93] whence, so the board of trade informed Drysdale, the proposal of remitting the quit rents for ten years was likely to encounter "very great Difficulties."[94] The treasury reported, however, in favor of remitting the quit rents and rights for a term of seven years from May 1, 1721, subject to the conditions that patentees holding land elsewhere in the colony by quit rent of the crown give security for its continued payment; that not more than one thousand acres be granted to any one person; and that the grants be made subject to the improvements required in other parts of Virginia. This report was approved on July 31, 1723, by the committee of the council, and was confirmed on August 6 by order of the lords justices.[95] The forts were never constructed. The immediate need for them may well be doubted, and a decade later the advance of settlement would have made them obsolete. The crux of the problem was the settlement of the west, and this the crown was fostering, albeit in a manner which partly defeated the end in view.[96]

The close of Spotswood's administration found the board of trade keenly alive to the menace of the French and, to a less extent, the Spanish settlements in America.[97] The conversion of the board must be credited to "the alarmist warnings of the little group of Anglo-American imperialists"[98] who had lost no opportunity of dinning into its ears the necessity for vigorous action. The anti-proprietary party in South Carolina had been the most ardent apostles of empire, but

[92] *C.O.5/1319*, pp. 173-179; *Ex. Jour. Coun.*, IV, 28.

[93] *Acts of Privy Coun., Col.*, III, 23; *C.O.5/1319*, p. 201.

[94] B. T. to Drysdale, June 19, 1723, *C.O.5/1365*, p. 246.

[95] *Acts of Privy Coun., Col.*, III, 23; *C.O.5/1319*, pp. 267-270.

[96] *Infra*, p. 294.

[97] The board, however, was a purely advisory body, and the privy council was less convinced of the necessity of a vigorous frontier policy.

[98] Crane, p. 224.

officials in the other colonies had caught the vision, the veteran Francis Nicholson as early as a quarter-century before.

What is Spotswood's rightful position in this group? Lack of knowledge of its other members[99] has led historians to take him at his own appraisal which, it must be confessed, is high. Spotswood did not lack the will to rule. Early in his administration he had suggested a plan which would have subordinated the rule of North Carolina to that of Virginia.[100] He evidently felt that the American coast could best be protected by a strong contingent of guardships in the Chesapeake, subject to orders from Williamsburg. He had urged his own fitness to lead expeditions to settle the Great Lakes region and to capture Florida. And with that provincial selfishness which he denounced so heartily in others, he coveted for Virginia a predominant part in the fur trade. But he overestimated Virginia's strategic position for the time being. Virginians were indeed to contend with the French for the mastery of the continent, but the hour had not yet struck. Every settler who moved west hastened its arrival. It seems that his encouragement of this comparatively prosaic process constitutes Spotswood's chief claim to greatness as an empire builder.[101]

[99] A lack which, so far as Carolina is concerned, Professor Crane's recent work has ably supplied.

[100] *Supra*, p. 24.

[101] *Infra*, p. 277 ff.

Chapter XII

RECONCILIATION AND DEVOLUTION

IT MUST have been apparent to the more thoughtful minds in the province that factional strife was being protracted at the expense of public welfare. Needed legislation was blocked in the assembly. The administration was diverted from the constructive work of government by political quarrels which promised to become chronic. The conviction therefore gained ground that the differences between the governor and his opponents must be ended. There were three possible ways in which this might be accomplished. Spotswood might be recalled. This, however, did not seem an easy matter to compass. No act of overt malfeasance could be laid to his charge, and the energetic, public-spirited governor was then high in the favor of the board of trade. Some of the more implacable spirits in the council might be removed. This, too, was not easy to bring about, and it is doubtful if it would have had the desired effect. Opposition to Spotswood certainly rested upon a broader base than the spleen of three or four councillors, and a wholesale removal at the governor's request was a strengthening of the prerogative more likely to arouse opposition than to allay it. The most sensible solution seemed to lie in an accommodation of differences.

The first cautious advances came from the council as early as May 1718. Nathaniel Harrison attempted to discover through the medium of William Robertson the attitude of the governor toward a cessation of all difficulties. Spotswood jumped at the opportunity, and after a series of conferences with Harrison proposed terms. He would not insist that his opponents ask his pardon or admit themselves to have been in the wrong, but stipulated only that in future they behave toward him, as their governor, with good manners. He would constitute none but councillors judges of oyer and terminer provided his opponents would recognize the king's prerogative upon this point. He would withhold all the papers which he had prepared indicting his enemies or defending himself provided the council would ask the board of trade to take no further notice of their accusations against him. He wished to include in this reconciliation the allies of both parties, and would therefore keep back the strong charge which he had prepared against Byrd,[1] provided that person would desist from further attacks upon his character and administration. He suggested that the council might give evidence of its desire for a reconciliation by addressing him upon his speech at the opening of the session of assembly.

According to Spotswood's story the councillors mistook his pacific attitude for an admission of weakness. They shunned the appearance of begging for peace, and tried to drive a hard bargain with the governor. Yet their terms, which Harrison delivered to Spotswood on May 9, do not appear so very unreasonable. The councillors were all very desirous of a general reconciliation and friendship, but were startled at the governor's actions in the meantime, particularly at his conduct at a recent meeting of the governors of the college, at his exposing the officers of the revenue in council the following day, and at the harsh characters which they were daily informed the governor gave them in common discourse. This led them to doubt the permanence of the peace if arranged in general terms which might later be misinterpreted. They therefore proposed, first, that all attempts at innovation upon the constitution of the government be laid aside and all privileges preserved which Virginia and they themselves enjoyed at the time of Spotswood's arrival; second, that all terms of reproach in common conversation be forborne and that they mutually endeavor to promote respect toward the governor and all others in authority in the colony; third, that all misunder-

[1] Spotswood may here be referring to his letter to the board of trade dated May 7, 1718. This, while it criticized the conduct of the former revenue officers, hardly amounted to a formal accusation. *Letters*, II, 265-272.

standings be forgotten, both parties so notifying the board of trade; and lastly, that a mutual word of honor be given for the performance of these articles which, memory being treacherous, were to be put in writing.[2] The governor took umbrage at these terms, expressing astonishment that after his taking so conciliatory an attitude he should be expected to subscribe to articles plainly admitting himself to be in the wrong, when the board of trade had decided all his disputes with the council in his favor. He plainly saw, so he informed Harrison, that the "party" was bent upon continuing their endeavors to embarrass his administration. He did not in the least fear their plots and contrivances, but would be upon his guard against them.

Some days later Mann Page, who had all along remained well affected toward the governor, attempted with Spotswood's consent to bring the insurgent group to accept the governor's terms. He reported to Spotswood that the only difficulty was the address, the council holding that this would be improper so late in the session. The governor said he would meet the council and propose something else in its stead. Accordingly, on May 16, he brought the matter up in a full council, narrating the steps already taken and attempting to reach an understanding. Stiffness and reserve greeted his proposal. The governor managed, however, to induce the council to accept an invitation to his house to drink a bowl of arrack punch. The gathering did not break up until midnight, but the council carefully avoided any overtures of peace. Since however, nothing passed which could give offense to anyone, the governor felt he had a right to expect, after all these advances on his side, that his opponents would change their attitude. Yet though they all remained in town during the rest of the session of assembly, not one paid him a visit. "Nay, when in Order to the Solemnizing his Maj'ty's Birth-day, I gave a publick Entertainment at my House, all Gent'n that would come were Admitted; These Eight Counsellors would

[2] A copy of the memorandum which Harrison gave Spotswood is to be found in *C.O.5/1318*, p. 561.

neither come to my House nor go to the Play w'ch was Acted on that occasion, but got together all the Turbulent and disaffected Burg's's, had an Entertainment of their own in the Burg's House and invited all ye Mobb to a Bonfire, where they were plentifully Supplyed with Liquors to Drink the same healths without as their M'rs did within, w'ch were chiefly those of the Council and their Associated Burg's without taking any Notice of the Gov'r, than if there had been none upon the place."[3] Spotswood attributed the reluctance of the council to make peace during the session to their alliance with the disaffected element in the lower house. They hesitated, he declared, to give the appearance of abandoning their fellow insurgents, the burgesses.[4]

On May 31, seven of the disaffected councillors[5] delivered a paper in response to the demand made by the governor the previous March for an explanation of the charges which they had made against him to the board of trade. They said that they did not think proper to meddle with that matter without directions from the board, especially since a reconciliation had been mutually proposed and accepted. The governor answered that he knew terms had been proposed on both sides, but he had rejected those of the councillors because of their unreasonableness, and they had neither written to the board of trade nor given any evidence during the session of assembly that they desired a better understanding. He declared that he took their evasive answer as a plain confession that they knew their accusations to be groundless.[6]

While thus showing a bold front in Virginia, Spotswood

[3] Spotswood to B. T., June 24, 1718, *Letters*, II, 284.

[4] The foregoing account is taken largely from a "Narrative" sent by Spotswood to Orkney. *C.O.5/1318*, pp. 541-553. The councillors may have had another version to relate.

[5] All but John Lewis.

[6] *Ex. Jour. Coun.*, III, 479, 480. At the next meeting of the council the governor caused his reply to be read. At the same time also, Secretary Cocke asked leave to withdraw his bond, since William Byrd had refused to continue as his security. He was permitted to give a new bond, with Edmund Jennings and Chichley Corbin Thacker as his securities. *Ibid.*, pp. 480, 481. Cocke's adherence to the governor had evidently terminated his friendship with Byrd.

was careful to guard his position in England. Writing both to Orkney and to the board of trade, he depicted the insurgent councillors as the fomenters of all the commotion in Virginia. These men, like Absalom of old, sought to secure the allegiance of the people by being the judges of every man's cause, and having in the commissary a "staunch Achitoful" they were determined not to leave in peaceful possession of his office any governor who disputed their position as the dominating influence in the public life of the colony. They it was who had instigated the burgesses to their late excesses. They already had to their credit the removal of two governors, yet they retained their own places at the council board. They were thus coming to be regarded as holding office for life, while the governor served only during their pleasure. For this situation there was a remedy. A recent removal of some of the councillors in New York and New Jersey had reduced those governments to obedience. There was ample occasion for pursuing the same course in Virginia. The governor was deprived of the advice of a council loyal to the interest of the crown while these men, false to the prerogative which they had sworn to uphold, were egging on the unruly elements in the colony to harass that faithful servant of the crown, the governor. In his letter to Orkney, Spotswood went further, proposing by name the desirable changes at the council board. If three or four turbulent spirits, such as Blair, Ludwell, Smith, and Byrd, were replaced by others of more peaceable and loyal principles, and Spotswood thought that Peter Beverley, Cole Diggs, John Robinson,[7] and Edward Hill were men of this stamp, the growing influence of the "party," so inimical to the peace of the province and the interests of the crown, might receive a decisive check.[8]

On August 19 Orkney appeared before the board of trade.

[7] It is possible that Spotswood, realizing that the bishop of London might oppose the removal of his commissary from the council board, sought to reconcile his lordship to the change by nominating his near relation and namesake. See Spotswood to Bp. of London, May 6, 1713, *Rawl., B 376*, fo. 26.

[8] Spotswood to B. T., June 24, 1718, *Letters*, II, 275-286; Spotswood to Orkney, July 1, 1718, *C.O.5/1318*, pp. 533-537.

He was informed, he said, by letters from Virginia, that great disputes had arisen between the lieutenant governor and the council, first occasioned, so he understood, by the way in which Colonel Spotswood had, in accordance with directions from the board, examined the accounts of the former receiver-general. He "had not only received some years ago a very good character of Col. Spotswood, but knew his personal good behaviour." The government of Virginia had been "put on a much better foot, by him than it had formerly been," and the titular governor saw no essential complaint against his deputy. Since, however, his efforts to compose these differences had been in vain, Orkney desired the board to investigate the situation and recommend to the crown the removal from office of the party at fault, since this seemed to be the only way of restoring peace in the government. Should the board decide upon a change in the council, his lordship had some new members to recommend.[9]

The "party" were not long in finding out that their removal was being considered. In December, Byrd requested that no action be taken against the councillors until they were given an opportunity to reply to the accusation against them. Byrd was in particular danger, for Spotswood had proposed his removal upon the ground that he had already been absent from Virginia three and a half years, and since he desired to become agent of the house of burgesses evidently intended to prolong his stay. The governor proposed in his place Cole Diggs, "a Gent. who lives very convenient to the seat of Governm't, of an ample Fortune, Good parts, and a fair Character and whose Father was also at that Board." He was "in no way related to that Luck of Hundred that sway the Bench in the General Court."[10]

After the close of the fall session of assembly Spotswood wrote once more to Orkney. Once again the burgesses had been disaffected by the machinations of the "party." The commissary working through his brother Archibald Blair ("Nor has

[9] *B. T. Jour.*, 1715-1718, pp. 425, 426.
[10] *C.O.5/1318*, p. 519; *Letters*, II, 304.

any Member," Spotswood had written previously, "shewn himself more violent against me than the Commissaries own Brother, whose Billingsgate expressions with regard to me on several Occasions I shall not offend your Lordships ears with"[11]), and Ludwell represented by his nephew Grymes, had directed the actions of the malcontents. Blair and his confederates were working for the removal not merely of Spotswood but of Orkney,[12] and it was to this end that the attempt had been made to appoint Byrd agent. Things were at a crisis in Virginia. If the hereditary faction which had been disturbing the government for nearly forty years did not receive a decisive check the royal authority in Virginia would be all but destroyed. Should the "party" succeed in securing the removal of another governor the consequences would be serious. Even those who now supported the executive would hesitate to oppose the men who appeared to possess for life both the supreme court of judicature and the administration of the government. "Wherefore I take ye Power, Interest and Reputation of the King's Governor in this Dominion to be now reduced to a desparate Gasp, & if the present Efforts of the Country cannot add new Vigour to the same, then the Haughtiness of a Carter, the Hypocrisy of a Blair, the Inveteracy of a Ludwell, ye Brutishness of a Smith, the Malice of a Byrd, the Conceitedness of a Grymes, and the Scurrility of a Corbin, with about a score of base disloyalists & ungrateful Creolians for their adherents must for the future Rule this Province." At all events, the "party" must be prevented from securing any more seats in the council. There was now a vacancy by the death of Berkeley, and Spotswood urged Orkney to support the candidacy of Cole Diggs.[13]

The tide of battle was turning in the governor's favor. Both

[11] Spotswood to Orkney, July 1, 1718, *C.O.5/1318,* pp. 533-537.

[12] Spotswood also stressed this point in a letter to Craggs. *Letters,* II, 306, 307.

[13] Spotswood to Orkney, Dec. 22, 1718, *C.O.5/1318,* pp. 565-571. Spotswood explained that by the present efforts of the country he meant the addresses which were coming in "of themselves" from the counties. *Supra,* pp. 186, 187.

Orkney and the board of trade were rallying to his support and Spotswood appeared confidently to expect the removal of four or five of his adversaries. It was not likely that this turn of events would escape the astute Byrd, and that gentleman appears to have been well aware of the way the wind was blowing, though it seems doubtful that he stooped, as Spotswood insinuated, to intercepting the governor's mail.[14] At all events, he realized that it would be well for the "party" to evince a desire for peace. He therefore promised to employ all his influence, either by writing or by going to Virginia, to persuade his fellow councillors to accept a reconciliation upon the plan which Spotswood had proposed. To facilitate these negotiations, however, Byrd proposed that the governor be instructed to comply with his own plan, to refrain from appointing other judges of oyer and terminer except in cases of extraordinary emergency, to cause the minutes of each council to be read at the next meeting, to consent to the repeal of the act which empowered him to expend what money he should think fit upon the governor's house, and to allow the councillors to express their opinions frankly in the council, the general court, and the assembly, and that both parties be instructed to send over no accusations without giving copies of them to the accused.[15] This hardly had the appearance of extending the olive branch. The board doubtless took particular umbrage that Byrd should have the temerity to raise once more the oyer and terminer question. The day after reading his peace proposals, therefore, it sent a memorial to the crown recommending Byrd's removal from the council, on the ground that he had been absent from Virginia for over three years without the requisite royal permission. Peter Beverley was proposed in his place.[16]

As we have seen, the Earl of Orkney had in August 1718

[14] Spotswood to Popple, Feb. 5, 1719, *C.O.5/1318*, pp. 615-618.

[15] *Ibid.*, p. 557. It is suggestive of the board's attitude towards Byrd that the latter did not present his proposals in person but gave them to Orkney. *B. T. Jour.*, 1718-1722, p. 51.

[16] *C.O.5/1365*, pp. 185, 186.

submitted to the decision of the board the differences between governor and council, with the proposal that the guilty be removed from office. In March 1719 he once more urged that the issue be settled. In April the board finally took up the matter, Orkney being called into conference.[17] Its decision was in the governor's favor, as its letter to Spotswood the following June plainly shows.[18] The address of the assembly received a rebuff in the letter which the board wrote at this time to Secretary Craggs.[19] The board indeed fell short of conceding the governor's desire for a wholesale purging of the council; aside from Byrd, none was recommended for removal. But it showed its desire to bring about a change in the composition of the council by its nomination to vacancies. As Spotswood had desired, Diggs succeeded Berkeley, and upon the death of Smith the following spring Beverley was given a place at the council board.[20] Thus the governor gained for his friends two seats of the opposition. He indeed lost a strong supporter when Dr. Cocke died suddenly during the October general court, 1720,[21] but the alignment in the council was not affected, for Cocke's place was filled by John Robinson.[22]

On December 9, 1719, Spotswood was able to present to his opponents tangible evidence that the British authorities were backing him. He laid before the council board copies of the opinion of Solicitor-General Sir William Thompson regarding collation, that of Richard West upon the power of proroguing assemblies under adjournment,[23] the representation of the board of trade on the address of the burgesses,[24] and that upon Byrd's petition for restraining the governor in the appointment of judges of oyer and terminer, the order in council appointing Cole Diggs to the council, and the representation of

[17] *B. T. Jour.*, 1718-1722, pp. 51, 54, 56.
[18] B. T. to Spotswood, June 26, 1719, *C.O.5/1365*, pp. 198-207.
[19] *Supra*, pp. 187, 188.
[20] *B. T. Jour.*, 1718-1722, p. 168.
[21] *Letters*, II, 8, *n.*, 343, 344.
[22] *Acts of Privy Coun., Col.*, II, 825.
[23] *Supra*, p. 183 *n.*
[24] *Supra*, pp. 187, 188.

the board of trade nominating Peter Beverley to that body, presumably the one proposing him in the place of Byrd.[25] The governor thus found himself in an enviable position. The very prospect of victory had tended to divide his opponents. Bassett and Harrison were both becoming palpably lukewarm.[26] "I consider," Harrison had written to Ludwell, "the consequences if Colo Byrd should ever obtain his end and Come here Governor and we should be so unfortunate as to Differ with him. Now that Colo. Byrd will come here in that Station I have much reason to think and therefore we should act so as not to give him any advantage against us by which he might keep us in awe."[27]

Harrison's misgivings were groundless. Byrd did not have the necessary influence in England to secure the governorship, though he had enough to keep the privy council from approving the board's memorial for his removal. Appearing in Virginia he presented on May 25, 1720 an order in council continuing him in the council, or restoring him to his former rank if dismissed or suspended. He had not been removed, and the next day he was sworn and took his seat.[28]

Three days later the reconciliation took place. Six of the insurgent group were present, Carter, Blair, Ludwell, Lewis, Byrd, and Harrison. Bassett was absent, while Smith and Berkeley were dead. The governor was also there, with his three supporters, Jennings, Cocke, and Page. Diggs was not present,[29] while Beverley had not yet been appointed. It was mutually agreed that all past controversies be buried in oblivion. Future differences between the governor and the major part of the council were to be referred to the board of trade by an impartial statement drawn up by both parties. If it were a question of law, the board was to be requested to take the

[25] *Ex. Jour. Coun.*, III, 517, 518.

[26] *Ludwell Paps.*, II, nos. 68, 74.

[27] Byrd, *Writings*, p. lxxiii.

[28] *Cal. Va. State Paps.*, I, 194, 195; *Ex. Jour. Coun.*, III, 524.

[29] Indeed Diggs does not appear to have taken his seat until the following October, although the news of his appointment had been received the previous December.

opinion of the law officers of the crown. No separate solicitations were to be made by either party. The unsettled dispute over the right of supplying ecclesiastical benefices was to be tried before the general court, with an appeal to the crown.[30] Letters were to be written to the board of trade to notify it of the reconciliation, and to request that no notice be taken of former representations made by either party against the other.[31] The letters were accordingly written,[32] and bore a ring of sincerity[33] which elicited from the board of trade a prompt reply, expressing satisfaction with what had taken place and hope that the reconciliation might prove lasting.[34] The currents of Virginia politics once more ran smoothly, on the surface at least.[35]

There were doubtless those in the colony who were little pleased at the pacific turn of events. To them the action of the council was a desertion of the "patriot" cause. Criticism therefore arose against those in high places. This the governor promptly stamped on. Invoking the provisions of a law which

[30] *Supra*, p. 200.

[31] *Ex. Jour. Coun.*, III, 524, 525. It will be observed that these are the terms proposed by the governor, without the qualifications demanded by the council in Virginia and by Byrd in England.

[32] Spotswood to B. T., May 5, 1720, *C.O.5/1318*, p. 847; Council to B. T., May 5, 1720, *ibid.*, p. 851. The letter of the council was signed by Jennings, Carter, Blair, Ludwell, Lewis, Byrd, Bassett, Cocke, Harrison, and Page, all the men then living who had been parties to the dispute as councillors.

[33] A letter from an anonymous writer in Virginia to Mr. King, a merchant of Bristol, represents Spotswood as being forced into a show of reconcilation by the fact that Byrd was empowered by Orkney, Argyle, and other great men to offer terms of peace, the non-acceptance of which on the governor's part would have resulted in his prompt removal. The letter, which was delivered to the board of trade by Joshua Gee, was violently hostile to the governor, and there seems little ground for giving it credence. *C.O.5/1319*, pp. 81-83.

[34] B. T. to governor and council, June 15, 1720, *C.O.5/1365*, p. 214. This reply was ordered entered in the council books. *Ex. Jour. Coun.*, III, 532.

[35] "We are now under an entire reconciliation & all parties seem resolved to forget the Past. Poor Nath. Burwell hath lost his place & is like to stand Concluded for w[t] I see. Tis well he can live without it." Robert Carter to Messrs. Perry, July 13, 1720. *Carter Letter Book*. Evidently the councillors had now abandoned the attempt to restore Burwell to the post of naval officer from which Spotswood had removed him.

had been passed during the troubled times following Bacon's Rebellion, he instructed the grand jury of the October general court to inquire into the agitation which had been on foot since the previous general court, designed to incite the people against the governor, councillors, judges, and other principal officers. This the grand jury promised to do.[36] The governor was prepared, if necessary, to enforce peace.

The reconciliation between governor and council may have been one of political expediency, rather than a hearty banishing of all ill will. Indeed it was hardly to be expected that the animosities of the past few years would immediately subside. Yet it was a boon of no little consequence that the government could now proceed to the expedition of necessary business, now much accumulated.

The 1720 elections resulted in a change in twenty-two seats in the house. Edwin Conway and George Marable were not returned, but Gawin Corbin, John Grymes, and Archibald Blair once more took their seats.[37] Due to a disputed election in Westmorland it was some days after the opening of the session that Daniel McCarty was seated.[38] In his absence, John Holloway and John Clayton were nominated to the speakership. These two had but recently been rivals in another connection. Holloway while judge of the court of vice-admiralty had been retained as attorney by William Howard and other pirates. This had led to a dispute between him and the governor, the upshot of which was that Holloway had either been removed from his office or had found it advisable to vacate it. Clayton had been appointed in his place. Holloway was now applying to the lords of the admiralty for reinstatement.[39] The nomination of these two was therefore of considerable political significance, and the choice of Holloway as speaker must have warned the governor that the spirit of resistance was not yet

[36] *C.O.5/1319*, pp. 27-30.

[37] *Jour. Burg.*, 1712-1726, pp. ix, x.

[38] *Ibid.*, pp. 294, 295. The election had evidently been close, and turned upon the qualifications of a few doubtful voters.

[39] *Letters*, II, 319, 352-354.

dead in the lower house.[40] Clayton was made chairman of the comittee for propositions and grievances, a post which he had held in 1715. Corbin headed the committee on elections and privileges, and Henry Harrison that for public claims.[41]

In his speech at the opening of the session the governor alluded to the recent restoration of harmony, philosophized upon the ideal relations which should subsist between colony and mother country, and referred to his lands, "the Stake I have among you," which he had by choice acquired in Virginia, as proof that he could have no designs against the welfare of the colony.[42] The governor called the attention of the assembly to the defenselessness of the harbors and frontiers, the disarmed condition of the militia, the inconvenient length of many counties, and the need for treaties with the Five Nations.[43] In a respectful yet cordial reply, the burgesses promised to take up these matters,[44] and their actions seconded their words.

The progress of western expansion, deemed of the utmost expediency as a protective measure against the encroachment of the French, was encouraged by the erection of two new counties, Spotsylvania and Brunswick. The inhabitants of these counties were exempted from all levies for ten years, and the crown was addressed to remit quit rents and "rights" for the same period of time.[45] The erection of these two counties and of two more, Hanover and King George, diminished the excessive size of the western counties. Several acts were also passed altering the boundaries of parishes. With regard to the problem of defense from attack by sea, the burgesses passed a resolution that the guardships would be of greater service if placed under the immediate direction of the gover-

[40] *Jour. Burg.*, 1712-1726, p. 249. Holloway was nominated by Nicholas Meriwether, who in November 1718 had introduced into the house the address to the crown and the instructions to Byrd.

[41] *Ibid.*, p. 251.

[42] *Infra*, p. 277 ff.

[43] *Jour. Burg.*, 1712-1726, p. 250.

[44] *Ibid.*, p. 254.

[45] *Supra*, pp. 244-246.

nor.[46] The problem of militia reform, involved as it was with the conflicting interests of class, was referred to the next session.[47] With the policy of negotiating with the Five Nations the house expressed its sympathy, but urged delay for a time.[48]

Several important pieces of legislation not proposed in the governor's opening address were also enacted. The act for the appointment of sheriffs was amended,[49] further provision was made to prevent the tending of "seconds," and several new ferries were authorized. The finishing of the governor's house, that vexatious problem, was provided for through agencies other than that of the chief executive, Spotswood declining to have anything more to do with the matter.[50]

That the era of concord so recently ushered in had been accompanied by a change of attitude on the part of the governor is perhaps best exemplified by the land laws which were enacted in 1720—laws better calculated to improve the lot of the colonial landholder than to increase the revenue of his royal landlord. One of these acts adapted the conditions of seating and planting to the more diversified uses to which land was now being put in Virginia. The other, while improving the method of quit rent collection, substituted for the penalty of forfeiture for three years' non-payment that of double quit rents for "concealed" lands. The prejudice to the crown was more apparent than real. Double quit rents were collectable by distress, while a colonial court could hardly be found which would condemn land for non-payment.[51] Thus Spotswood was

[46] *Supra*, p. 211.

[47] *Supra*, p. 205.

[48] *Supra*, p. 104.

[49] The amending act, which imposed a penalty upon those who refused to accept the office of sheriff, was similar to one of 1710. Being again made temporary it would have been contrary to the governor's instructions to pass it had the penalty not been raised from 3000 to 5000 pounds of tobacco. This afforded a loophole of which Spotswood readily took advantage, since he did not want any more differences than he could help with the assembly, and since it was necessary, if justice were to be administered and quit rents collected, that those appointed sheriff be compelled to assume office. Spotswood to B. T., March 6, 1721, *C.O.5/1319*, pp. 90, 91.

[50] *Jour. Burg.*, 1712-1726, pp. 283, 284.

[51] *Supra*, pp. 149, 150, 155.

by no means betraying the trust of his royal master. Yet he no longer posed as the defender of the interests of the crown against a turbulent populace. Why should he estrange the Virginia landholding class, among whom he had already cast his own lot?

Several disputed elections led the burgesses into what the governor considered a flagrant abuse of their right to determine their own membership. The house assumed the judicial function of deciding who possessed the freehold qualification for voting. Sheriffs were ordered to summon persons before it, and servants were called upon to report the intimate conversations of their masters. A law was then passed, compelling voters to take oath to their freehold if so required at the poll, those taking a false oath being subject to a penalty. Not until this point did Spotswood interfere. The governor held that it would be unjust to have the qualifications of voters questioned before the house until they had been convicted of taking a false oath, since this would be compelling them to testify against themselves in a case for which a penalty was prescribed by law. But an amendment to safeguard this inherent right of Englishmen was rejected, and Spotswood declined to sanction the bill "without some provision to secure the Rights & Libertys of ye people." Since the house was apt to become embroiled with the governor whenever designing men inspired the burgesses with thoughts of enlarging their power, Spotswood proposed to the board of trade that the crown be moved to ascertain what rights and privileges the house should be allowed, that a governor might not transgress in abridging what was justly their due, nor they in assuming that to which they had no right.[52] Conscious,

[52] Spotswood to B. T., March 6, 1721, *C.O.5/1319*, pp. 92-95. At the same time the governor expressed to the board his disapproval of the new custom of paying the burgesses out of the treasury instead of by county levies. He had permitted this payment, but insisted upon issuing the warrants himself in accordance with his instructions, and refused to sanction a resolution placing £2000 in the hands of the speaker for that purpose. The burgesses had doubtless adopted this new policy partly because there was plenty of money in the treasury, partly because Spotswood had questioned the legality of the old method of payment. *Supra*, pp. 130, 131.

doubtless, of its ignorance of colonial traditions, the board of trade contented itself with cautioning Spotswood's successor that since his predecessor had had so many disputes with the house upon this score, he should take care that no innovations be made either upon the prerogative or upon the ancient usage of the assembly.[53] This, of course, begged the whole question.

On December 14 John Grymes introduced into the house a resolve that it was necessary to appoint some proper person in Great Britain to solicit matters agreed upon "by this General Assembly."[54] This clear note of opposition revived for the time the old division between the friends and the enemies of the governor. The resolution was adopted only by the casting vote of the speaker, but once committed to this course of action the burgesses voted to appoint William Byrd,[55] and to pay him £400 "in consideration of his Expences Trouble and Services." The governor was empowered and desired to issue his warrant for this sum.[56] Naturally the latter objected. He proposed two amendments, that the instructions to the agent be signed by the governor, and that the agent give bond to the governor not to meddle with any affairs of the government of Virginia not contained in his instructions.[57] This would have silenced Byrd more effectually than ever. The matters contained in the instructions might equally well have been negotiated by Blakiston. What the burgesses wanted was a man of Byrd's views and abilities, qualified to appear before the board of trade with a free hand as to the course he pursued. Therefore, although the

[53] B. T. to Drysdale, June 19, 1723, *C.O.5/1365*, p. 246.

[54] Later, at the instance of the council, this was changed to "by the Lieut. Governour Council and Burgesses of this General Assembly." The change is significant. It was necessary, every so often, for the upper house to remind the burgesses that they were merely a part, and not the whole, of the general assembly. *Jour. Burg.*, 1712-1726, pp. 299, 308.

[55] Byrd was again bound for England.

[56] *Ibid.*, p. 300. This, at least, was the sense of the burgesses' resolve, though no such power could be given the governor without the concurrence of the council.

[57] *Ibid.*, p. 308.

governor defended his position in an able message, the house remained obdurate, and the matter fell through[58] without, however, giving rise to that bitterness which had characterized the two preceding assemblies. "I take my leave of you," said Spotswood at the close of the session, "with abundant Satisfaction hoping that the next time we met we shall accord Stil more and more in our Sentiments."[59]

This hope was realized when the assembly convened in May 1722.[60] In his opening speech the governor recommended that it second the encouragement which parliament had recently given to the production of naval stores in the plantations, and that it provide for an embassy to negotiate with the Five Nations at Albany. He also communicated to the assembly an unfavorable reply from the government of Maryland to a proposal for the joint erection of a lighthouse upon Cape Henry.[61]

As the governor had expected, it was decided to do nothing about the lighthouse until Maryland showed more of a disposition to cooperate. Six thousand pounds, however, was appropriated as a bounty upon naval stores, a measure which accorded not only with the governor's public policies but with his private interests. A proposal, however, to place a bounty upon pig iron, of which Spotswood was the sole producer in Virginia, was voted down.[62] Into the governor's plans for a conference with the Five Nations the burgesses entered readily. Not only did they appropriate £1000 to defray the cost of the negotiations; they also insisted that the Virginia em-

[58] *Jour. Burg.*, 1712-1726, pp. 309, 310, 313, 314. Spotswood suggested to the board of trade that if the crown should yield, before Byrd arrived in England, the quit rents and rights in the new counties, it would help to convince the people than an agent was not needed. Spotswood to B. T., Jan. 16, 1721, *C.O.5/1319*, pp. 16-18. See also same to same, March 6, 1721, *ibid.*, p. 97.

[59] *Jour. Burg.*, 1712-1726, p. 316.

[60] During the second session the house consisted of fifty-six members, Hanover and King George being represented for the first time. The standing committees of the former session were all revived.

[61] *Ibid.*, pp. 319, 320.

[62] *Supra*, p. 236.

bassy be headed by Spotswood in person.[63] This action must have been as gratifying to the pride as it was favorable to the policies of the governor. Legislation was also passed providing for the enforcement of the treaties to be made with the northern Indians.[64]

Several other matters were dealt with by the assembly. Provision was made for the punishment of mutinous seamen, for the quarantining of ships coming from the plague-swept regions of southern Europe, for the improvement of transportation by the clearing of rivers and creeks, for improving the breed of horses, and for freeing the public thoroughfares of the colonial capital from the depredations of hogs.[65] Another act, besides regulating servants and slaves, attempted to cope with the problem created by the policy of the mother country of shipping her criminals to the plantations. This policy naturally met with little favor in America, but colonial efforts to put a stop to the traffic were always nullified by the British authorities. The Draconian penal code of the time must be remembered in this connection. Those convicted of the grosser forms of crime expiated their offenses for the most part upon the gallows. Those transported were not necessarily hardened criminals; they were apt to be victims of economic depression and arbitrary laws. Yet to the colonists, provisions such as those incorporated in the Virginia act of 1722 were but necessary precautions to protect society from a wave of crime. In England, however, the contractors for the transportation of convicts complained that the act made their business impossible. It was therefore disallowed.

The perennial question of the allowance to Byrd was raised upon the second day of the assembly. A motion to adjourn the debate was lost by the casting vote of the speaker, and Byrd was voted £300.[66] This time Spotswood withdrew his

[63] *Supra*, p. 105.
[64] *Jour. Burg.*, 1712-1726, pp. 346, 347, 350-353.
[65] *Ibid.*, p. 353.
[66] *Ibid.*, pp. 322, 323.

opposition. Several things may have prompted this change of policy. He was doubtless tired of wrangling. That the burgesses had allowed him a similar sum for his expenses in going to Albany in 1717 must have had a mollifying influence.[67] Furthermore, the death of Blakiston had left the place of Virginia agent vacant. Two candidates were proposed, John Carter, son of the councillor, and Byrd. Spotswood had appointed Carter, but it was doubtful if he would accept the office.[68] Byrd might thus become the regularly appointed agent of Virginia, and it would therefore be well for the governor not to repudiate too overtly his former extra-legal services in that capacity.

"Such Concord, and application to Business," declared the governor at the close of the session, "Such good Temper and generous disposition and Such deference to a Governor's Reccomendation have been manifested in this Session of Assembly that I cannot in Justice part with you without rendering my public Acknowledgements and for my own particular must Return you my Thanks for what you have voted in consideration of my Journey to *New York* in the year 1717 not so much valuing the Quantum that you have given, as the Regard which you have now Shewn to my Services in those daies."[69]

It was indeed a favorable account of his province which Spotswood was able to send to the board of trade. The return of prosperity had brought a surplus in the standing revenue of government as well as in the fund at the disposal of the assembly. The people were contented. All branches of government had cooperated upon constructive policies. The perfect concord of 1722 justified the protection which the board had afforded him during the "angry proceedings" of 1718. "And as to myself, I have the pleasure of seeing my whole twelve Years administration receive so ample a Testimony of the approbation both of the Council and the Repre-

[67] *Ibid.*, p. 343.
[68] Spotswood to B. T., June 23, 1722, *C.O.5/1319*, p. 155.
[69] *Jour. Burg.*, 1712-1726, p. 354.

sentatives of the People, that I hope whatever imputations have been on my conduct heretofore will be looked upon as the effects of some people's private passions rather than any real occasion given on my part."[70]

In July 1722 Spotswood set out upon his embassy to the Five Nations. Never had the situation in Virginia appeared more favorable to his administration. Yet it would seem that he departed with the knowledge that his governorship was at an end. This is borne out, not merely by his own declaration[71] and by that of one of his most inveterate opponents,[72] but by his actions during the summer of 1722. A number of patents were pending for surveys which had been made in Spotsylvania County, some of them those of the governor under borrowed names. The government had decided to withhold the patents until the crown passed upon the remission of rights and quit rents. In April 1722, however, before the crown had made its ruling, upon the advice of the council, many of whom were also interested, Spotswood issued patents of a somewhat anomalous nature which, it was hoped, might be sustained in law, whatever contingency should arise. The only reason for the issuing of such doubtful patents, when by waiting a short space of time good ones might have been secured, seems to have been the one later offered by Spotswood, that he and the others interested, expecting the arrival of a successor who would not favor these proceedings, preferred poor titles to the prospect of receiving no titles at all.[73]

The cause or causes of Spotswood's removal have never been determined with any accuracy, nor can such a determination be hoped for here. The evidence is circumstantial and by no means conclusive. Several possible explanations present themselves.

Spotswood's post may have been desired for a British placeman. His successor, Hugh Drysdale, was an English major and an Oxford man, having been associated with Bishop Gib-

[70] Spotswood to B. T., June 11, 1722, *C.O.5/1319*, pp. 131, 132.
[71] *Ibid.*, pp. 533, 534.
[72] John Grymes to Peter Leheup, May 25, 1724, *C.O.5/1320*, p. 63.
[73] *Infra*, pp. 281, 282.

son at Queen's College.[74] It is significant that he was recommended to the Earl of Orkney by Sir Robert Walpole.[75] But these contacts notwithstanding, he does not seem to have had particular influence, and there is little reason for thinking that the vacancy was made for his benefit.

In the second place, the authorities in England might have felt that Spotswood was unfit to be continued in office. The removal can hardly have been made in the interest of harmony. While reproving him at times for tactlessness, the board of trade had supported the governor during a bitter struggle with the most influential men of the colony, and now differences had been accommodated so that the government was administered almost without a hitch. Of its belief in Spotswood as an energetic and faithful servant of the crown the board had given frequent evidence. It will be noted, however, that Spotswood's attitude was mellowing, and there is a bare possibility that the board felt that he was becoming too colonial in his sympathies. The theory has recently been advanced[76] that Spotswood was removed because the government disapproved of the large tracts of land which he had taken up. A letter containing an account of his speculations had been presented to the board of trade but its tone was not calculated to inspire confidence and the bearer, Joshua Gee, was informed that when proof of its allegations was received the board would consider the matter.[77] No such proof appears to have been submitted.[78] The governor's iron works were an equally likely source of trouble. To this enterprise Byrd had, with all the appearance of innocence, called the attention of the board.[79] But that Spotswood's presumed unfitness to continue in office was the motivating force behind his removal is rendered highly improbable by the fact that the board of

[74] Drysdale to Bishop of London, Nov. 26, 1723, *Fulham MSS., Virginia*, 1st Box, No. 67.

[75] Orkney to [Newcastle?], May 5, 1726, *C.O.5/1344*.

[76] By Dr. H. R. McIlwaine. *Jour. Burg.*, 1712-1726, pp. xlv, xlvi, *n.*

[77] Letter from Virginia to Mr. King, Oct. 5, 1721, *C.O.5/1319*, pp. 81-83; *B. T. Jour.*, 1718-1722, p. 336.

[78] It is not to be supposed, however, that when his removal was urged his opponents would overlook so good a talking point against him.

[79] *Ibid.*, p. 328.

trade, to which such considerations would inevitably have been submitted, seems to have had no part in displacing him.

Thirdly, the theory most generally accepted is that Spotswood's removal was contrived by personal enemies, chief among them the commissary. In this instance, the orthodox view would seem to be correct. Spotswood's reconciliation with the council had indeed restored harmonious coordination between the various branches of the government, but in some hearts rancor still lingered. Nor were all the matters at issue settled. Certain it is that Spotswood and Deputy Auditor John Grymes were still at odds,[80] and it is doubtful if the governor's reconciliation to Byrd and Ludwell was more than superficial. Yet these were opponents whom the governor might have withstood had he been both willing and able to placate the commissary. Apparently he was neither.

In 1721, Byrd and Blair both left for England.[81] Byrd was doubtless called thither by private business. He appeared before the board of trade to discuss the problem of encouraging naval stores, and far from appearing hostile to the governor, suggested that bounties be placed upon sow and pig iron, which he informed the board the governor was producing at his iron works.[82] Spotswood wrote to Bishop Robinson that Blair was leaving, "(as he gives out)," upon college affairs, particularly about his pretensions to the president's salary. In this affair the governor asserted that he was not in the least concerned. He had told the commissary that as he could neither alter his opinion in Blair's favor, nor approve of the general management of the college he would, to avoid contention, stay away from the meetings of the governors, and meddle as little as possible with the affairs of that foundation. "We accord at present so well," Spotswood continued, "that he is continually assuring me of all the Service he can do me at home; but as I take him to be clearer sighted than not to

[80] *Letters*, II, 325; Grymes to Leheup, May 25, 1724, *C.O.5/1320*, p. 64.

[81] *B. T. Jour.*, 1718-1722, p. 328; Dell [?] to Berriman, Oct. 28, 1721, *Fulham MSS.*, *Virginia*, 1st Box, No. 141.

[82] *B. T. Jour.*, 1718-1722, p. 328. Whether Byrd was making these revelations with the object of getting the governor into trouble it is impossible to say.

perceive that ye chief motive of my agreement is for Peace and Quietness sake, I shall be contented with his not offering to do me any Disservice."[83]

Thus, by his own confession, Spotswood retained his hostility to Blair, and believed (and who will doubt it?) that the animosity was mutual. It thus seems plausible that the commissary when in England worked for the removal of the governor, but the steps which he took can be stated only hypothetically. He knew the board of trade to be friendly to Spotswood. Byrd had tried repeatedly to turn it against the governor without success. Blair apparently did not make the attempt. He doubtless worked through personal interviews with individuals who, unlike the board of trade, kept no record of their proceedings.[84] Just what his actions were, it is therefore difficult to say. He may have obtained the influence of the bishop of London. And it seems quite likely that he won the ear of Auditor-General Horace Walpole, who was displeased with both the quit rent law of 1720 and the demands that rights and quit rents be remitted in the new counties. This Walpole appears to have regarded as part of a land-grabbing conspiracy, a frame of mind which some judicious prompting from Blair may well have induced. That the auditor-general's more famous brother recommended Drysdale increases the probability that he had some hand in the passing of Spotswood. But the actual removal was probably made through Orkney, who may well have been persuaded that the strenuous tactics of his lieutenant were compromising his own position.[85] He it was who appointed Spotswood's successor, and Spotswood's subsequent hostility to Orkney indicates that he considered the governor-in-chief responsible for his removal.[86] Orkney, entertaining as he did so high an opin-

[83] Spotswood to Bishop of London, May 26, 1721, *Rawl. B. 376*, fo. 260b.

[84] If this be indeed the case, the question of Spotswood's removal is probably one which can never definitely be determined.

[85] "But he was recalled, because it had been probably whispered to Lord Orkney by the agent, 'that if he did not remove his lieutenant, the burgesses would certainly address the king to remove him.'" Chalmers, *Revolt of the Colonies*, II, 78.

[86] Spotswood to Orkney, March 22, 1727, *C.O.5/1320*, p. 245. See also *ibid.*, p. 241; *C.O.5/1365*, pp. 311-313.

ion of Spotswood in 1718, would hardly have embarked upon this course without some strong influence. The close relations between Blair and the new governor from the very time of the latter's appointment seem to indicate that this influence was supplied by the commissary. That Blair would control the new administration was rumored in Virginia before Drysdale's arrival.[87] Drysdale and Blair appeared together before the board of trade to discuss the current problems of government in Virginia.[88] When, on September 27, 1722, Drysdale met his first council and published his commission, Blair was present.[89] They had evidently arrived from England upon the same ship. Drysdale's panegyrics upon Blair[90] and Blair's upon Drysdale[91] indicate that the commissary was having his own way with the new governor,[92] and it is quite evident that the "persecution" of Spotswood over his lands was initiated not by Drysdale but by the former governor's old opponents, among them certainly Grymes and, almost as certainly, Blair.[93]

The unadorned facts of Spotswood's removal are that on April 20, 1722, Drysdale presented to the board of trade a royal commission, dated April 3, appointing him lieutenant governor of Virginia.[94] Upon September 27 his commission was read in Virginia, and Spotswood, then absent in New York, ceased to be governor. His salary was paid up to September 26.[95] This being all that is definitely known, perhaps no more should be stated. Yet the evidence seems to warrant the belief that his undoer was his fellow Scot, the commissary.

[87] "*. . . it was rumoured yt a new Governor was coming over. . . .* But more especially when it was understood yt Parson Blair was likely to act as Prime Minister . . ." *C.O.5/1319*, p. 533.

[88] *B. T. Jour.*, 1718-1722, p. 368.

[89] *Ex. Jour. Coun.*, IV, 19.

[90] Drysdale to Bishop of London, Nov. 26, 1723, *Fulham MSS., Virginia*, 1st Box, No. 67.

[91] Blair to Bishop of London, July 22, 1723, *ibid.*, 2nd Box, No. 113.

[92] See also Byrd to John Custis, London, July 29, 1723, Byrd, *Writings*, pp. 397, 398.

[93] *Infra*, p. 283 ff.

[94] *B. T. Jour.*, 1718-1722, p. 351; *C.O.5/1319*, pp. 85, 86.

[95] *Ex. Jour. Coun.*, IV, 19, 20, 23.

There thus appears justification for the sweeping assertion that throughout his long residence of more than fifty years in Virginia, Blair succeeded in securing the removal of every governor who thwarted his will. A color of romance attaches itself to the unlovable figure of the commissary. The triumph of the spiritual over the temporal authority was indeed not new in history, but the eighteenth century was not a religious age, and there is room for doubt whether this un-maker of governors was a religious man. Blair was popular neither with the people nor with the clergy of Virginia. He waged his battles in the matter-of-fact realm of politics, where he had to rely upon his own shrewdness, persistence, and courage to outdo his adversaries.

"The historian," says Chalmers, "will dwell with pleasure upon the merits of Spotswood. There was a utility in his designs, a vigor in his conduct, and an attachment to the true interest of the kingdom and the colony, which merit the greatest praise. Had he attended more to the courtly maxim of Charles the Second 'to quarrel with no man, however great might be the provocation, since he knew not how soon he should be obliged to act with him,' that able officer might be recommended as the model of a provincial governor."[96] A contemporary has passed similar judgment. "That Gentleman," wrote Blakiston, "has really Capasity and Tallents to manage in a high Sphere but he adheres to much of his Own sentiments Sometimes and thinks him Selfe ill treated if everybody will not think as he does."[97] From these opinions it is difficult to dissent. A greater tact would have increased Spotswood's usefulness and might well have prolonged his administration indefinitely. But more than the lack of a spirit of conciliation stood between the governor and complete success.

Spotswood had made a vigorous fight to uphold the prerogatives of the crown. This he had done not from disinterested loyalty alone, but because the royal authority was inextricably bound up with his own. The struggle had been

[96] Chalmers, *Revolt of the Colonies,* I, 78.

[97] Blakiston to Ludwell [?], July 2, 1716, *Ludwell Paps.,* II, no. 40.

waged over the courts of oyer and terminer, the right of presentation, and countless lesser issues. Since the final word lay with Britain the governor had been upheld in theory. But that his nominal victories brought him little accretion of power indicates that the center of political gravity now rested in the colony itself. The governor's penchant for efficiency seems to have had a salutary effect, but he had been able in the matter of quit rents to win only a partial victory for the crown, and the virtue of his land reforms lies in their conformity to local conditions. Behind the failure of such schemes as his regulation of the tobacco trade lay the colonial proclivity to reduce governmental activity to a minimum. His humane Indian policy miscarried, as similar projects were to miscarry in the future, because it was not to the material interests of the white population to support it. His efforts to arouse a spirit of intercolonial cooperation produced meager results. American nationalism was to come, but its realization involved the snapping of the bonds between colonies and mother country.

Virginia was sufficiently close to the frontier process to have retained in large measure the pioneer's self-reliance and impatience of external control. But a century of unbroken occupation had created in the tidewater area a society which had attained a fair degree of political, economic, and social stability. Her people had developed a consciousness of identity of interests and ideals which amounted to a local patriotism. While there is little reason to believe that this separatist tendency was deliberately fostered, Virginia was pursuing a path which led away from Britain. Spotswood held an exalted conception of the position of His Majesty's governor. His inability fully to realize this conception demonstrates the difficulty of bridging the widening rift between colony and mother country. The vicissitudes attending his efforts thus have a significance far broader than the twelve years of his administration, or the bounds of the province which he administered. They foreshadow the disruption of one empire, the birth of another.

Chapter XIII

THE PLANTER

EVERY Man that is endued with a common Share of Thought & understanding to forecast his Worldly Affairs (& I presume none that know me will exclude me from that number) certainly forms to himself Some apparent Comforts, when he unconstrainedly embarks in an Undertaking that must quite change the Scene of his Life."[1] In so writing at the close of his administration Spotswood indicates his frame of mind at its inception. His friends, he tells us elsewhere, had attempted to dissuade him from abandoning an army career for that of a colonial governor on half-pay. But if the rewards which the colonies offered to shrewdness and energy were hidden from his comrades, to Lord Cadogan's canny subordinate they soon became apparent.

As we have already seen, the year 1714 brought to Virginia some forty Germans sent over from England by Blakiston to further an enterprise in which Spotswood, de Graffenried, and probably others were interested. Before they arrived the baron, whose fortunes in Virginia had gone awry, had returned to Switzerland, leaving Spotswood to take care of the immigrants. Making a virtue of necessity, the governor concealed his part in bringing the Germans over, paid the balance of £150 sterling due on their passage in default of which they would have been sold as servants, and settled them at Germanna on the Rappahannock, then a part of Essex County. Twelve miles beyond the patrol of the rangers, their settlement defended one of the most exposed parts of the frontier. The 3229 acres upon which they were located, known as the Germanna Tract, was granted by patent on October 31, 1716, to William Robertson, clerk of the council, by whom it was

[1] Spotswood to Nathaniel Harrison, March 28, 1724, *C.O.5/1319*, p. 386.

conveyed the following month to Spotswood,[2] the first land in Virginia which the governor held in his private capacity. According to Spotswood the Germans, who as aliens could not leave property to their children, preferred leasing their land from the governor for life to owning it outright. When they needed more land he acquired the Wilderness Tract of 3065 acres by granting it on November 2, 1719, to Richard Hickman,[3] clerk in the secretary's office, who transferred it to the governor a month later. Shortly thereafter the Germans became dissatisfied and moved off Spotswood's land. The governor thereupon purchased servants and slaves to develop it.[4] Not far distant was the Fork Tract of 1920 acres located in the fork of the Rappahannock and the Rapidan. This had been granted to Harry Beverley by patent on November 2, 1705, and was conveyed by him to Spotswood on April 22, 1720. Spotswood also held in the vicinity the Barrows Tract of 177 acres, though how this came into his possession is not known.[5]

In February 1717 Sir Richard Blackmore wrote to Secretary Cocke that he and several other men in England intended to establish iron works in Virginia, and asked him to interest the governor in the project. Spotswood thereupon set his Germans to hunt for ore, spending in this way over £60. Two years later Sir Richard decided to drop the project, and Spotswood resolved to carry it on with nine or ten Virginians as partners. The Mine Tract of 15,000 acres was taken up, the patent being issued to Robert Beverley and Thomas Jones on February 20, 1719. This tract appears finally to have come into the exclusive possession of the governor.[6]

[2] *C.O.5/1318*, p. 484; *C.O.5/1319*, p. 367.

[3] Spotswood later justified his practice of granting land to others in trust for himself on the ground that he did it in good faith, making no secret of the fact to the council, in the belief that he could not be both grantor and grantee. Spotswood to Harrison, March 28, 1724, *Ibid.*, pp. 385, 386.

[4] *Ibid.*, pp. 367, 387.

[5] *Ibid.*, p. 367; *C.O.5/1320*, p. 193.

[6] *C.O.5/1319*, pp. 367, 387, 388. The letter written by Spotswood to Nathaniel Harrison in 1724 from which most of the details of the circumstances under which the former acquired his various holdings are drawn,

Further down the Rappahannock, on Massaponax Creek, some distance below the present city of Fredericksburg, Spotswood acquired some other holdings. A tract of 3650 acres there had been mortgaged for 1000 years by Charles Smith to Messrs. Micajah and Richard Perry, and assigned by them on April 27, 1720, to Spotswood, Thomas Jones, John Baylor, and Robert Beverley. Out of this the governor eventually obtained the Lower Massaponax Tract of 1350 acres and the Upper Massaponax Tract of 500.[7]

Thus at the time of the erection of Spotsylvania County, Spotswood controlled, if he did not own outright, some 25,000 acres, all of which appears to have been located in what was theretofore Essex County. Upon some of this quit rents had been paid for several years, and either importation or treasury rights must have been furnished for all of it. The boundary of Spotsylvania, as we have seen, started from Snow Creek. This was just below Massaponax Creek, and all the holdings of the governor thus fell within the new county, as did the holdings of a number of other men, a total of about 125,000 acres. According to Spotswood this was done because of the great distance, in some cases ninety miles, from court houses and churches in the old counties,[8] while Drysdale contended that it was "artfully contrived" to secure exemption from quit rents.[9] In any case, since the boundary was fixed by act of assembly the blame cannot be placed upon the governor alone. From the assembly, too, came the representation to the crown which, conveying as it did the decided impression that all land in the new counties still remained unpatented, fell short

---

gives the impression that the lands came into his possession by a chain of events over which he had very little control, and almost in spite of what he could do. This may well be doubted. Several years later Byrd gossiped with Chiswell "of Colo. Spotswood, and his Strategems to shake off his Partners, and secure all his Mines to himself." Byrd, *Writings*, p. 351. But Spotswood's statement of the bare facts of the case is probably sufficiently accurate, for he was well aware that Harrison was in a position to verify it.

[7] *C.O.5/1319*, pp. 367, 368; *C.O.5/1320*, pp. 193, 194.

[8] *Ibid.*, p. 225.

[9] Drysdale to B. T., June 6, 1724, *C.O.5/1319*, p. 350.

of scrupulous honesty. Yet if these actions be worthy of censure, the greater part must fall upon the king's representative.

On December 23, 1720, the very night that the governor signed the act erecting the two new counties, the council granted a number of petitions for land in Spotsylvania, amounting in all to 91,500 acres.[10] No patents, however, were issued for some time, since the crown had not yet acted upon the assembly's petition. Otherwise, the governor had at this time as complete control over the granting of titles as his heart could well desire. The council had authorized him to issue patents when it was not in session,[11] and upon the death in 1720 of Secretary Cocke, Spotswood neglected to appoint anyone to succeed him, and continued until the close of his administration to exercise that office himself.[12] Richard Hickman, clerk in the secretary's office, was a willing tool. Among the licences to take up land approved by the council was one to Hickman and his partners for 20,000 acres adjoining the Germanna and Iron Mine Tracts, which Spotswood desired for the production of naval stores.

Robert Beverley had, previous to 1710, surveyed some 13,000 acres of "excellent Land among ye little Mountains." For this he had paid rights, but had not taken out patents before the proclamation of 1710 imposed terms of seating and planting which could only be fulfilled in so isolated a location by a settlement sufficiently strong to resist Indian attack. His rights therefore lay in abeyance until the opportunity presented itself of forming such a settlement by freeing a number of German families imported under indenture in 1717. He invited the governor to join in the enterprise, and with some other partners the Spotsylvania Company was formed. Beverley assigned his surveys to the company, being reimbursed for the rights he had paid. Some seventy Germans

[10] *Ex. Jour. Coun.*, III, 538, 539. Both Ludwell and Byrd were absent during these proceedings.

[11] *Ibid.*, p. 401.

[12] Grymes to Leheup, May 25, 1724, *C.O.5/1320*, p. 64.

were settled upon the tract as free men in twenty-odd tenements, close together for purposes of defense. They were provided with cattle, and Spotswood declared in 1724 that they had not up to that time been charged any rent. Other Germans, whose terms of service were expiring, desired to settle here also, and it was later decided to enlarge the tract to 40,000 acres so as to include within it contiguous pine land suitable for the production of naval stores. As in other enterprises, all the other partners either died or withdrew, and the governor was left in possession of the 40,000 acre Spotsylvania Company Tract,[13] all of which was doubtless surveyed shortly after the erection of Spotsylvania. Thus the surveys which had been made in Spotsylvania, the patents for which were being held up pending the action of the crown upon the assembly's memorial, included some 60,000 acres of the governor's.

Just when it was that certain tidings of his removal reached Spotswood is not known, but it cannot be doubted that by the spring of 1722 he realized that he was about to be superseded, and that Commissary Blair had the ear of his successor.[14] Delay seemed hazardous and the council, several of whose number were also interested, advised the governor to grant the

[13] *C.O.5/1319*, pp. 368, 388, 389; *C.O.5/1320*, pp. 193, 194. Spotswood later declared that he spent over £5000 in buying up the rights of his partners and of others who had pretensions to his holdings. *C.O.5/1320*, p. 225.

[14] "*Afterwards when it was rumoured yt a new Governor was coming over*, some Persons apprehending yt Difficulties might arise from a Gentleman who was entirely a Stranger to ye Constitution & Practice of ye Colony, press'd to have their Patents sign'd: but more especially when it was understood yt Parson Blair was likely to act as Prime Minister, those who dreaded ye exercise of any Power lodged in him, & were sensible yt he could less injure them by his open Vote on ye General Court, than by his Secret Advice to ye Governor, chose to secure in time their Lands by a Title, wch nothing but ye Law could set aside, & where they had a dernier Resort to his Majesty's Justice; rather than venture to let them lye any longer unpatented, & consequently depend upon his Courtesie for a Grant of them." *C.O.5/1319*, pp. 533, 534. In another place, Spotswood declared that in view of the conduct of his successor, he could not but think it a lucky precaution on his part to have secured his land before Drysdale took over the government. *Ibid.*, pp. 539, 540. See also Grymes to Leheup, May 25, 1724, *C.O.5/1320*, p. 63.

patents forthwith, taking security for the payment of rights in case the crown should not remit them.[15] Accordingly, between May 8 and July 27, 1722, he issued patents for nearly 179,000 acres of new land in Spotsylvania.[16] By one of these, dated June 22, the 40,000 acre Spotsylvania Company Tract was granted to Thomas Jones, John Clayton, and Richard Hickman in trust for Spotswood, while on July 21 there was granted to Richard Hickman a tract of 28,000 acres.[17] Since, however, this grant included the Germanna, Wilderness, and Fork Tracts, only 19,786 acres of new land was involved, this being evidently the 20,000 the survey of which was authorized in 1720. Thus at the termination of his administration Spotswood held 85,027 acres in Spotsylvania County.[18] His title to only 25,000, granted before the erection of Spotsylvania, was above dispute in point of law.

Immediately upon their erection Hanover and King George became full-fledged counties, and sent burgesses to the assembly of 1722. County government was not organized in Spotsylvania until 1723, and Brunswick remained unorganized until 1732.[19] The first burgesses from Spotsylvania, Larkin Chew and Francis Thornton, took their seats in May 1723,[20] William Bledsoe being appointed sheriff during the same month.[21] No quit rents had been demanded by Spotswood from the county which bore his name, not even for land

[15] *Ex. Jour. Coun.*, IV, 11. Part of this entry is rewritten over an erasure. Any serious misinterpretation of the council's action would, however, assuredly have been detected.

[16] *C.O.5/1319*, p. 363. Before the arrival of the order in council of the lords justices, Drysdale added some 30,000 acres more. *Ibid.*, pp. 363, 364.

[17] This came later to be known as the Alexandria Tract. *C.O.5/1320*, p. 273.

[18] *Ibid.*, pp. 193, 194. This is the account given by Spotswood, and followed by the board of trade in its representation to the crown. *C.O.5/1365*, p. 329. Drysdale placed the total at 86,650, leaving out the Barrow Tract and including all the Massaponax Tract, though stating that Spotswood probably did not own it all. *C.O.5/1319*, pp. 367, 368. The colonel also had an interest in some land at Christanna, but permitted it to lapse with the termination of his administration. *Ibid.*, pp. 389, 390.

[19] *Ex. Jour. Coun.*, IV, 9, 266.

[20] *Jour. Burg.*, 1712-1726, p. 364.

[21] *Ex. Jour. Coun.*, IV, 34.

which had paid rents before its erection, and soon after Drysdale's arrival the council unanimously advised that this policy be continued until the royal pleasure was known.[22] Here the matter rested until the arrival of the order of the lords justices.[23] The council then decided that land in Spotsylvania and Brunswick which had paid quit rents before their erection was still liable to these payments, and that all those who had taken up more than 1000 acres were excluded from the benefits of the recent remission and must therefore pay both quit rents and rights. Surveyors were ordered for the future not to receive entries for more than 1000 acres, or to make surveys for land already entered in excess of that quantity.[24] The action of the council merely confirmed the policy which the government had already decided to adopt, and which had been communicated to Spotswood three days before by Nathaniel Harrison, the deputy auditor.

Faced thus with the prospect of exclusion from any remission of rights or of quit rents, the colonel surmised "that aim has been taken at my Possessions, by those who have first broached the Notion that a Restriction of Lands peculiar to these two Counties would be most for his Majesty's Interest."[25] Replying to Harrison he denied that he had been prompted by self-interest alone in acquiring his lands, and described the manner in which these had come into his possession, saying that if the auditor, who had been closely in touch with his administration, did not contradict his statements, others ought to be satisfied of their truth.[26] He then gave his own interpretation to the order of the lords justices, namely that all persons settling within the two counties were to be exempted from the payment of rights and quit rents from May 1, 1721 to May 1, 1728, and that the restriction as to acreage was an instruction to the governor not to grant larger

[22] *Ibid.*, IV, 27.
[23] *Supra*, p. 249.
[24] *Ex. Jour. Coun.*, IV, 61, 62.
[25] Spotswood to Nathaniel Harrison, March 28, 1724, *C.O.5/1319*, p. 385.
[26] *Ibid.*, pp. 385-395. This material has already been drawn upon in the preceding account.

patents. This applied to future grants, for it could not be observed before it was received. As interpreted by the council, the order would exempt only two grants, totalling 1400 acres. These would pay a nominal quit rent of 28*s.*, which according to the usual mode of payment would yield about 10*s.* That the remission of such a trifle should have provoked so much discussion before three great government boards in England was in Spotswood's opinion preposterous. The board of trade, the ex-governor declared, knew from reports which he had sent them of the large grants which had been made in Spotsylvania. Had they intended that these be excluded from the benefit of the exemption, they would expressly have said so in their representation. The established maxim was to construe acts of charity and bounty in the most liberal sense. The object of the order was to encourage the thick settlement of the frontier. This the large landholder would be compelled to do as effectively as the small, in order to make the improvements on his property enjoined by the conditions of seating and planting. Many people believed, Spotswood declared after striving to reconcile his conduct with the established custom of Virginia and with his instructions, "that I am the Jonas that brings all these Storms & hard Constructions upon them; & if I must be thrown overboard before all those who have embarked with me can be saved, . . . I was not in the Prophets Case, Guilty of Wilful Disobedience."[27]

Everything considered, Spotswood's interpretation of the order appears to have been well designed to produce the results desired by the British authorities,[28] and that a council of landholders should have placed a different construction upon it indicates the satisfaction derived in some quarters from seeing the former governor in difficulty. At that, the council was not long in awakening to the fact that the interests of Spotswood were now one with their own, for on April 23

[27] *C.O.5/1319*, p. 395.

[28] Since the latter were in obvious ignorance of the conditions prevailing in Spotsylvania, it is impossible to state, in terms of the situation on the spot, precisely what their meaning was. The provisions of the royal concession certainly went far to defeat its purpose.

they decided that limiting the size of land grants was contrary to the interests of the crown, and therefore proposed that the board of trade be requested to secure the removal of that restriction.[29] The governor held that it was the pleasure of the crown that no one hold more than 1000 acres in the new counties.[30] To this the council agreed, but it was decided that since no instructions had been received concerning the large tracts the whole matter should be referred to the board of trade. In the meantime no rights or quit rents were to be demanded from the large tracts, since this might be construed as conferring a title to them. At the same time William Bledsoe, sheriff of Spotsylvania, was called to account for having failed to comply with the governor's warrant for receiving the quit rents of Spotsylvania. Appearing before the board, he stated that he was advised by Colonel Spotswood not to meddle with the collection of quit rents, but to write a letter of excuse to the auditor, the colonel drawing up a letter for him, a copy of which he produced to the council. It being apparent that Bledsoe had received no quit rents for which to account, he was dismissed. On the same day Thomas Chew was appointed to take his place.[31]

Sorely perplexed by the Spotsylvania land situation, Drysdale resubmitted the problem to the board of trade. Not only was he at a loss to know whether the exemption of quit rents and rights extended to the larger grants; he doubted the validity of these grants themselves. If the order in council were retroactive must not all grants over 1000 acres be void? If it were not, did not the failure to pay rights invalidate them? The latter consideration did not seem so serious from the point of view of Virginia precedent. The practice of accepting treasury rights in lieu of importation rights had no legal founda-

[29] Drysdale to B. T., July 10, 1724, *C.O.5/1319*, p. 397; *Ex. Jour. Coun.*, IV, 64.

[30] In other words, he considered the larger grants invalid. This view had been suggested to him by the receiver-general, John Grymes, who made no secret of the animosity which existed between himself and the ex-governor. Grymes to Leheup, May 25, 1724, *C.O.5/1320*, pp. 63, 64.

[31] *Ex. Jour. Coun.*, IV, 63, 64, 68.

tion save the executive action of the council,[32] which therefore contended (as if one act of usurpation were just ground for another) that it might waive the treasury rights altogether without consulting the crown.[33] It thus appears not unreasonable that Spotswood should waive the rights temporarily upon the advice of the council. Yet Drysdale was technically correct in calling such action illegal. The bonds which had been furnished in lieu of rights presented another problem. Only two, it was said, had been drawn up in accordance with the council's recommendation, the patentees promising to pay the rights upon demand.[34] Thereafter Spotswood had authorized the substitution of bonds which gave the patentees the option, if rights were demanded, of paying them or of surrendering their patents. Most questionable of all the new grants were the two which Spotswood had made upon his own behalf, for he had omitted to give any bond at all,[35] and the patent for the Alexandria Tract was not even recorded in the secretary's office.[36] Were not these grants therefore void? These and many other questions arose in Drysdale's mind, and it was doubtless with much relief that he referred them to his superiors.[37] He said nothing at this time of the council's opposition to restricting the size of land grants, but reported it the following month.[38]

[32] *Supra*, p. 140 n.

[33] Memorial of Coun. to B. T., Dec. 12, 1722, *C.O.5/1319*, pp. 175, 176. Curiously enough, this claim provoked no comment from the board of trade.

[34] *Ibid.*, p. 346.

[35] According to Spotswood, this was an inadvertency. Upon his return from New York, he had offered to pay any demands of the government, but Grymes had refused to receive either rights or quit rents, lest this should make good his title. *C.O.5/1320*, pp. 193, 194. In March 1724, while protesting against his construction of the order of the lords justices, Spotswood renewed the offer to Harrison. *C.O.5/1319*, p. 390.

[36] This, Spotswood declared, was probably due to the fact that he had told the clerk not to record it until he had checked up an error which he suspected in the survey. *Ibid.*, p. 389.

[37] Drysdale to B. T., June 6, 1724, together with five enclosures, *Ibid.*, pp. 345-373, particularly in this connection, enclosure no. 5, pp. 371-373.

[38] Drysdale to B. T., July 10, 1724, *Ibid.*, p. 397.

The prospect of exemption from quit rents and rights had led Spotswood to take up more land than he would otherwise have done. Especially was this true of the extensive pine lands and uplands upon which he intended to produce naval stores. The hostile attitude of the government of Virginia now filled him with misgivings. His grants might be declared illegal, thus depriving him of his land, but even if held valid but subject to the payment of rights and quit rents, this might entail so great an expense that their use for the production of naval stores would be unprofitable. Should this prove the case, Spotswood had made it clear that he intended to surrender some of his land.[39] But here lay another difficulty, for the government had entertained the opinion that even though the patents were surrendered the rights would still be due, since in the case of land lapsing for non-seating and planting, rights were never refunded to the patentee. It might also be difficult to surrender part of a patent, and retain the rest.[40] His position was precarious, and in the spring of 1724 Spotswood prepared to go to England to defend his interests.[41]

Spotswood informed the board of trade that he was deterred from returning to England to give an account of his conduct promptly upon the close of his administration by the danger of exposing himself in an unarmed vessel to the mercies of the pirates, who were determined to be revenged upon him. Anxious to avoid all appearance of interfering with the administration, he had removed as far as possible from the seat of

[39] *C.O.5/1319*, p. 390. Experience had shown, Spotswood later declared, that tar could not be made according to the directions of the act of parliament without the skill of the Finland tarburners, nor could hemp be raised to perfection from English or East Country seed. Memorial of Spotswood to Crown, *C.O.5/1320*, p. 57. Yet it was declared after testing a sample of Virginia hemp, furnished by Spotswood, that it was considerably superior to the best Russia, and equal in strength to the best Riga. Officers of Woolwich Naval Yard to [Admiralty?]. Oct. 27, 1725. *C.O.5/1321*, p. 23. In 1723 Spotswood produced nineteen hundredweight of hemp. *Spotsylvania Co. Order Book*, 1722-1724, p. 29.

[40] *C.O.5/1319*, pp. 371-373.

[41] This was not the sole reason for his voyage. He was married shortly after his arrival in the mother country.

government and devoted himself to the production of naval stores.[42] In this retreat he had hoped to remain unmolested, but Drysdale had employed Larkin Chew to spy upon him and his neighbors. Chew, whom Spotswood had formerly employed as a common carpenter,[43] had gone so far when drunk as to lay violent hands upon the ex-governor at his own door and before his servants. For this Spotswood had "sufficiently corrected him," but had nevertheless hoped that Drysdale would support the dignity of the chief executive by showing some displeasure at insults offered to one who had so recently held that position. Instead, Larkin Chew and his "saucy son," both of whom lost no opportunity of openly affronting the ex-governor, were showered with new marks of favor. Chew had threatened all the sober justices, and had finally succeeded in having them turned out of the commission of the peace.[44] He had induced people to sign papers reflecting upon Spotswood's character. He had contrived a petition to the assembly proposing that the sites upon which Spotswood was erecting wharves and warehouses for shipping his naval stores be taken for town lands.[45] He had prompted the surveyors of highways not to repair roads and bridges used by the ex-governor's carriages, and had instigated his tenants not to discharge any of their obligations to him, but to "run with idle stories to this Governor, who will be sure to stand by them."[46] Since

[42] It is to be noted that he made no mention at this time of his iron industry.

[43] The extensive licences to take up land granted to Chew during Spotswood's administration suggest that he was a man of means. *Ex. Jour. Coun.*, *passim.*

[44] Commissions of the peace for Spotsylvania were issued with marked frequency. *Ibid.*, IV, *passim.* It seems, however, that Chew was not alone in interfering with the county court, for about this time the council received from several of the justices a letter "complaining of sundry interruptions given them in the Administration of Justice by Col° Spotswood." A copy of this complaint was ordered transmitted to the colonel. *Ibid.*, p. 72.

[45] In 1726 the burgesses referred to the next session a petition from Spotsylvania for laying out two towns, one of which was to be on fifty acres of land at the mouth of Massaponax Creek. *Jour. Burg.*, 1712-1726, p. 410.

[46] A petition of "Zeriechias Flishman and George Ouds in behalf of themselves and fourteen other high-Germans," residing in Spotsylvania County near Germanna, was read in council in April 1724, complaining that Spotswood had unjustly sued them in the county court for breach of an agree-

the conduct of Chew was countenanced by the governor, and those in authority seemed bent upon ruining both his reputation and his fortune, he thought it high time to return home to lay his case before the board of trade. He was therefore about to obtain passage to the northward incognito in order to escape the pirates, intending to proceed thence to England.[47]

The Spotsylvania land question was referred by the board of trade to Attorney-General Yorke and Solicitor-General Wearg, who after hearing what Spotswood and the Virginia agent had to offer upon the subject made their report in January 1726. The grants for more than 1000 acres were not on that account void, there being no law or instruction restricting grants at the time they were made. However, they were not entitled to exemption from rights or quit rents. These were due on the entire tract. The patentee must pay for all or surrender all but 1000 acres. Where patents had been granted upon the consideration of rights, and neither rights nor adequate security for them had been given, such grants were a deceit upon the crown, and might be repealed by law if the crown so desired, but it would be inadvisable to take advantage of patents issued since May 1, 1721, for non-payment of rights if they otherwise conformed to the order of the lords justices.[48] Where bonds were given either to pay rights or to surrender the patent, if the patent were surrendered the crown had no remedy to secure the rights. The large grants made by Spotswood to others in trust for himself without paying or giving security for rights, were in point of law a deceit upon the crown, and might be repealed. However, they might be made good if the crown saw fit to accept the rights, though

---

ment made with them upon consideration of money advanced to them upon their transportation. The council ordered that since the petitioners were poor and ignorant of the law they be represented by the person acting as deputy attorney for the crown in Spotsylvania, in order to insure them a fair trial. A new commission of the peace was issued at the same time, this doubtless being the change which Spotswood complained was engineered by Chew. *Ex. Jour. Coun.*, IV, 64, 65.

[47] Spotswood to B. T., June 16, 1724, *C.O.5/1319*, pp. 379-382.

[48] That is, were 1000 acres or less per person.

not by a mere tender of these rights by the former governor. The failure to enter a patent upon record did not invalidate it.[49]

The law as laid down by Yorke and Wearg not merely excluded Spotswood from all the benefits of the order of the lords justices, but placed it within the power of the crown to annul his title to somewhat more than half of his holdings. That the colonel was very active in setting forth his actions in their most favorable light is therefore not surprising. His land had not been acquired at the expense of the interests of others. Grants of land in large quantities were common in Virginia,[50] and had proved the most effective way of settling the frontier. The rapidity with which Spotsylvania had developed as compared with Brunswick was due, not as Drysdale had stated to the better facilities of water transportation, for the contrary was the case, but to the protection from the Indians which the strong settlements planted by Spotswood afforded to the inhabitants.[51] "And to deprive a Man of his Possessions, after he has bore ye Brunt of ye Danger, & maintained them 'til the Terror of the Indians is over; after he had Expended thereon more than double their prime Value; After he has cleared Grounds, fenced Fields, builded Houses, made Roades & Bridges, Set up Mills, drove out Stocks of Cattle, transported Household Goods, removed Families of Women and Children, with all ye Necessaries of Life to support People in the wild Woods; & in short, after he has passed through ye immense Troubles, Fatigues, Dangers, & Expences, wch are inseparable from new Settlements in America, whenever they are made at any distance from ye Seated part of ye Country: to Dispossess him then of his Lands, for a meer Chicane in Words, & to transfer his Improvements to Others, who never had the Courage or Industry, to gain an Acre of Land out of the Woods, where there was either Danger or

[49] *C.O.5/1319*, pp. 479-487.

[50] At this very time, Drysdale was frequently making grants of 10,000 acres and above in other parts of Virginia. *Ex. Jour. Coun., passim.*

[51] By 1726 the militia of Spotsylvania numbered 75 horse and 294 foot. *C.O.5/1320*, p. 111.

Difficulty; would be such an Oppressive Act & cruel Proceeding, as would in no wise resemble Royal Justice."[52]

In May 1727, after numerous deliberations upon a voluminous quantity of material,[53] the board sent a representation to the crown recommending that Spotswood be allowed to hold all his lands free from rights and quit rents for the seven-year period. This they proposed the more readily because he had imported some three hundred white persons into Virginia, and had made upon his lands improvements which would have entitled him to hold an even greater quantity had it been taken up upon the conditions enjoined by Virginia law.[54] Two months later the representation of the board was referred to a committee of the council.[55] The committee, after both the agent for Virginia[56] and counsel for Spotswood had appeared before it, and the lord president had discussed the matter with Townshend and Walpole, recommended in December 1728 that Spotswood be permitted to retain possession of his land. The governor should issue new patents in place of the two of questionable validity issued in 1722 for a total of 59,786 new acres, and upon this much of his holdings Spotswood should be exempt from quit rents for the seven years, now expired, following May 1, 1721, but in accordance with his own proposals he should when the new patents were issued supply the customary rights.[57] This recommendation, which was confirmed by an order in council in February 1729, was prompted by the considerations that the revenue would

[52] *C.O.5/1320*, p. 201.

[53] *C.O.5/1319*, pp. 531-541; *C.O.5/1320*, pp. 5-226, *passim; C.O.391/33*, pp. 307, 308; *C.O.391/34*, pp. 8, 9; *C.O.391/35*, pp. 17-369, *passim; C.O.391/36*, pp. 26-116, *passim.*

[54] *C.O.5/1365*, pp. 325-335; *C.O.5/1320*, pp. 273, 274.

[55] *Acts of Privy Coun., Col.*, III, 168.

[56] The agent offered no objection to Spotswood's retaining his lands. *Ibid.*, p. 170.

[57] It was perhaps the necessity for additional funds occasioned by this order which led Spotswood to put in a claim for the balance of his expenses on his embassy to Albany. Payment was delayed until 1733 when, the council being in a generous mood, he was given over half as much again as he had claimed. *Ex. Jour. Coun.*, IV, 225-314, *passim; C.O.5/1322*, pp. 114, 137-141, 427, 429; *C.O.5/1366*, p. 84; *C.O.391/39*, p. 253; *C.O.391/41*, p. 73.

suffer by taking land from the colonel, for in that case it would not begin to pay quit rents so soon, Spotswood being obliged to pay from then on; and that despite irregularities Spotswood had done more than any other to further the work for which the frontier counties had been erected and granted special privileges. He was doubtless more willing, or at least in a better position, to carry on the work of populating the frontier region and producing naval stores than those to whom his patents would otherwise pass.[58]

The question of Spotswood's lands was thus settled, but the status of the other holders of large patents in Spotsylvania still remained undetermined. In November 1728 Governor Gooch had written to the board of trade of the difficulty which was being encountered in forming a rent roll for Spotsylvania. The period of exemption from quit rents and rights had now expired, but the government was still at a loss to know how to treat the large patentees. Hitherto it had refrained from demanding either rights or quit rents, and had declined to accept them when tendered, lest this should be construed as confirming the patents.[59] What course was it now to pursue? Gooch, whose attitude towards this situation was in striking contrast to that of Drysdale, stated that while these patentees had done wrong in proceeding so far without the crown's approval, they had nevertheless made improvements, impossible upon small tracts, in the absence of which the settlement of the country must have proceeded at a much slower rate. He therefore hoped that the favor which Spotswood appeared to deserve might be extended to the other patentees also. He thought that it would be equitable to exempt them from rights but to demand quit rents from the time of the patent. To demand rights would occasion lawsuits over the bonds given for their payment.[60] Before this suggestion reached the board of trade, the order in council concerning

[58] *Acts of Privy Coun., Col.*, III, 168-171; *C.O.5/1321*, pp. 201-206.

[59] See also in this connection Drysdale to B. T., July 10, 1726, *C.O.5/1320*, p. 134.

[60] Gooch to B. T., Nov. 6, 1728, *C.O.5/1321*, pp. 213-215.

Spotswood's lands had been issued. Upon hearing of this the Virginia council, supposing that a similar course would be pursued in the case of the other patentees, ordered that rights be immediately demanded from them also, together with quit rents from May 1, 1728. The arrears of quit rents before that date were not to be demanded until the royal pleasure was known.[61] Contrary to expectations, however, in the case of the other grants the crown acted in accordance with the suggestion of Gooch, not with the precedent set in Spotswood's case. The quit rents were to be demanded, but upon the payment of the arrears of quit rents, all holders of not more than 6000 acres were excused from the payment of rights. Holders of more than 6000 acres were to pay both quit rents and rights for all land in excess of that amount.[62] The Virginia council had therefore to reverse itself, and with this final flurry in 1730 the vexatious land question in Spotsylvania and Brunswick came to an end.[63]

While the growth of Brunswick was slow, that of Spotsylvania was phenomenal. In 1726 the former had 160 tithables, the latter 950.[64] The clearest evidence of frontier expansion is to be found in the quit rent accounts. At the time of its division by the erection of Orange County, Spotsylvania had a patented acreage far greater than that of any other county, and was paying one-sixth of the royal quit rents of the province.[65] The account of the sale of treasury rights is also suggestive,

[61] *Ex. Jour. Coun.*, IV, 208. In Spotswood's case rights and quit rents from May 1, 1728, were ordered demanded upon the entire 59,728 acres mentioned in the order in council. But this included the two surveys of Robert Beverley, amounting to between 13,000 and 14,000 acres, upon which it was claimed rights had already been paid.

[62] *C.O.391/38*, pp. 121, 122, 218, 219; *C.O.5/1366*, pp. 38-47.

[63] *Ex. Jour. Coun.*, IV, 214, 228, 229.

[64] *C.O.5/1320*, pp. 107, 111. Three years later these had increased to 1394. *Spotsylvania Co. Order Book*, 1724-1730, p. 355. The fact that Brunswick produced Oronoco tobacco and Spotsylvania sweetscented doubtless had something to do with the relatively rapid growth of the latter.

[65] From £45.8.10½ on 45,444 acres in 1723-1724, the quit-rent revenue from Spotsylvania grew in ten years to £496.0.4¼ on 551,289. Brunswick first appears upon the rent roll in 1729 with 51,427 acres, which by 1735 had grown to 164,537. *C.O.5/1319-1323*, *passim*.

for while land continued to be taken up in the older counties, the great increase in the sale of rights was unquestionably due to the westward movement.[66]

In 1730 the sheriffs of Spotsylvania and Hanover were allowed thirty per cent on the quit rent tobacco they collected, since many of the plantations were sixty and even eighty miles from navigable water, a plain indication of the advance of settlement into the interior.[67] The exemption from the payment of public levies for ten years had expedited this movement, as had also the remission of rights and quit rents by the crown, though the effectiveness of the latter concession had been greatly impaired by the long delay attending its final explanation.[68] The efforts made by Spotswood to secure the frontier from attack, not only by erecting fortified settlements, but by his negotiations with the Five Nations together with his policy of settling people upon his extensive holdings, had militated in the same direction. The conclusion is unavoidable, however, that underlying economic forces were thrusting the population westward. The low price of tobacco made imperative its large-scale production upon unexhausted soil. Such soil was to be found in unlimited quantities only in the west.

It is improbable that Spotswood ever held office in Spotsylvania County. To do so after once having occupied the position of chief executive of the province would have been an anticlimax little to the liking of so proud a spirit. Yet that he

[66] The revenue from the sale of treasury rights was as follows:

Average for years 1709-1717	£ 84.14. 9¼
Average for years 1717-1721	205. 4. 6¼
For the year ending April 1722	228.19. 0¼
For the year ending April 1723	338.14.10
For the year ending April 1724	416.10. 6
For the year ending April 1725	723. 1. 5¼
For the year ending April 1726	460.13. 3¾
For the year ending April 1727	737. 7. 7½
For the year ending April 1728	699.17. 7¾

C.O.5/1316-1320, passim.

[67] *Ex. Jour. Coun.*, IV, 214.

[68] The discouragement from this source was great, and some who had secured patents failed to prosecute their undertakings. The 12,000 acres granted on June 21, 1722 to Cole Diggs, Peter Beverley, and John Robinson was permitted to lapse by non-cultivation. *Ibid.*, p. 180.

should passively resign all share in the direction of the affairs of a locality in which he was so vitally interested was not to be expected. As we have seen, the money appropriated by the assembly for erecting public buildings in Spotsylvania and for providing the settlers with arms was placed in his hands, and the way in which this was spent soon gave rise to complaint. The court was held in a room of Spotswood's house;[69] the church, also on his own property, seemed likely to benefit few inhabitants other than the Germanna Germans; while both, almost entirely surrounded for a distance of eight or ten miles by land belonging to the colonel, were inconviently located for four-fifths of the people.[70] In 1726 the assembly authorized the erection by subscription of a courthouse in Spotsylvania at a more convenient place.[71] The burgesses declined to make any allowance for the buildings erected by the colonel until they were legally conveyed to county and parish respectively.[72] They also held that Spotswood had overcharged for the arms he had imported. The account of the £500 appropriated for buying arms for Brunswick County was only settled when, in 1738, the attorney-general obtained a judgment against Spotswood for nearly half that sum.[73]

As we have seen, Spotswood became engaged in exploiting

[69] When in April 1724 Spotswood announced that the courthouse, prison, pillory, and stocks were practically finished, he specified which *rooms* he was prepared to surrender to the county. The county court then appeared well satisfied. *Spotsylvania Co. Order Book*, 1722-1724, p. 67.

[70] *Cal. Va. State Paps.*, I, 208, 209. In 1732 the assembly changed the county seat to Fredericksburg (Hening, IV, 364, 365), while as to the church, William Byrd records the same year that "some pious people had lately burnt it down, with intent to get another built nearer to their own homes." *Writings*, p. 356.

[71] Drysdale to B. T., July 10, 1726, *C.O.5/1320*, p. 127. In October 1726, when one of the numerous commissions of the peace was issued for Spotsylvania, instead of the usual terse statement of the fact, the council minutes record that the board, having had under consideration the settling of the commission of the peace for Spotsylvania, had nominated such persons as seemed most fit for the office of justice and most likely to attend to their duty. *Ex. Jour. Coun.*, IV, 116. Evidently the problem presented difficulties.

[72] In 1733 Spotswood purchased the courthouse and prison at Germanna from the county for ten pounds. *Spotsylvania Co. Order Book*, 1730-1738, p. 183.

[73] *Jour. Burg.*, 1727-1740, pp. 34, 35, 331, 377.

Virginia's iron deposits at least as early as 1717. Fifteen years later, when Byrd called him "the Tubal Cain of Virginia," Spotswood "corrected me a little there, by assuring me he was not only the first in this Country, but the first in North America, who had erected a regular Furnace. That they ran altogether upon Bloomerys in New England & Pennsilvania, till his Example had made them attempt greater Works."[74] Jones described Spotswood's undertakings with the zeal of a promoter. The facilities for the iron industry were excellent. "This Iron has been proved to be good, and 'tis thought, will come at as cheap a Rate as any imported from other Places; so that 'tis to be hoped *Col. Spotswood's Works* will in a small Time prove very advantageous to *Great Britain*, which undoubtedly will be carried to greater Perfection and universal Benefit, by his skilful Management and indefatigable Application to such noble Undertakings and glorious Projects."[75] In a somewhat different spirit, but testifying even more positively to the progress which had been made, Drysdale wrote to the board of trade in 1723, "I judge it part of my duty to inform your Ldspps. of an affair, that is at present the common Theme of peoples Discourses, and employs their thoughts. Coll Spotswoods Iron workes; he has brought itt to that perfection that he now sells by publick auction at Wms:burgh, backs and frames for Chymnies, Potts, doggs, frying, stewing, and baking panns, some of these utensils, are sett up at 2d per pound. others at 3d per pound, and so rise in their price as peoples inclinations or wants encourage them to bidd."[76]

Gooch realized that he could best serve the Virginia iron industry by minimizing its importance. In 1734 he wrote to the board of trade that there were four furnaces in Virginia,

[74] Byrd, *Writings*, p. 358. Spotswood is mistaken here. Not bloomeries alone, but blast furnaces and forges had been in operation in New England some seventy years earlier. To Spotswood, however, would seem to belong the credit for erecting the first air furnace in America. *Massachusetts Historical Collections*, Fourth Series, VII, p. 403; *Proceedings of the Massachusetts Historical Society*, Second Series, VIII, p. 13 ff.

[75] *Present State of Virginia*, pp. 57, 58.

[76] Drysdale to B. T., May 16, 1723, *C.O.5/1319*, pp. 208, 209.

all employed in running pig iron which, being sent to Britain to be forged, was considered beneficial to trade. Forges for making bar iron had long been discussed and one was now built, though not yet in operation.[77] There was no intention of manufacturing for exportation. Pots, andirons, and backs for fireplaces were made for local use. There was one air furnace where they made a variety of articles. This had cost the owner a great deal of money.[78] Two years later the governor wrote that iron works might continue in Virginia for a time, since the persons employed in that industry were prevented by the act of 1727 from raising tobacco. However, there was so little encouragement for the importation of pig iron into Britain that he doubted if it would continue for long. The forge was now turning out bar iron to supply the local market, brisk in the winter time when the shipments from Britain were exhausted. If this trade were encouraged, a large quantity of bar iron might be furnished by Virginia for the British markets. The products of the air furnace (boxes for cart wheels were now also made) were sold to people calling for them at the furnaces, and were also marketed elsewhere in the colony. When opportunity offered, they were exported to other parts of America and to the British West Indies but this, Gooch thought, did not have any considerable effect upon the trade of Great Britain.[79] In 1739 the four furnaces for pig iron, the forge, and the air furnace were still in operation, but Gooch assured the board of trade that there was little profit in these enterprises. There was sent to London and Bristol about 1500 tons of pig iron a year, while the output of the forge amounted to twenty tons of bar iron. The import duty im-

[77] In 1732 Chiswell questioned the wisdom of producing bar iron, for "he doubted the Parliament of England would soon forbid us that Improvement, lest after that we should go further, and manufacture Our Bars into all Sorts of Iron Ware, as they already do in New England & Pennsylvania." Byrd, *Writings*, p. 355.

[78] Gooch to B. T., May 24, 1734, *C.O.5/1323*, pp. 241, 242. One furnace had, the previous year, run some iron of a different shape for ballast. This was seized at London by the customs officials, and only cleared after the owners had proved that it was "only Runn, no way Manufactured."

[79] Gooch to B. T., May 19, 1736, *C.O.5/1324*, pp. 40, 41.

posed in Britain greatly discouraged the production of the latter.[80] Gooch did not mention the name of Spotswood in describing the iron industry to the board of trade, but we know that the air furnace and at least one of the smelters belonged to him.

As we have seen, in 1724 Spotswood went to England, where he was to remain six years. In 1725 he appointed his cousin, John Graeme of Middlesex, England, manager of his estate in America.[81] The scope of the enterprise which Graeme was to manage (not altogether to the satisfaction of the absent owner[82]) is indicated by the report of three sworn appraisers appointed on October 5, 1725 by the county court, to see if the improvements made upon the colonel's land met the conditions of seating and planting. Upon the 28,000-acre Alexandria Tract there were twenty-one plantations or tenements. The houses were valued at £9,063.16.6, the enclosures at £511.17, the orchards and gardens at £647, and the mills with their dams at £1200. The cleared land was estimated at 630 acres, while 263 head of cattle and 16 horses were kept upon the tract. Upon the 40,000-acre Spotsylvania Tract there were thirty plantations. The houses were valued at £791.3.6., the enclosures at £435.10.4., the orchards and gardens at £139, and the slate quarry, with its bridges and road, at £150. Forty-five horses and 208 head of cattle were kept upon it, and 750 acres had been cleared.[83] On the Iron Mine Tract of 15,000 acres there were six plantations. The houses, furnace,

[80] Gooch to B. T., July 3, 1739, *C.O.5/1324*, p. 336.

[81] *Spotsylvania County Records*, W. A. Crozier, ed. (N.Y., 1905), pp. 97, 98.

[82] Spotswood told Byrd "That what with Neglect and Severity, above 80 of his Slaves were lost while he was in England, and most of his Cattle starved. That his Furnace stood still great part of the time, and all his Plantations ran to ruin. That indeed he was rightly serv'd for committing his Affairs to the care of a Mathematician, whose thoughts were always among the Stars." Byrd, *Writings*, pp. 359, 360.

[83] These improvements were not sufficient to save the tract, which had therefore to depend upon the improvements made in excess of the required amount upon neighboring tracts. This would not have been permissible but for the land act of 1720.

dams, bridges, and so forth, were valued at £6949, the enclosures at £200.14, and the orchards and gardens at £38. About 300 acres had been cleared, and 154 head of cattle and twelve horses were kept upon the tract. The improvements upon the three tracts as thus appraised would have sufficed to keep from lapsing 142,360 acres, or two-thirds as much again as Spotswood actually held.[84] In 1729 Blair wrote to Bishop Gibson, saying that he was sending him six Virginia hams by the ship *Spotswood*, James Bradley master.[85] One would like to know if the enterprising colonel was the owner of this vessel, or whether it had merely been named in his honor by an admirer. Spotswood's undertakings certainly needed shipping, and the former seems the more probable explanation.

Shortly after his return to Virginia Spotswood adopted the policy of leasing land in small allotments for two generations, subject to a rent which varied somewhat, but of which 800 pounds of tobacco for 150 acres was typical. The policy was continued after his death, and in all 14,369 acres was leased in 104 separate allotments,[86] an extensive tenantry indeed for a country in which we are told renters were not common.[87]

Spotswood was married in 1724 to Anne Butler Brayne, daughter of Richard and Anne Brayne of St. Margarets, Westminster. When the family proceeded to Virginia in 1730 they were accompanied by Mrs. Spotswood's sister, Dorothea, who three years later married Elliott Benger in Spotsylvania County.[88] Thanks to the visit which William Byrd paid to Germanna in 1732 we have a charming picture of the home which Spotswood established in the wilderness.[89] The inven-

[84] *C.O.5/1320*, pp. 273, 274.

[85] Blair to Bishop of London, July 5, 1729, *Fulham MSS. Va.* Box 2, no. 165. Blair hoped the hams would be allowed to pass the customs house since the duty would be more than they were worth.

[86] *Spotsylvania Co. Recs.*, pp. 136-140; *Orange Co. Deed Books*, I-X, *passim.*

[87] Jones, *Present State of Virginia*, p. 61.

[88] *Wm. & Mary Quar.*, X, 143, 144; *Spotsylvania Co. Recs.*, p. 84, Green, *Culpeper*, pp. 2, 3.

[89] Byrd, *Writings*, pp. 356-370, *passim.*

tory of his personal effects made after his death indicates that his *menage* was not unworthy of a former governor.[90]

Spotswood's will, which was dated April 19, 1740, reveals his interest in his iron works. All his lands were entailed upon his eldest son John, or in the event of the latter's death without male heirs, upon his second son Robert. The executors were empowered to continue Spotswood's policy of leasing his lands, but it was provided that the Iron Mine Tract should be set apart for carrying on the iron industry. Eighty slaves and twenty slave children were entailed upon it, and it might be leased for a period of twenty-one years, but only as a unit, with all its equipment intact. It was evident that Spotswood wished his estate to descend in accordance with the British law of primogeniture. Robert was to receive a younger brother's portion of £3000 sterling, while two daughters, Anne Catharine and Dorothea, were to receive £2000 each. All his children being minors at the time of Spotswood's death, it was provided that they should come into their heritage when they reached the age of twenty-one or, in the case of his daughters, at their marriage should it occur earlier. These legacies, and some other smaller ones, were to be paid out of his estate, to be raised by the mortgage or sale of lands.[91]

While Spotswood was still in England, John Hamilton of New Jersey, who in 1722 had resigned under fire as Deputy Postmaster-General, bespoke the colonel's good offices to aid him in recovering his post. "But the Colo. considering wisely that Charity began at Home, instead of getting the Place for Hamilton, secured it for a better Friend: tho', as he tells the Story, that Gentleman was absolutely refus'd before he spoke the least good word for himself."[92] At all events in 1730 Spotswood was appointed Deputy Postmaster-General for ten years at a salary of £300 per annum and a commission of ten per cent of the clear profits. This office he seems to have executed with customary vigor and more than customary tact, for he

[90] *Orange County Will Book*, I, 181-186.
[91] *Ibid.*, p. 131 ff.
[92] Byrd, *Writings*, p. 370.

successfully dissipated the strong antagonism which the southern colonies had thitherto accorded the postal system. By 1732 Spotswood had extended to Williamsburg a service which had previously stopped short at Philadelphia.[93] He appointed his cousin and former manager, John Graeme, postmaster at Massaponax, "with a Salary of £60 a Year, to reward him," gibed Byrd, "for having ruin'd his Estate while he was absent."[94] A more famous appointment reveals that time had not modified Spotswood's meticulousness where the accounts of his subordinates were concerned. "In 1737," writes Benjamin Franklin, "Colonel Spotswood . . . being dissatisfied with the conduct of his deputy at Philadelphia respecting some negligence in rendering, and inexactitude of his accounts, took from him the commission and offered it to me."[95] The Philadelphia post office was accordingly located "at B. Franklin's in Market Street."[96]

If Spotswood maintained other official connections after 1722 next to nothing is known of them. Morley states that shortly after the failure of the excise scheme of 1733 a retired deputy governor of Virginia came over to Walpole with a plan for an American tax. "No," said the minister, "I have old England set against me, and do you think I will have the new England likewise?"[97] With the very dubious exception of Robert Hunter, who in any event would surely have been referred to as governor of Jamaica, Spotswood was the only retired deputy governor of Virginia then alive. It would be instructive to know the nature of his proposal. Direct parliamentary taxation it cannot have been, for even in the bitter days of 1715 he had upheld the right of the colonists to tax themselves;[98] and in 1732 while discussing with Byrd an attempt to force a New England assembly to establish a civil

[93] Fairfax Harrison, "The Colonial Post Office in Virginia," in *Wm. & My. Quar.*, Ser. 2, IV, 78-88; *New Jersey Archives*, First Series, IX, 289.

[94] Byrd, *Writings*, p. 378.

[95] *The Autobiography of Benjamin Franklin* (Boston, 1906), p. 107.

[96] Harrison, *op. cit.*, p. 81.

[97] *Works of Lord Morley* (15 vols., London, 1921), XIII, 156.

[98] *Letters*, II, 125.

list, he declared "that if the Assembly in New England would stand Bluff, he did not see how they cou'd be forct to raise Money against their Will, for if they shou'd direct it to be done by Act of Parliament, which they have threaten'd to do, (though it be against the Right of Englishmen to be taxt, but by their Representatives,) yet they wou'd find it no easy matter to put such an Act in Execution."[99]

Spotswood retained to the end his interest in an aggressive policy against Spanish America. We have already seen how, while still governor, he had cast himself for the leading rôle in an expedition against Florida.[100] Later, when talking of Spanish treasure fleets with William Byrd, he showed proper indignation at a ministry which tamely endured, at the behest of the South Sea Company, "all the late Insolences of the Spaniards." The colonel was convinced, it seems, that this pacific policy had cost him an important post, for when at one time the ministry had practically decided upon war, "they pitch't upon him . . . to be Governor of Jamaica, that by his Skill and Experience in the Art Military, they might be the better able to execute their design of taking the Havanna. But the Courage of these worthy Patriots soon cool'd, and . . . When the Scheme was drop't, His Government of Jamaica was drop't at the same time, and then General Hunter was judg'd fit enough to rule that Island in time of peace."[101]

His chance came when Walpole was forced into war with Spain in 1739. Quick to seize it by proposing that a regiment be recruited in British America, he was rewarded with the task of raising it. He was commissioned brigadier general, appointed quartermaster general and second in command under Lord Cathcart, and made colonel of the American regiment. Late in March 1740 his orders reached him, and with the hearty cooperation of Governor Gooch, who was named as his alternate, he grappled with the problems of recruiting, settling

[99] Byrd, *Writings*, pp. 365, 366.
[100] *Supra*, pp. 242-244.
[101] Byrd, *Writings*, pp. 368, 369. Hunter was appointed governor of Jamaica in 1729, holding the post until his death in 1734. *Dictionary of National Biography*, *s.v.* Robert Hunter.

rates of pay, billeting and, not the least difficult, coordinating the efforts of the various colonial governments. In two months 400 men had been raised in Virginia alone. Spotswood started north to confer with the other colonial executives, but had gone no further than Annapolis before he was stricken by sickness. He struggled, it seems, against the death which would snatch from his grasp the opportunity awaited for so many years. His illness was concealed, and no one was allowed to see him. As so often where knowledge is not available, rumor rushed in to fill the vacuum. The day before his death Gooch, who was entitled to know the truth if ever a man was, received word that Spotswood was too ill to be shown the letter which the governor had written him, that his doctors declared he could not live more than a day or two, and that he was to sail for Virginia the following day! But on June 7, 1740, the end came to Spotswood, at the age of sixty-four.[102]

By a peculiar turn of fate, Spotswood's death elevated his old rival to the supreme executive power of Virginia. Gooch now assumed command of the colonial forces, and when he left with his troops for Cartagena the government devolved upon Blair as president of the council.[103] But the commissary, who had already rounded out full eighty-five years, cared no longer for power, and it was with relief that he wrote to his bishop that his ten months' administration was at an end, thus permitting him to enjoy more retirement from company and business in which to end his days.[104]

[102] *C.O.5/1337*, Nos. 123-133; Cathcart to Newcastle, Aug. 2, 1740; Cathcart to Lord Harrington, Aug. 13, 1740; *C.O.5/41; The Works of Tobias Smollett* (N.Y. 1901) XII, 189; Fortescue, *History of the British Army*, II, 55-60.

[103] Blair to Bishop of London, Oct. 11, 1740, *Fulham MSS., Virginia*, 1st Box, No. 93; Blair to B. T., Oct. 15, 1740, *C.O.5/1325*.

[104] Blair to Bishop of London, Sept. 17, 1741, *Fulham MSS., Virginia*, 2nd Box, No. 212.

Appendix I

ORKNEY'S APPOINTMENT

WITH the appointment of Orkney the conferring of the government of Virginia upon absentees becomes a permanent policy. It is therefore of some importance to determine its date. Upon this point writers have shown marked divergence of opinion. Brock merely states that Orkney held office for "quite forty years" (*Letters*, I, vii), which, since his Lordship unquestionably died in 1737, has led some to place his appointment at 1697. So reliable an authority as the *Dictionary of National Biography* indicates in one place (*s.v.* George Hamilton, Earl of Orkney) 1714 to 1737, and in another (*s.v.* Robert Hunter) 1704 to 1734 as the period of Orkney's governorship. Campbell (*History of the Colony and Ancient Dominion of Virginia*, p. 375), Flippin (*Royal Government in Virginia*, pp. 60-62), and Osgood (*Eighteenth Century*, II, 161) give 1704 as the date. The *Virginia Magazine of History* points out that Orkney received no official commission before 1710 (xxx, 62, 63). This is incontestably true (*C.O.5/1361*, p. 81; *C.O.5/1362*, p. 124; *Harl. 2264* fo. 110), but does it end the matter? Orkney's appointment was rumored both in London and Williamsburg early in 1705 (*Cal. State Paps., Col.*, 1704-1705, p. 432; *Va. Mag. Hist.*, v, 52, 53), and Daniel Parke's complaint to the board of trade that the Duke's promise of the government of Virginia to him at the battle of Blenheim had been disregarded in favor of the Scottish earl (*Cal. State Paps., Col.*, 1706-1708, p. 519) would seem to establish the fact beyond doubt. It therefore appears that while Orkney's commission was not issued until 1710 (officially to give the government to a general on active duty in Flanders would have looked full ugly) and while he does not figure in the board of trade papers before that time, he was tacitly granted the government in 1704, possibly in 1705. Burk (*History of Virginia*, II, 329) is doubtless right in stating that from the first he received part of the salary. Why else would Orkney be interested? The accounts of the two shillings a hogshead do not aid us upon this point, for even after Spotswood's arrival the entire £2000 was debited against the acting governor. The beginning of Spotswood's administration furnishes a useful exception. Orkney's salary began from the date of his commission, Spotswood's from his arrival in the colony. We are thus in a position to determine their respective shares, another mooted point. Sir William Keith, a personal friend of Spotswood, says that Orkney received £1200 (*History of the British Plantations*, p. 171) and Osgood makes the same statement (*Eighteenth Cent.*, II, 161). But Keith is not always accurate. He puts the date of Spotswood's transmontane expedition at 1714 and that of his removal at 1723 (*op. cit.*, pp. 173, 174). The documents show that each received £1000. *C.O.5/1316*, O. 79; *Ex. Jour. Coun.*, III, 252; *Letters*, II, 333. The perquisites of office, placed by Keith at £600 per annum (*op. cit.*, p. 175) seem to have gone to the lieutenant governor.

Appendix II

REVENUE FROM THE DUTIES OF TWO SHILLINGS PER HOGSHEAD, ONE SHILLING AND THREEPENCE PER TON, AND SIXPENCE PER POLL

THIS table does not include the revenue from the sale of treasury rights and from fines and forfeitures, though this went into the same fund. The figures given are the gross receipts, before the fees of naval officers, receiver-general, and deputy auditor were deducted. They are taken from the following sources: *Blathwayt's Virginia Papers* (MS. volume in Library of Congress); *Colonial Papers, 1710-1720* (Loose MSS. in Virginia State Library); *C.O.5/1316*, O. 79, 101, 130, 172; *C.O.5/1317*, pp. 57, 116, 249, 475; *C.O.5/1318*, pp. 139, 349, 767, 769, 875; *C.O.5/1319*, pp. 119, 147, 151, 169.

REVENUE FROM THE DUTIES OF TWO SHILLINGS PER HOGSHEAD, ONE SHILLING AND THREEPENCE PER TON, AND SIXPENCE PER POLL

	Upper James	Lower James	York	Rappahannock	Potomac	Accomac	Total
Year ending Oct. 1710	£480. 3. 1½	£ 89. 9. 5	£1364.17. 4½	£ 803. 9. 1¼	£ 298. 1.10½		£3036.10.10¾
Oct. 1710–Jul. 1711	241.10. 4¾	204.17. 4	1396.16. 4¼	683. 9. 7½	316.12. 0½		3043. 5. 9
Jul. 1711–Apr. 1712	75. 4. 0½	89.14. 6	134. 8. 4½	183. 9. 3½	106. 6.10½	£ 52. 6. 6	601. 9. 7
Year ending:							
Apr. 1713	624. 1. 3¾	163. 8.11	1418.12. 3½	821. 5. 8	731. 7. 5½	60. 4. 1¼	3818.19. 9
Apr. 1714	469. 9. 4¼	219. 8. 1	1073.16. 9½	692.17. 3¼	544.14. 1	38.10. 4½	3038.15.11½
Apr. 1715	449.11. 6¼	99.16. 1¼	1186. 7. 3¾	698.16.11¼	585.12. 1¾	8. 9. 3½	3028.13. 3¾
Apr. 1716	291. 4. 7¼	224. 9. 9¾	955.10. 3½	727. 8. 0¼	272.14. 1	36.14.10¾	2519. 1. 8½
Apr.–Oct. 1716							
Year ending:							
Oct. 1717	573. 8. 0½	320. 5. 3¾	1281.18. 4½	915.16. 1½	536.18. 3½	53. 7.11¼	3681.14. 1
Oct. 1718	724. 7. 9½	354. 1. 4½	1343. 4.10¾	1115. 5. 7½	542.16. 4¼	60. 9. 4¼	4150. 4. 6¼
Oct. 1719	787.19. 7	380.11. 8	1587.11. 3¼	898. 1. 1¼	550. 4. 6½	120. 8. 8¼	4325. 6.11¼
Oct. 1720							
Oct. 1721	763. 8.10½	38. 5. 1¼	1705. 3.11	1347. 3. 9¾	600. 1. 2	90. 6. 7½	4543.19. 6
Oct. 1722	524.16. 9½	304.10. 0½	1351.16. 2¼	960. 8. 5½	516. 1. 5		3657. 2.11¼

Appendix III

THE ROYAL QUIT RENTS IN VIRGINIA

THE figures which follow are not copied directly from the accounts. In places they are arrived at by rather involved computation. The form of the quit rent accounts changes several times during this period, and into any attempt to reduce them to a common form the personal equation enters to some extent. Therefore, while it is believed that the following table conveys a generally accurate impression, those desiring strict accuracy are referred to the quit rent accounts themselves. Compositions for escheats and the annual rent of £6.13.4 from the Northern Neck are omitted from this table. The following sources have been used: *Blathwayt's Virginia Papers; C.O.5/1316,* O. 100, 131, 170; *C.O.5/1317,* pp. 484, 485; *C.O.5/1318,* pp. 135, 136, 495, 496, 760-764; *C.O.5/1319,* pp. 113, 114, 143, 144, 243, 244.

The Royal Quit Rents in Virginia

	Acreage paying quit rents			Quit rent receipts			
Year	Paying current rent	Paying, arrears[1]	Total	Paid when due[2]	Total, including arrears received during the year	Per cent paid in money	Price per cwt. brought by quit rent tobacco
1710[3]	2,450,998		2,450,998	£1050.10. 7½	£1050.10. 7½	0	2*s*. – 5*s*.
1711	2,493,252		2,493,252	832. 4.10[4]		0	2*s*.6*d*.– 5*s*.6*d*.
1712[5]				188.19. 8½[6]			
1713	2,619,775		2,619,775	1286. 5. 9½	1286. 5. 9½	0	3*s*. – 6*s*.
1714	1,145,925		1,145,925	1306. 2. 4½	1306. 2. 4½	65	12*s*.11¾*d*.
1715	1,808,939	706,930	2,515,870	1815. 2. 0½	2540. 2. 6¼	97	11*s*. 8⅓*d*.
1716	1,684,910	582,418	2,267,329	1814. 2. 8½	2457. 2.11¼	78	12*s*. 9⅝*d*.
1717	2,216,881	619,122	2,836,003	2240.16. 7¾	2861. 9. 2½	98	14*s*. 7¾*d*.
1718	2,385,228	416,573	2,801,801	2388.13. 4¾	2805. 8. 3	98	9*s*. 1*d*.
1719[5]							
1720	2,757,163	679,730	3,436,893	1835.17. 0½	2106.13. 2½	69	2*s*.6*d*.–10*s*. 6*s*.
1721	2,803,732	347,794	3,151,526	2042. 4. 3½	2275. 6. 4	61	2*s*.6*d*.– 9*s*. 6*d*.
1722	2,726,847	9,560	2,736,407	2086. 6.11¼	2092.15. 3	61	3*s*. – 9*s*.

1. That is, paying during the year indicated rents unpaid in previous years.
2. Rents collected one year and sold another are credited to the year when collected.
3. The date given is that of the year for which the quit rents were due. They were accounted for in the April of the year following.
4. This does not include the rents for four counties, sold the following year.
5. The accounts for these years have not been located.
6. Sold in 1713 and 1716.

BIBLIOGRAPHY

Manuscript Sources

THE present work has been based to a very large extent upon manuscript material preserved in Great Britain. To this the writer has had indirect access through notes very kindly placed at his disposal by Professor T. J. Wertenbaker, through transcripts in the Library of Congress and in the Historical Society of Pennsylvania, and through other transcripts procured direct from London. The originals have been used to a slight extent. The material from the Public Record Office is listed below.

C.O.5/41. Cartegena Expedition. Throws light upon the closing incident of Spotswood's public career.

C.O.5/210. Plantations General: Despatches to Governors. Contains the text of several sets of instructions.

C.O.5/1316-1325. Original Papers, Letters, and Enclosures relating to Virginia, sent to the Board of Trade by the Governors, or received by them from other sources. A wealth of information upon all phases of the subject is to be found in this series, including a number of Spotswood's unpublished letters.

C.O.5/1341-1344. Papers relating to Virginia sent to the Secretary of State. Fragmentary, but containing some items of value.

C.O.5/1363-1365. Entry Books of the Board of Trade. This useful series includes the out-letters of the board relating to Virginia.

C.O.5/1386-1387. Acts of the Virginia Assembly. Since no printed collection of Virginia laws approximates completeness for the colonial period, this collection is invalable for the text of acts not to be found elsewhere.

C.O.323/6-8. Plantations General, Original Papers. This useful collection contains a variety of papers relating to the plantations as a whole.

C.O.324/9-11. Plantations General, Entry Books, The subject matter of these entry books parallels that of the *C.O.323* series.

C.O.391/33-41. Journal of the Commissioners for Trade and Plantations.

Treas. 64/88-90. Entry Books of William Blathwayt, Auditor-General of the Plantations. Blathwayt's Journal, as it is frequently called, is an important source for colonial administration, particularly its fiscal side.

The British manuscript sources also include the *Fulham MSS. Virginia*, 1st and 2nd Boxes, containing letters and other useful papers relating to Virginia sent to the bishop of London. The *Harleian* and *Additional MSS.* of the British Museum, together with the *Rawlinson MSS.* of the Bodleian Library, Oxford, yielded several useful papers.

The following manuscript material was used in Virginia:

Executive Journals of the Council of Virginia. Two manuscript volumes, 1705-1721 and 1721-1734, preserved in the Virginia State Library. This material has since been printed, and all citations have been changed to refer to the printed volumes.

The *Ludwell Papers* in the library of the Virginia Historical Society include several important letters to and from Philip Ludwell, Jr.

Colonial Papers, preserved in the Virginia State Library. A miscellaneous manuscript collection.

The *Orange County Deed Books*, *Will Books*, and *Order Books*, and the *Spotsylvania County Order Books*, found in the offices of the clerks of the respective circuit courts, are important for Spotswood's career after his return to private life.

Some useful manuscript material, listed below, was found in the Huntington Library:

Letter Book of Robert Carter, 1720-1721. This correspondence of "King" Carter throws some light on political developments, but is especially valuable in revealing the business enterprises of a wealthy Virginia planter.

Blathwayt's Colonial Papers, Virginia, 1664-1712. A collection of papers belonging to the auditor-general.

Huntington Library. A classification of manuscripts, several of which proved of value.

Blathwayt's Virginia Papers, 1675-1717. This collection, similar to the one in the Huntington Library, is to be found in the Library of Congress.

Printed Sources

The Official letters of Alexander Spotswood, Lieutenant-Governor of the Colony of Virginia, 1710-1722, ed. by R. A. Brock (2 vols., Richmond, 1882-1885). This printed edition of the manuscript letter book of the governor in the possession of the Virginia Historical Society, while by no means a complete collection of the letters written by the governor during his administration, contains the majority of the more important ones.

Journals of the House of Burgesses of Virginia, 1619-1776, ed. by J. P. Kennedy and H. R. McIlwaine (13 vols., Richmond, 1905-

1915). This indispensable source contains the proceedings of the lower house, together with the text of messages exchanged between it and governor and council. It is well indexed, and a good summary of the proceedings of each session is to be found at the beginning of each volume.

Legislative Journals of the Council of Colonial Virginia, ed. by H. R. McIlwaine (3 vols., Richmond, 1918-1919). These supplement the journals of the burgesses, containing a few messages not found in the latter, and giving more exact information as to the legislative proceedings of the council which, however, can in most cases be inferred from the journals of the lower house.

Executive Journals of the Council of Colonial Virginia, ed. by H. R. McIlwaine (4 vols., Richmond, 1925-1930). One of the most important sources for the history of colonial Virginia, and the one which furnishes the clearest and most complete picture of the workings of the colonial executive.

The Statutes at Large: being a Collection of all the Laws of Virginia, ed. by W. W. Hening (13 vols., Richmond, 1819-1823). The standard printed collection of Virginia statutes has proven of the greatest service. It has evidently been edited, however, to serve the lawyer rather than the historian. It thus happens that a number of laws are omitted which, while only in force for a short period of time, were temporarily of paramount importance. The editorial notes are generally, but not always, reliable.

Acts of Assembly passed in the Colony of Virginia from 1662 to 1715, Vol. I (London, 1727).

Abridgement of the Public Laws of Virginia in force and use, June 10, 1720 (London, 1728). This and the preceding collection supplement Hening to a limited extent.

Calendar of Virginia State Papers and other Manuscripts, ed. by W. P. Palmer, Vol. I (Richmond, 1875). Fragmentary, but contains a number of useful documents.

Acts of the Privy Council of England, Colonial Series, ed. by W. L. Grant and James Munro (6 vols., Hereford, 1908-1911). This most useful series gives the actions of the privy council with reference to colonial affairs. It unfortunately falls short of completeness.

Calendar of State Papers, Colonial Series, America and West Indies, ed. by Cecil Headlam, *et al.* (30 vols., London, 1860-1930). In this series is to be found the gist of the more important documents in the Public Record Office, many of which are reproduced verbatim. Unfortunately, the volumes covering Spotswood's administration are only now appearing.

Journal of the Commissioners for Trade and Plantations (8 vols.,

London, 1920-1931). The journal not only indicates the matters which came up before the board, but where it received verbal information tells a great deal about colonial affairs. More often than not, it does not indicate the action of the board upon the matters considered. The journal and the board of trade papers must thus be studied in conjunction.

Chalmers, George, *Opinions of Eminent Lawyers on Various Points of English Jurisprudence, chiefly concerning the Colonies, Fisheries, and Commerce of Great Britain* (Burlington, 1858). Contains several opinions bearing upon Spotswood's administration. Many others, however, are not to be found here, and must be sought in the board of trade papers.

Archives of Maryland (47 vols., Baltimore, 1883-1930). Contain suggestive material upon the relations between Virginia and her sister tobacco colony of the Chesapeake.

Documents relative to the Colonial History of the State of New York, ed. by E. B. O'Callaghan (11 vols., Albany, 1853-1858). Here are found a number of printed documents, the originals of which are in the Public Record Office, which throw light upon intercolonial relations, and particularly upon Indian affairs.

The Colonial Records of North Carolina, ed. by William L. Saunders (10 vols., Raleigh, 1886-1890). Particularly useful in connection with the boundary dispute, the Cary Rebellion, and the Tuscarora War.

Minutes of the Provincial Council of Pennsylvania, more commonly known as Pennsylvania Colonial Records (16 vols., Philadelphia, 1852-1853). Contain material upon the intercolonial phase of the frontier problem.

Wraxell, Peter, *An Abridgement of the Indian Affairs*, ed. by C. H. McIlwain (Cambridge, 1915). Supplements the fuller accounts to be found in the *New York Colonial Documents*. Has an excellent introduction.

Historical Collections relating to the American Colonial Church, ed. by W. S. Perry (5 vols., Hartford, 1870-1878), Vol. 1, Virginia. Useful, though by no means complete.

The Writings of "Colonel William Byrd, of Westover in Virginia, esq^r", ed. by John Spencer Bassett (New York, 1901). The engaging "writings" of one of Spotswood's foremost opponents are later than his administration, and do not shed much direct light upon it. Yet their oblique rays are illuminating. The excellent introduction contains an able summary of the quarrel between Byrd and Spotswood.

Memoirs of a Huguenot Family, trans. and ed. by Ann Maury (New

York, 1872). The diary of John Fontaine gives a first-hand account of some of Spotswood's activities in the west.

The Letters and Dispatches of John Churchill, First Duke of Marlborough, ed. by Sir George Murray (5 vols., London, 1845). For Spotswood's military career.

Periodicals

Tyler's Quarterly Historical and Genealogical Magazine (Richmond, 1919-).

The Virginia Magazine of History and Biography (Richmond, 1893-).

William and Mary College Quarterly Historical Magazine (26 vols., Williamsburg, 1892-1919), 2nd Series (Williamsburg, 1921-).

The above-cited magazines, while containing suggestive articles, have been particularly useful because of the reprints of documents which they contain.

Carpenter, A. H., "Habeas Corpus in the Colonies," in *American Historical Review,* VIII (Oct., 1902), pp. 18-27.

Wertenbaker, T. J., "The Attempt to Reform the Church of Colonial Virginia," in *Sewanee Review,* XXV (1917), pp. 257-282.

Secondary Works

Burk, John Daly, *History of Virginia from its First Settlement to the Present Day* (3 vols., Petersburg, 1804-1805).

Beverley, Robert, *History of Virginia, in Four Parts* (2d ed., London, 1722).

Campbell, Charles, *Genealogy of the Spotswood Family in Scotland and Virginia* (Albany, 1868).

Campbell, Charles, *History of the Colony and Ancient Dominion of Virginia* (Philadelphia, 1860).

Chalmers, George, *An Introduction to the History of the Revolt of the American Colonies* (2 vols., Boston, 1845).

Keith, Sir William, *History of the British Plantations in America* (London, 1738).

Oldmixon, John, *The British Empire in America* (2 vols., London, 1741),

The foregoing "classical" historians are of value less for the light which they shed upon the subject than for the opportunity which they afford for tracing current ideas concerning it. At times, however, it is clear that they have made use of sources which are no longer available.

Beer, George Louis, *The Old Colonial System*, Part I, (2 vols., New York, 1912). Deals primarily with an earlier period, but is the best treatment extant of the conditions under which the commerce of Virginia was conducted.

Bond, Beverley W., Jr., *The Quit-Rent System in the American Colonies* (New Haven, 1919). A Comprehensive study of a very significant problem.

Bruce, Philip Alexander, *Economic History of Virginia in the Seventeenth Century* (2 vols., New York, 1896). The standard work upon the subject.

Buford, Edward P., *Fort Christanna* (Lawrenceville, 1924). An account of one of Spotswood's most cherished undertakings, written with a wealth of local color.

Clowes, Sir William Laird, *et al.*, *The Royal Navy, a History from the Earliest Times to the Present* (7 vols., London, 1897-1903).

Corbett, Sir Julian S., *England in the Mediterranean* (2 vols., London, 1917). For the English occupation of Tangier.

Crane, Verner W., *The Southern Frontier* (Durham, 1928). An excellent study.

Dictionary of National Biography, ed. by Leslie Stephen and Sidney Lee (53 vols., New York, 1885-1900).

Fortescue, Sir John William, *History of the British Army* (13 vols., London, 1899-1930). Furnishes the background for Spotswood's military career.

Gordon, Armistead Churchill, *Men and Events, Chapters of Virginia History* (Staunton, 1923.) Contains a suggestive essay upon Spotswood, with useful bibliographical notes.

Jones, Hugh, *The Present State of Virginia* (London, 1724; reprinted, New York, 1865). This contemporary work, written by a clergyman who had lived for several years in Virginia, is particularly valuable for the light which it sheds upon social conditions. Jones was a loyal supporter of Spotswood, and his laudatory picture of the governor must be accepted with caution.

Osgood, Herbert L., *The American Colonies in the Eighteenth Century* (4 vols., New York, 1924). The standard political history of the period.

Scott, William Wallace, *History of Orange County in Virginia, 1734-1870* (Richmond, 1907). A history of the region which saw many of Spotswood's enterprises written by one possessing an enviable knowledge of its topography and history.

INDEX